NEW RECIPES FROM MOOSEWOOD RESTAURANT

7-04/01

NEW RECIPES FROM MOOSEWOOD RESTAURANT

New Edition

The Moosewood Collective

Ten Speed Press
Berkeley Toronto

1☺
TEN SPEED PRESS
P.O. Box 7123
Berkeley, California 94707
www.tenspeed.com

Distributed in Australia by Simon & Schuster Australia,
in Canada by Ten Speed Press Canada, in New Zealand
by Southern Publishers Group, in South Africa by
Real Books, in Southeast Asia by Berkeley Books,
and in the United Kingdom and Europe by Airlift Books.

Interior design and typography by Fifth Street Design

Appearing in the handtinted photographs on the back cover
of this book are workers, families, and friends of Moosewood.
The photos are the work of Al Karevy and Patti Harville.

The Library of Congress has assigned this and the previous
editions the following catalog card number: 87-050179

This paperback edition: ISBN 1-58008-148-7
First paperback edition: ISBN 0-89815-208-9
First cloth edition: ISBN 0-89815-209-7

Printed in the United States of America

1 2 3 4 5 — 04 03 02 01 00

ACKNOWLEDGMENTS

Besides the 17 present members of the Moosewood Collective who have made this cookbook possible, there is a host of other supporters behind-the-pages and between-the-lines. Without the astute advice, encouragement, and excellent help of these friends and professionals, our book could not have taken shape with nearly the ease or careful consideration that was possible, thanks to their willingness to add their skills to ours.

First we must thank many of the "ex-Moosers," former members of the collective, and others who contributed time and energy to our restaurant or this book. Many have traveled to distant places, have hitched their wagons to other stars, but we still remember them fondly and recognize their valuable contributions. Hello out there, Judy Barringer, Jonathan Kline, Julie Knie, Kris Miller, Jori Ross, Yvonne Fisher, Andi Gladstone, Cary Joseph, Jim Legott, Tom Mank, and Shevek Hertzendorf.

And of course the world-at-large knows Moosewood because of the *Moosewood Cookbook* compiled by Mollie Katzen from the first four years of the restaurant. Ten years later, over a million copies have been sold, and many millions more people have joined in eating food prepared from those recipes.

We would like to mention Ithaca's Somadhara Bakery, a local business with which we've had a strong relationship. They have supplied us with fresh-baked, whole grain breads for over ten years now. They are good neighbors.

For their beautiful work and admirable patience during the hectic scheduling of people and places, our photographers Al Karevy and Patti Harville deserve the highest praise.

For editing with a fine-tooth comb, Andrea Clardy cannot be thanked enough. She corrected mistakes and inconsistencies and provided objective critiques. She also offered us zest and structure at critical stages of this manuscript's development. Her special blend of good humor and serious work has endeared her to us.

We also appreciate the generous cooperation of Susan J. Brown and Holly Carlson-Lau in sharing office space. Carl Lagoze, thanks for your technical advice.

Michael Aman, our typesetter, we thank for hours and hours at the keyboard, typing and deciphering our scribbles. His careful, attentive eye caught many a discrepancy, and his advice and organization were helpful far beyond the call of duty.

For long-term friendship and creative advice, we would like to thank Jeff Furman and Fred Rolfe.

Our agents, Arnold and Elise Goodman, have given us support, consideration, and excellent advice from start to finish. Their clear-sighted direction and impeccable judgment were influences that helped to revitalize our efforts during the course of our work on this cookbook. They have been strong and flexible throughout, and we admire their professional expertise. They have made us feel well taken care of. Thank you.

Greetings to our restaurant "regulars," fans of Moosewood who come to eat several times a week (some come every day!) and have favorite tables and favorite dishes. Their honest feedback and long-lasting, loyal support enrich our days and contribute to the family feeling of Moosewood Restaurant.

Photography by Kathy Morris

Row 1 (top l to r): *David Hirsch, Tony Del Plato*

Row 2: *Bob Love, Laura Branca, Lisa Wichmann*

Row 3: *Ned Asta, Eliana Parra, Nancy Lazarus, Linda Dickinson, Maureen Vivino*

Row 4: *Tom Walls, Maggie Pitkin, Susan Harville, Wynelle Stein*

The Moosewood Collective

All of these people, past and present members of the Moosewood Collective, have created this book by their various efforts in developing and testing recipes and in research, writing, editing and general support.

Joan Adler

Ned Asta

Laura Branca

Linda Brecht-Torn

Carol Cedarholm

Susan Jane Cheney

Linda Dearstyne

Tony Del Plato

Linda Dickinson

Susan Harville

David Hirsch

Roseann Iacovazzi

Nancy Harville Lazarus

Bob Love

Flora Marranca

Celeste Tischler Materi

Fouad Makki

Ashley Miller

Eliana Parra

Maggie Pitkin

Ira Rabois

Sara Robbins

Wynelle Stein

Therese Tischler

Maureen Vivino

Tom Walls

Allan Warshawsky

Mitch Weiss

Lisa Wichman

TABLE OF CONTENTS

SOUPS

SALADS

SANDWICHES AND DIPS

MAIN DISHES

MAIN DISHES (continued)

Pastas

Fish

SAUCES, SIDE DISHES, AND CONDIMENTS

Sauces

Side Dishes

Condiments

BREADS

DESSERTS

INTRODUCTION

Eating is one of life's sweet pleasures – so is cooking and serving good food to others. And that's what we've been doing at Moosewood since 1973. The Moosewood cuisine is continually evolving. In this new cookbook, we introduce the latest and the greatest, the leanest and the greenest, the best and the rest of the recipes from Moosewood Restaurant.

People from all corners of the world have made their way to Moosewood, and what they usually expect is a much bigger restaurant with much taller waiters. Moosewood is a small place, and our kitchen, in particular, is tiny with no special equipment: no microwave, no high-speed oven, no grinder, no griddle, no deep-fat fryer. Our menu is different at every meal, and we do a lot of cooking in a short time in this small space with no last-minute madness. The happy result of these limitations is that our recipes are straightforward and easy to prepare. Over time each dish has been tested and refined so that these recipes should not intimidate a beginning cook and yet will interest the more experienced chef.

More than a decade ago, we were just discovering how to be vegetarians. Soybeans and brown rice were a challenge. Yogurt was a little exotic, remember? Well, since then we've found the world full of foods and flavors to taste and savor. And you know, this vegetarian food is not just loved by vegetarians. Many of us are not strict vegetarians and neither are most of our customers, who come to Moosewood for the good food.

We're excited to be part of the developing American vegetarian cuisine. We think that the real inspiration for our cooking is an openness to ethnic and regional foods – and a readiness to mix and match in the American melting-pot tradition, taking the best and most interesting and throwing it together in new ways to create something unique and wonderful.

Take the case of Japanese Braised Eggplant. Linda and Joan returned from a local Japanese restaurant swooning over a gingery eggplant appetizer called Nasu No Ok Yaki. They wanted to find a way to bring the essence of this sweetly rich delicacy to a heartier main dish. In the end, our cooks came up with a succulent braising marinade that crosses the culinary borders of Japan, Polynesia, and American barbeque, and a rich tempeh filling that borrows from Indonesia – and Bulgaria! We knew we'd happened on something terrific when we discovered what braising can do for eggplant. We experimented with that as a first step in some of our classic eggplant dishes and now it's standard procedure.

Moosewood, the restaurant, has drawn much of its character from the town in which it has grown up. Ithaca, New York, is perhaps the most cosmopolitan little city on the continent. Nestled at the foot of Cayuga Lake between Cornell University and Ithaca College, it more closely resembles a cleaned-up, stripped-down version of Manhattan's Upper West Side than other sleepy towns in the Finger Lakes region. In the late '60s, Ithaca was home to a number of counter-cultural communes; today a network of collectives, cooperatives, and community action groups influences the political and economical climate.

Our restaurant is a worker-owned, worker-operated business. Management decisions are made by group consensus which at times may seem laborious, but is actually surprisingly effective. Fourteen years of continuous operation have worked many of the bugs out of the system and several fourteen-year veterans are still around to lend their expertise.

Each owner (and that's all 17 of us) is also a worker who may be a cook, waiter, menu planner, or dishwasher. Our salaries are based on an equal wage, and we have a flexible schedule with options to work a variety of jobs or to learn new skills. In addition, there are apprentices and substitutes who frequently join the collective when there are openings. There's no one boss, much to the wonderment of those who come in asking to see the manager and are shown into the offices of the dishwasher. We're interested in helping each other, so if your waiter's very busy, the cook may serve your dinner.

Moosewood workers are very active outside the restaurant. Among us are artists, dancers, farmers, musicians, writers, political activists, architects, anthropologists, storytellers, students, teachers, and parents. Collectively, through benefit brunches and direct contributions, we are able to further our contributions to the community.

Now to the recipes: they're organized in an obvious, common-sense way, so that if you have a yen for pasta, you can flip through that section and find something that will satisfy. Follow recipes closely the first time and read them over at least twice before starting. Before you put the book away, make notes on the meal – you may have wished for a hint of dill to be more dominant, or you might prefer lemon juice to vinegar. That's how we work with our own recipes, which are covered in a thicket of scribbles from the cooks. Then play with the recipe a bit next time – follow your intuitions and whims. Recipes are to be tampered with, and we all can become more than tenacious recipe followers.

Most of all, taste as you go along. Add a little of a particular ingredient to a small portion before you're generous with it. A good hand with the herbs, spices and salt and pepper is an acquired thing, and it makes all the difference in the final sparkle of your food.

You'll find a few familiar recipes here – good old guacamole and good old hummus, for instance – but they are requested so often at the restaurant that it was unthinkable to leave them out of this book. And there are a few at the other extreme; if wasabi, wakame, nori, annato, kuzu, and tamarind aren't in your kitchen repertoire, check them out in the appendix and give them a try.

At Moosewood, we're always creating new dishes while keeping the old ones alive and well on the main menu. If someone asks what keeps us going, the answer is, first of all, we love food. But also, over the years, we've learned that sharing wonderful food with friends and family is only the tangible reward. It's the care and imagination we give daily to our food that yields a sustaining nourishment for the spirit. If we have a secret, that's it – and it's also why we work gladly. For us, good food and good spirits are inseparable.

SOUPS

Soups

Soup has many nostalgic associations for us – historical, cultural, and literary. We think of grandma's kitchen, Old World peasants' harvest, new age communal meals, after-the-opera supper at midnight, stone soup, and all those fairytale cottages in the woods with a cauldron of soup on the fire and a generous old couple at the door bidding welcome to the weary wanderer.

Because it is basic, inexpensive, nutritious, and almost infinitely flexible, soup is a metaphor for all food. Soup can be hearty or delicate, simple or extravagant, hot or cold, soothing or spicy, serious sustenance or light divertissement. Some soups are almost instant, and most can be conveniently prepared ahead of time. The aroma of soup simmering in the kitchen evokes the spirit of caring – of home and hearth.

You can confidently create a good soup with almost anything, with or without a recipe, if you follow certain guidelines and procedures. Begin by sautéing onions and other vegetables in oil or butter. Most dried herbs, such as bay leaf, thyme, oregano, and basil, should be gently sautéed with the vegetables before liquid is added. But the essential oils of fresh herbs and of some dried herbs, such as dill, tarragon, and chervil, are more fragile and may easily be cooked away; add these herbs toward the end of soup making.

Add liquid and simmer the soup until the vegetables are tender. We recommend vegetable stock as the liquid base, although water may be used. Simmer soups gently. Don't boil a soup or you may alter the color and flavor, destroy vitamins and nutrients, and lose the fragrance of the herbs. If you're using milk or tahini, over-heating the soup will make them curdle. Dairy products, such as milk, yogurt, and sour cream, should be added gradually when the soup is off the heat. Any soup should be reheated slowly.

There are several ways to thicken soup. You can mix a roux – a mixture of butter and flour – with some hot stock or milk and blend it into the soup. Cream cheese and sour cream are good ingredients to mellow the flavor and thicken cream soups. You can use leftover cream and cheese sauces as a base for many soups. Or, to avoid butterfat, you can purée a portion of the soup with cooked potatoes and then combine the puréed and chunky parts of the soup for a thick, rich texture.

One of the most obvious and economical rewards for maintaining a whole foods kitchen is that most of the snippings and peelings and unused parts of raw vegetables can be used to make a good stock with little effort. The water left over when vegetables are steamed is not only tasty but full of vitamins. And in many leftovers you have the beginnings of soup. You can use leftover Spicy Peanut Sauce in Mushroom-Sesame-Tofu Soup or leftover filling from North Indian Stuffed Eggplant as a base for Potage St. Cloud.

We thought we had learned to cook when we made soup in kindergarten class. And on a basic level we had. All artistry in cooking is using techniques and ingredients to create a new blend, just as instruments combine their different voices to make music together. The principle is the same whether we're contemplating a mixture of vegetables and barley, as wholesome and simple as "Good Morning to You" played on kazoos, or the sophisticated Chilled Cantaloupe-Amaretto Soup, as refined and rarified as a Miles Davis combo.

Chilled Cantaloupe-Amaretto Soup

Serves 4 to 6

This soup is just short of divine ecstasy – but only if the cantaloupe and peaches are in season, fragrant and ripe.

1 fresh, ripe cantaloupe, peeled, seeded, and cubed

2 fresh, ripe peaches, peeled, pitted, and chopped

1 teaspoon pure almond extract

2 cups heavy cream (or milk or half-and-half)

¼ cup amaretto liqueur

2 tablespoons fresh lemon juice

pinch of ground nutmeg or cinnamon (*optional*)

In a blender, purée small amounts of the fruit with the liquids until all the ingredients are used. The soup should be very smooth. Stir in the nutmeg or cinnamon. Chill several hours before serving.

Here's a pleasant summer meal:

Chilled Cantaloupe-Amaretto Soup
An antipasto platter
Fettucine with pesto sauce
Crusty Italian bread
A light white wine

Chilled Avocado-Grapefruit Soup

Serves 6

A slightly sweet and unusual soup that should be served in small bowls as an appetizer or possibly for dessert.

3 small to medium ripe avocados	¼ teaspoon cinnamon
2 cups grapefruit juice	1¼ cups water
½ teaspoon salt	¼ cup apple juice or apple-apricot juice
¼ teaspoon ground allspice	maple syrup or other sweetener to taste

In a blender or food processor, purée the avocado pulp with the grapefruit juice until very smooth. Pour the purée into a bowl and stir in the rest of the ingredients. Chill for several hours. Serve cold.

Serve with French Rice Salad *(p. 36)* or Mexican Corn and Cheese Stuffed Peppers *(p. 102)*.

Chilled Crème De Crécy

Serves 4 to 6

A brilliantly orange first course or summer luncheon soup.

2 tablespoons butter

⅓ cup chopped scallion bulbs (white part only)

1 teaspoon grated fresh ginger root (½ teaspoon powdered ginger)

½ teaspoon ground cinnamon

4 medium carrots, peeled and sliced

3 tablespoons grated orange peel

3 cups water

salt and black pepper to taste

1½ cups orange juice

½ cup heavy cream

2 teaspoons fresh lemon juice

Gently sauté the scallions, ginger, and cinnamon in butter for several minutes. Stir in the carrots and orange peel and sauté 3 or 4 minutes more. Add the water, salt, and pepper. Bring to a boil, then reduce the heat and simmer covered until the carrots are just tender.

Purée the carrot mixture with the orange juice, cream, and lemon juice. Adjust salt and pepper to taste.

Chill several hours before serving.

This soup is an appropriate introduction to Vegetable Ragoût *(p. 120)* or Garden Vegetable and Tempeh Sauté *(p. 116)*.

Chilled Spinach-Yogurt Soup

Serves 4 to 6

A smooth, green soup with a bright, tart-edged taste.

2 tablespoons vegetable oil

1½ cups chopped onions

1 medium potato, chopped

1 teaspoon salt

dash of black pepper

1½ to 2 cups Vegetable Stock *(p. 30)* or water

10 ounces spinach, washed and stemmed

2 cups milk

2 to 3 teaspoons chopped fresh dill (1 teaspoon dried)

1 cup plain yogurt

□

nutmeg, preferably freshly grated

Sauté the onions in the oil on low heat. After about 10 minutes, add the potatoes, salt, pepper, and stock or water. Bring to a boil, then reduce the heat and cover. Simmer until the potatoes are tender, about 10 to 15 minutes. Add the spinach.

When the spinach is wilted but still bright green (2 or 3 minutes), remove from the heat and stir in the milk and dill. Blend in a food processor or blender, in batches, until it is very smooth. Whisk in the yogurt.

Chill for about 4 hours. The soup will thicken as it cools. If it is too thick, whisk in some milk, stock, or water. Adjust the seasoning after it has chilled. Serve garnished with a pinch of nutmeg.

Accompany with Armenian Stuffed Cabbage *(p. 90)*, Moroccan Stew *(p. 121)*, or Kolokithopita *(p. 140)*.

Scandinavian Apple Soup, Hot or Cold

Serves 4 to 6

A simple soup that works for any season – cold in summer, hot in winter. It's particularly good for brunch. The disarming simplicity of this soup will delight your family or guests at any time of year. This is a popular soup on our brunch menus.

2 tablespoons butter

¾ cup chopped onions

10 tart eating or sauce apples, about 3 pounds

3½ cups Vegetable Stock *(p. 30)* or water

½ teaspoon cinnamon

⅛ teaspoon ground cloves

pinch of nutmeg, preferably freshly grated

1 cup heavy cream or milk

honey *(optional)*

fresh lemon juice *(optional)*

□

unsweetened heavy cream, whipped

ground cinnamon

Melt the butter in a small skillet and slowly sauté the onions, stirring occasionally, until they are translucent. Meanwhile, core and seed the apples and cut them unpeeled into bite-size chunks. Place the apple chunks in a soup pot with the stock or water and simmer covered on medium heat until the apples are soft, about 15 minutes.

Using a blender or food processor, purée the onions, apples, and stock. Return the mixture to the soup pot and add the spices and cream. The amount of cream used determines the richness of the soup. To serve hot, reheat the soup, keeping it under a boil to avoid curdling. Just before serving, remove the soup from the heat and adjust the sweet-tart ratio with honey and/or lemon juice.

To serve cold, taste after the cream is added, and adjust sweetness-tartness with honey and/or lemon juice. Chill at least 2 hours.

Ladle the soup, hot or cold, into cups or bowls and top with a spoonful of unsweetened whipped cream and a dusting of ground cinnamon.

Serve for brunch with Mushroom-Leek Frittata *(p. 110)* or as a prelude to Mushroom-Tofu-Pecan Stuffed Squash *(p. 103).*

Miso Broth

Serves 4 to 6

This recipe is for a basic miso broth, a staple of Japanese cuisine. Miso Soup is simple and nutritious and is especially satisfying during the depths of winter, when it can warm you from the inside out. Move over, chicken soup!

Moosewood's Andi Gladstone, who also produces films and quiz shows for Japanese media, has miso soup for breakfast every morning, as per custom in Japan.

6 cups water	□
2 tablespoons tamari soy sauce	**chopped scallions**
1 medium carrot, julienned *(see Appendix)*	**toasted sesame seeds**
	dark sesame oil *(see Appendix)*
1 cup thinly sliced onions	□
1 teaspoon grated fresh ginger root	**1 5 × 2-inch strip of wakame** *(see Appendix)*
2 tablespoons miso *(see Appendix)*	

Place the wakame in a bowl, cover it with hot water, and set it aside to soak.

Bring the 6 cups of water and the soy sauce to a gentle simmer. Add the carrots, onions, and ginger and simmer covered for several minutes. Drain the wakame, chop it, and add it to the soup. Simmer the broth on low heat for 30 minutes.

Add a small amount of the vegetable broth to the miso and stir it into a paste. Then add the miso paste to the soup, stirring until it is dissolved. Simmer the soup gently just a few minutes longer, taking care that it does not come to a boil.

For variation, try adding broccoli spears, chopped cabbage, sliced mushrooms, tofu, or tofu kan *(see Appendix)*. You may prefer to sauté the vegetables lightly in a spoonful of vegetable oil before adding them to the broth. For a heartier soup, add ½ cup of cooked rice or soba noodles *(see Appendix)*.

Garnish each serving with chopped scallions and toasted sesame seeds and add a few drops of dark sesame oil for its wonderful fragrance.

We consider this soup the perfect prelude to Japanese Braised Eggplant *(p. 96)* or Sweet and Sour Vegetables and Tofu *(p. 119)*.

Tomato-Garlic Soup

Serves 6

This simple soup can be made in ten minutes and yet it always receives raves. Served with plenty of warm bread and fresh salad, it makes a lovely dinner for unexpected company.

3 tablespoons olive oil

3 to 6 large garlic cloves, minced or pressed

8 cups tomato juice or undrained canned tomatoes puréed in a blender

1 tablespoon Hungarian sweet paprika
(see Appendix)

¼ to ½ cup red wine or dry sherry
(optional)

☐

croutons

freshly grated Parmesan cheese

chopped fresh parsley

Sauté the garlic in the olive oil very briefly, taking care not to brown it. Stir in the paprika and sauté for another minute, stirring continuously, and taking care that it doesn't scorch. Stir in the tomato juice and heat. Add the wine. Simmer 5 to 10 minutes.

Garnish with croutons, freshly grated Parmesan cheese, and chopped fresh parsley.

Variations:

- *Mediterranean:* Add cooked garbanzo beans and garnish with shredded feta cheese and chopped fresh parsley.
- *Mexican:* Add Tabasco sauce and garnish with shredded cheddar cheese and tortilla chips.

Maureen's Tomato Soup

Serves 4 to 6

This is our own Maureen Vivino's favorite tomato soup. It is especially nice with summer-fresh, ripe tomatoes just off the vine. The addition of eggs, cream, and cheese creates a rich first course.

3 tablespoons olive oil

1 cup chopped onions

8 garlic cloves, minced

7 medium fresh tomatoes, quartered, or 5 cups canned tomatoes

2 cups Vegetable Stock *(p. 30)* or water

1 to 2 teaspoons fresh basil (½ teaspoon dried)

1 teaspoon vinegar

¼ cup dry red wine

1 to 2 tablespoons dry sherry *(optional)*

salt and black pepper to taste

□

2 egg yolks

½ cup heavy cream or milk

⅓ cup freshly grated Parmesan cheese (1 ounce)

Sauté the onions and garlic in the olive oil, stirring often, until the onions are translucent. In a blender or food processor, purée the sautéed onions and garlic and the tomatoes with the stock. Heat the purée in a soup pot and simmer for 10 minutes. Stir in the basil, vinegar, wine, sherry, and salt and pepper. Simmer for 15 minutes more. Remove from the heat.

In a bowl beat the egg yolks with the cream and Parmesan cheese. Stir in ½ cup of the hot soup, mixing well. Gradually pour this mixture back into the soup, whisking or stirring constantly. Heat carefully for a few minutes and serve.

Serve with Eggplant Provençale *(p. 94)*. Or for a light luncheon soup, omit the egg yolks and cream and serve with Herbed Cream Cheese sandwiches *(p. 70)* or salad.

Hungarian Vegetable Soup

Serves 6 to 8

As appropriate for lunch with the kids as for late night suppers. Adding a cup of cooked egg noodles will create an even heartier soup.

3 tablespoons vegetable oil or butter

2 cups chopped onions

2 garlic cloves, minced or pressed

2 tablespoons Hungarian sweet paprika *(see Appendix)*

½ teaspoon Hungarian hot paprika *(optional)*

¼ teaspoon dried marjoram

2 small carrots, cut into ½-inch rounds

2 cups thinly sliced cabbage

1 cup cut green beans

2 green peppers, chopped

1 small zucchini, cut in half lengthwise and sliced in half-moons

2 cups sliced mushrooms (8 ounces)

2 large tomatoes, chopped

salt to taste

5 cups Vegetable Stock *(p. 30)* **or water**

2 cups tomato juice

½ cup dry red wine

2 tablespoons tamari soy sauce

1 tablespoon dried dill

□

sour cream or yogurt

In a large soup pot, sauté the onions and garlic in oil until the onions are translucent. Add the paprika, marjoram, carrots, and cabbage and cook on medium heat for 5 minutes. Add the remaining vegetables and salt, reduce the heat, cover, and cook for 5 more minutes. Finally, add the liquids and seasonings and simmer until all the vegetables are tender, about 25 minutes.

Serve with a dollop of sour cream or yogurt and a crusty black bread.

Yogurt-Barley Soup

Serves 4 to 6

This appealing Middle Eastern soup is a little tart and brightened with fresh mint.

⅔ cup uncooked barley*

5 cups Vegetable Stock *(p. 30)* or water

□

2 tablespoons butter

2 cups chopped onions

1 medium carrot, diced

1 tablespoon chopped fresh mint
  (½ teaspoon dried)

1½ teaspoons salt

black pepper to taste

2 cups plain yogurt

2 tablespoons minced fresh parsley

Combine the barley and stock or water in a soup pot and bring to a boil. Simmer the barley, covered, while preparing the vegetables in a separate pan.

Sauté the onions in the butter until translucent. Add the carrots and continue to cook, stirring frequently, until the carrots are tender. Add a little water if necessary to prevent the vegetables from sticking.

When the barley is tender, add the vegetables, mint, and seasonings to the soup pot. Simmer for an additional 10 minutes, then stir in the yogurt and parsley. Carefully warm the soup on low heat, adding more stock if it is too thick.

This soup tastes even better the next day, but reheat it gently, or the yogurt will curdle. As the barley cooks and later as it cools, it releases starch which thickens the soup. If the soup becomes too thick, add more stock or water to thin it.

Yogurt Barley Soup works well as part of a Middle Eastern-style array of foods – olives, tomatoes, hard-boiled eggs, and pita with spreads.

------

* 2½ cups of cooked barley and 3 cups of stock or water may be substituted for the uncooked barley.

Spicy Peanut Soup

Serves 4 to 6

An exceptional soup that transports peanut butter from the mundane world of school lunches to the highly seasoned cuisine of Southeast Asia.

2 tablespoons vegetable oil	**1 cup peanut butter**
2 garlic cloves, minced or pressed	**¾ teaspoon ground coriander**
1 tablespoon grated fresh ginger root	**pinch of cayenne**
2 cups diced onions	**¾ teaspoon freshly ground lemon grass,**
2 green peppers, diced	**if available** *(see Appendix)*
2 cups coconut milk *(see Appendix)*	**½ teaspoon salt**
3½ cups Vegetable Stock *(p. 30)* **or water**	**1 to 2 tablespoons fresh lemon or lime juice**

Heat the oil in a soup pot. Carefully sauté the garlic and ginger, stirring until the garlic is tender. Add the onions and peppers and sauté, stirring occasionally, for 5 minutes, until the peppers are brightly colored. Add the coconut milk and 2½ cups of stock or water and bring to a boil.

Lower the heat and simmer covered for 20 minutes. Blend the peanut butter and remaining cup of stock into a smooth paste and whisk it into the soup with the spices and salt. Simmer about 15 minutes longer, whisking occasionally to avoid lumping or sticking. Just before serving, remove the soup from the heat and stir in the lemon juice or lime juice.

An excellent Spicy Peanut Soup can be made with leftover Spicy Peanut Sauce *(p. 191)*, thinned with stock or water.

Serve with any Pita Sandwich *(p. 66)*, Asian Asparagus Salad *(p. 48)*, or Broccoli-Mushroom-Tofu Salad *(p. 47)*.

Pistou

Serves 4

Pistou is the French word for pesto. This soup is a must for pesto lovers and stone soup aficionados.

2 tablespoons olive oil

¾ cup diced onions

1 medium carrot, sliced

1 small green pepper, chopped

1 medium potato, diced

1½ cups cut string beans

1 cup sliced zucchini

4 cups Vegetable Stock *(p. 30)* or water

1 cup cooked, drained navy beans *(see Appendix)*

½ to ¾ cup Pesto Genovese *(p. 151)*, Winter Pesto *(p. 154)*, or Tofu Pesto *(p. 153)*

salt and black pepper to taste

Sauté the onions and carrots in olive oil for 3 or 4 minutes. Add the green peppers, potatoes, and string beans and sauté for another 4 minutes. Add the zucchini and stock or water, cover, and bring to a boil. Add the navy beans and lower the heat.

Simmer the soup for about 15 minutes or until the vegetables are tender but not overcooked. Stir in the pesto. Add salt and pepper to taste.

Try this soup with Cheese Tart *(p. 132)* or pasta and a light sauce such as Ramatuelle *(p. 147)*. This meal can be appropriately topped off with Wine-Poached Pears *(p. 245)* and your best Maurice Chevalier imitation.

Mushroom-Sesame-Tofu Soup

Serves 6

A classic of eclectic post-hippie cuisine, this chunky protein-rich soup is a complete meal with bread and a crisp salad. This is one of our favorite soups (and non-dairy, to boot!).

2 tablespoons peanut oil or vegetable oil
1½ cups chopped onions
1 teaspoon grated fresh ginger root
3 celery stalks, sliced
2 cups sliced mushrooms (8 ounces)
⅛ teaspoon cayenne
½ teaspoon salt
2 or 3 bay leaves

4 cups undrained whole tomatoes, chopped
1 cup Vegetable Stock *(p. 30)* or water
2 tablespoons tahini *(see Appendix)*
3 tablespoons peanut butter
1 cake of tofu, pressed *(see Appendix)* and cut into ¾-inch cubes

Sauté the onions and ginger in the oil for about 4 minutes. Add the celery and continue to sauté for about 5 minutes. Stir in the mushrooms, cover, and cook on low heat for about 10 minutes. Stir in the cayenne, salt, and bay leaves. Add the tomatoes, their juice, and the stock or water.

Simmer covered for about 20 minutes. Add the tahini and peanut butter, stirring briskly to dissolve. Finally, add the cubes of tofu. Continue to simmer on very low heat for 20 minutes, stirring occasionally to prevent scorching.

Mediterranean White Bean Soup

Serves 6

Because of their delicate flavor and smooth texture, white beans are wonderful soup beans, combined here with Mediterranean seasonings.

1 cup dried navy beans, soaked *(see Appendix)*

Vegetable Stock *(p. 30)* **or water**

2 tablespoons olive oil

2 bay leaves

4 whole garlic cloves

3 sprigs fresh thyme (½ teaspoon dried thyme)

¼ teaspoon fennel seeds

□

2 tablespoons olive oil

2 cups chopped onions

2 large carrots, chopped

2 green peppers, chopped

½ cup water

□

½ teaspoon dried mint

¼ cup chopped fresh parsley

1 to 2 tablespoons fresh lemon juice

salt to taste

Put the drained beans into a 4-quart pot and add stock or water until it reaches a point an inch above the level of the beans. Add the oil, bay leaves, garlic, thyme, and fennel seeds and simmer covered until the beans are tender, about 1 hour. Replenish the liquid occasionally, keeping the beans covered with an inch of liquid. When the beans are tender, discard the bay leaves, garlic cloves, and thyme twigs, if you're using fresh thyme.

Meanwhile, sauté the onions in 2 tablespoons of olive oil for 5 minutes. Add the carrots and sauté another 5 minutes. Stir in the peppers and sauté 5 minutes more. Add ½ cup water and cook the vegetables covered until the carrots are just tender.

Stir the vegetables into the pot of cooked beans and simmer 15 to 20 minutes to blend the flavors. Add the mint, parsley, and lemon juice. Salt to taste and serve.

In the Mediterranean mode: serve with Pissaladière *(p. 133)* or Zucchini-feta Casserole *(p. 114)*.

Potage Plaisance

Serves 4 to 6

A judicious pinch of saffron enlivens this interesting tomato soup.

3 tablespoons olive oil

¾ cup finely chopped leeks *(see Appendix)*

⅓ cup chopped onions

4 small garlic cloves, minced or pressed

1 bay leaf

¼ teaspoon ground fennel seeds

¼ teaspoon dried thyme (1 scant teaspoon fresh)

½ teaspoon dried basil (1 tablespoon fresh)

□

3 cups chopped fresh or undrained canned tomatoes

3 cups Vegetable Stock *(p. 30)* **or water**

⅔ cup cooked rice *(see Appendix)*

¼ cup chopped fresh parsley

small pinch of saffron *(see Appendix)*

salt and black pepper to taste

Sauté the leeks, onions, garlic, bay leaf, fennel, thyme, and basil in the olive oil. (If fresh basil and thyme are used, they should be added later with the liquids.) When the onions are translucent, add the tomatoes to the pot along with the stock or water. Cook covered on low heat for about 15 minutes. Add the rice, parsley, fresh herbs if used, saffron, salt, and pepper. Reheat and serve.

Saffron is an essential ingredient in this soup, but be careful not to add too much or it will overwhelm the other flavors.

Serve with Stuffed Zucchini Bretonne *(p. 92)* or Mushroom-Leek Frittata *(p. 110)*.

Coconut-Bean Soup

Serves 6

A hybrid of Southeast Asian and Moosewood cuisine. Coconut milk adds sweetness and texture to this delicately seasoned soup.

1 cup dried navy beans, soaked *(see Appendix)*

Vegetable Stock *(p. 30)* **or water**

2 bay leaves

2 large whole garlic cloves

1 tablespoon vegetable oil

☐

3 tablespoons vegetable oil

1½ cups chopped onions

2 garlic cloves, minced

2 teaspoons curry powder *(see Appendix)*

¼ teaspoon cayenne *(optional, depending on hotness of curry powder)*

1 medium green or red bell pepper, chopped

2 medium tomatoes, chopped

1 teaspoon salt (or to taste)

1 tablespoon brown sugar

3 tablespoons fresh lemon juice

1¼ cups unsweetened coconut milk *(see Appendix)*

½ cup cooked rice *(see Appendix)*

☐

toasted coconut

Put the drained beans into a 4-quart pot and add stock or water until it reaches a point an inch above the level of the beans. Add the bay leaves, garlic, and 1 tablespoon of oil and simmer covered until the beans are tender, about 1 hour. Replenish the liquid occasionally, keeping the beans covered with an inch of liquid. When the beans are tender, discard the bay leaves and garlic cloves.

While the beans are cooking, sauté the onions, minced garlic, and spices in 3 tablespoons of oil on low heat until the onions are translucent. Add the peppers, tomatoes, salt, sugar, and lemon juice and simmer for 5 to 10 minutes until the peppers are tender. Stir in the coconut milk and rice and set aside. When the beans are tender, stir in the vegetable-spice mixture and more stock or water if the soup seems too thick. Heat gently for 10 to 15 minutes to blend the flavors. Adjust the salt and spices.

Serve garnished with toasted coconut.

Wonderful with Mixed Vegetable Curry *(p. 124)* or North Indian Stuffed Eggplant *(p. 98)*.

Armenian Lentil Soup

Serves 6

Most lentil soups are healthful, but can be a little boring. This one is healthful and exotic. The addition of aromatic herbs, spices, and – surprise! – apricots transforms a homey classic into something excitingly eccentric.

1½ cups dried lentils

6 cups Vegetable Stock *(p. 30)* or water

½ cup chopped dried apricots (4 ounces)

□

3 to 4 tablespoons vegetable oil

1 cup chopped onions

2 to 3 cups cubed eggplant

1½ cups chopped tomatoes, fresh or canned

1 green pepper, chopped

¼ teaspoon cinnamon

¼ teaspoon ground allspice (or another ¼ teaspoon cinnamon, if preferred)

¼ teaspoon cayenne or crushed red pepper

1 tablespoon paprika

1½ teaspoons salt

3 tablespoons chopped fresh parsley

1 tablespoon chopped fresh mint

Rinse the lentils, and then bring them to a boil in the stock or water. Reduce the heat and simmer covered for 20 minutes. Add the chopped apricots and simmer covered for another 20 minutes.

Meanwhile, sauté the onions in the oil until translucent, then add the eggplant and 4 or 5 tablespoons of water. Cook covered on medium heat, stirring occasionally, until the eggplant is almost tender. Add the remaining vegetables, dried spices, and salt. Cover and cook until tender, about 10 minutes.

Stir the sautéed vegetables into the cooked lentil-apricot mixture and simmer for 15 minutes. Add the parsley and mint and serve.

Armenian Lentil Soup is perfect with dark bread, sharp cheese, and a crisp salad.

Egg-Lemon Soup
with Spinach

Serves 6

Inspired by the classic Greek avgolemono soup, our variation includes spinach and garbanzo beans for added color, nutrition, and taste.

2 tablespoons vegetable oil

2 cups finely chopped onions

1 large garlic clove, minced or pressed

2 medium carrots, finely chopped

½ teaspoon dried dill

5 cups Vegetable Stock *(p. 30)* or water

3 eggs

4 tablespoons fresh lemon juice

1 cup cooked brown rice *(see Appendix)*

1½ cups stemmed and chopped fresh spinach

½ cup cooked garbanzo beans *(see Appendix)*

salt and black pepper to taste

In a soup pot, sauté the onions and garlic in oil until the onions are translucent, about 10 minutes. Add the carrots, dill, and 4 cups of the stock or water, cover, and bring to a boil. Reduce to a simmer and cook until the carrots are tender, about 10 minutes. While the carrots are cooking, whisk together the eggs, lemon juice, and remaining one cup of liquid.

Remove the pot from the heat and whisk in the egg mixture. Then reheat gently, stirring continuously, until the egg mixture thickens. Do not allow the soup to boil or it will curdle. Stir in the rice, spinach, and garbanzo beans and season to taste with salt and pepper.

When the soup is hot, serve at once. The spinach should still be bright green, contrasting nicely with the bits of orange carrot.

We suggest serving with Zucchini-feta Casserole *(p. 114)* or Cheese Börek *(p. 138)* or as a lovely first course for Fish à la Grecque *(p. 171)*.

Potage St. Cloud

Serves 6 to 8

A vivid chartreuse-colored soup. The sweet pea potage provides a perfect backdrop for the light curry.

3 tablespoons butter

1½ cups chopped onions

1 garlic clove, minced or pressed

3 medium potatoes, sliced

1 medium parsnip, sliced *(optional)*

1 large carrot, sliced

2 teaspoons turmeric

½ to 1 tablespoon curry powder *(see Appendix)*

5 cups Vegetable Stock *(p. 30)* or water

6 cups green peas, fresh or frozen

2 cups half-and-half or milk

salt and black pepper to taste

Sauté the onions and garlic in butter until golden. Add the potatoes, parsnips, carrots, turmeric, curry powder, and stock or water and simmer until the vegetables are tender, about 20 minutes. Reserve 1 cup of the peas for garnish and add the rest to the pot. Cook frozen peas for 10 minutes, fresh ones for 5 minutes. In a blender or food processor, purée the hot soup with the half-and-half until very smooth. Add salt and pepper to taste. Cook the reserved peas until just tender to garnish individual servings.

Leftover filling from North Indian Stuffed Eggplant *(p. 98)* is the perfect "scratch" from which to start this soup (replacing the first eight ingredients). Purée the filling in a blender or food processor with the peas and hot stock or water and the half-and-half. Finish the soup as directed.

Serve with Corn Bread *(p. 235)* and Artichoke Heart and Tomato Salad *(p. 40)*.

Potage à la Bretonne

Serves 6

A comforting, homey soup from Brittany.

1¼ cups navy beans, soaked *(see Appendix)*

□

¼ cup butter

2 garlic cloves, pressed or minced

3 leek bulbs (white parts only), well rinsed *(see Appendix)* **and thinly sliced**

2 cups diced onions

2 bay leaves

¾ teaspoon dried thyme

¾ teaspoon salt

⅛ teaspoon black pepper

3 medium tomatoes, chopped

⅓ cup fresh lemon juice

1 cup heavy cream or half-and-half

3 to 4 cups Vegetable Stock *(p. 30),* **bean stock, or water**

Cook the beans in water to cover (adding more water as needed) until they are tender.

Sauté the garlic, leeks, and onions in the butter until the onions are translucent. Add the herbs and seasonings and continue to sauté for 5 to 10 minutes more, until the onions begin to brown. Add the tomatoes and half of the lemon juice and simmer covered for 10 minutes. Stir in the beans and their juice and cook for another 10 minutes on low heat. Stir occasionally to prevent sticking. Remove the bay leaves.

Purée the soup in a blender or food processor adding the cream and stock or water as you blend. Stir in the remaining lemon juice. Add more stock or water if the soup needs to be thinned. Adjust the seasonings. Gently reheat on very low heat.

We like to serve this soup with French Rice Salad *(p. 36)* and a wedge of Brie.

Creamy Squash Soup

Serves 4 to 6

A lovely, slightly sweet soup, the essence of autumn. This soup can become a non-dairy one by using oil or margarine instead of butter and apple juice instead of cream.

1 acorn squash or a small buttercup or butternut squash (about 2 cups, cooked)

3 tablespoons butter, vegetable oil, or margarine

2 cups chopped onions

1 small carrot, diced

1 medium potato, diced

2 cooking apples, peeled, cored, and chopped

3½ cups water

1½ cups milk or apple juice or 1 cup heavy cream

⅛ teaspoon cinnamon

salt and black pepper to taste

Clean the squash, cut it in half, and scoop out the seeds. Place it, cut side down, on a lightly oiled baking pan, cover, and bake at 350° about one hour, until soft. Butternut squash may be peeled, cubed, and boiled rather than baked, if you prefer, but baking is easiest and heightens the flavor.

Meanwhile sauté the onions in the butter until they are translucent. Add the carrots, potatoes, apples, and water. Bring the vegetables to a boil, lower the heat, and simmer about 20 minutes, until all the vegetables are tender.

When the baked squash has cooled, scoop out the soft insides and discard the skins. Combine the squash, vegetables, and stock with the milk, cream, or apple juice in a blender or food processor and purée in several batches to a smooth, creamy consistency.

Heat the soup on low heat until it is hot, but not boiling. Add the cinnamon. Season to taste with salt and black pepper.

Serve this soup with a hearty dark bread and a soufflé. If you have baked squash left over, you might use it in Squash Rolls *(p. 231)*.

Creamy Onion Soup

Serves 4

A smooth and rich soup enhanced by the sweetness characteristic of gently sautéed onions.

2 small potatoes, sliced	1 cup milk
3 cups potato water and/or Vegetable Stock *(p. 30)*	1 teaspoon salt
	¼ teaspoon black pepper
1 tablespoon vegetable oil	□
2 tablespoons butter	chopped fresh parsley
3½ cups chopped onions	croutons *(see Appendix)*
⅓ cup dry white wine	grated cheddar cheese
6 ounces cream cheese at room temperature, cubed	

Boil the potatoes in the stock or water until soft. Reserve the liquid. Sauté the onions in the butter and oil on low heat for 10 minutes. Add the wine and simmer for 5 minutes. In a blender (a food processor does not work well for this), purée the cream cheese cubes, sautéed onions, and cooked potatoes with a cup or two of the liquid in which the potatoes were cooked. Pour the purée into a soup pot and stir in the rest of the potato liquid, the cup of milk, salt, and pepper. Heat carefully, stirring occasionally.

Garnish with chopped parsley, croutons, or grated cheddar cheese.

This soup is an ideal first course for an elegant dinner. Its pleasing light texture will not upstage an elaborate entrée.

Very Creamy
Potato-Cheese Soup

Serves 4 to 6

This is our customers' all-time favorite soup and probably the richest soup we offer. Cream cheese is our secret for giving it a velvety texture.

3 to 4 tablespoons butter

2 cups chopped onions

1 large garlic clove, minced or pressed

2 large potatoes, unpeeled and coarsely chopped

1 large carrot, unpeeled and coarsely chopped

3 cups Vegetable Stock *(p. 30)* **or water**

1 teaspoon dried dill (2 tablespoons of fresh dill)

4 ounces cream cheese

1½ cups milk (or part cream)

1 cup grated sharp cheddar cheese (3 ounces)

salt and black pepper to taste

☐

chopped fresh parsley

In a large soup pot, sauté the onions and garlic in the butter until the onions are translucent. Add the potatoes and carrots and sauté for 5 to 10 minutes longer. Add the stock or water and dill and simmer until all the vegetables are tender.

Purée the vegetables with the cream cheese and milk in a blender or food processor. Return the soup to the soup pot. Season with salt and pepper. Stir in the cheddar cheese and reheat gently.

Serve each cup or bowl garnished with chopped fresh parsley. A simple green salad is the perfect complement because opposites attract.

Potage Jacqueline

Serves 4 to 6

A soothing soup, gently seasoned to emphasize the innate goodness of sweet potatoes. This recipe was created by our own Jacqueline Lisa Wichman.

2 tablespoons butter	1 bay leaf
2 cups chopped onions	½ teaspoon salt
1 celery stalk, chopped	black pepper to taste
1 teaspoon grated fresh ginger root	1 cup milk
3 medium sweet potatoes, peeled and thinly sliced	½ cup heavy cream
4 cups water	

Melt the butter in a heavy saucepan and sauté the onions until translucent, stirring occasionally. Add the celery and ginger and continue to cook until the onions begin to brown. Add the sweet potatoes, water, bay leaf, and salt and pepper and bring to a rapid boil. Reduce the heat, cover, and simmer 15 to 20 minutes, until the sweet potatoes are tender.

Remove and discard the bay leaf. Purée the soup mixture with the milk and heavy cream in small batches in a blender or food processor. Adjust the salt and pepper to taste and reheat gently. Take care not to boil the soup.

Garnish Potage Jacqueline by floating a thin lemon round on each serving. Offset the sweetness of this soup with the tart zing of Antipasto Pita *(p. 66)*.

Crème Andalouse

Serves 6

Leeks, tarragon, and cream add a French touch to this sophisticated version of a Spanish soup.

2 tablespoons butter

3 leek bulbs (white part only), rinsed *(see Appendix)* **and chopped**

6 fresh tomatoes, chopped, or 4 cups undrained canned tomatoes

7 cups Vegetable Stock *(p. 30)* **or water**

4 medium potatoes, cubed

1 teaspoon salt

½ teaspoon dried tarragon

⅛ to ¼ teaspoon cayenne

1 teaspoon fresh lemon juice

½ cup heavy cream

□

herbed croutons *(see Appendix)*

¼ cup chopped fresh parsley

Sauté the leeks in the butter until soft. Add the tomatoes and simmer for 10 minutes. Add the remaining ingredients, except the lemon juice and cream. Simmer until the potatoes are thoroughly cooked.

Purée the cooked vegetables in a blender, adding the lemon juice and cream. Gently reheat, taking care not to boil which could cause it to curdle.

Garnish with croutons and parsley. This pretty pastel soup is nicely accompanied by Salat Tangiers *(p. 37)* or Mushroom Pâté *(p. 77)* and crackers.

Vegetable Stock

Yields 2 quarts

Vegetable Stock is a broth made by simmering vegetables in water until they are soft and their flavors and nutrients have been released into the liquid. Then the stock is poured through a strainer and the vegetables are either discarded or used, puréed, to thicken a soup.

The best vegetables to use in stock are carrots, peeled onions, celery, zucchini, potatoes, parsley, parsnips, sweet potatoes, and squash. We often throw in chunks of apples or pears to sweeten the stock a little – especially if the carrots we're using aren't very sweet. It's wise to avoid the strongly flavored vegetables of the cabbage family, such as broccoli and cauliflower, and turnips, rutabagas, and kohlrabi – and vegetables with bleeding colors, such as beets, red cabbage, and greens (unless you intend to make a borscht or cream of green soup). Green peppers and eggplant will make the stock bitter. Be cautious about adding lots of tomatoes or other acidic fruits or vegetables to the stock, because they may curdle the soup if you add milk or other dairy products later on.

Wash all vegetables thoroughly, especially root vegetables. Making stock is the perfect solution for vegetables that are too unattractive cosmetically to be used in other ways. Leftover carrot sticks, parsley stems, and unused halves of onion can all be tossed into the pot.

2 large unpeeled potatoes, quartered	1 apple or pear, seeded and quartered
2 large carrots, peeled and sliced thickly	1 bay leaf
1 large onion, peeled and quartered	12 peppercorns
1 celery stalk, chopped	10 cups water (2½ quarts)

Put all of the ingredients into a large pot, bring to a boil, and simmer for 45 minutes to an hour. Strain and use.

For a spicier stock throw in some garlic cloves, skins and all, and a small amount of tomato. For a specifically Asian broth, add ginger, scallions, and shiitake mushrooms *(see Appendix)*. Or, make it sweet for a carrot purée or Scandinavian fruit soup with the addition of sweet potato or winter squash.

SALADS

Salads

S alads at Moosewood are much more than a mere healthy appetizer for "real food." They may serve as a first course, as the main meal itself, as a side dish, or even as dessert.

Salad making lends itself to creative experimentation. You don't have to consider the formulas necessary for baking or worry about some small oversight causing an eleventh hour failure. There are only a couple of common-sense principles for salad making such as using only the finest, freshest vegetables you can find, cutting them to an agreeably similar size, and never overwhelming the salad with too much marinade or an incautious dressing. Within that framework you can dream up intriguing innovations, mixing tastes, textures, and colors to create an appealing dish, different every time. We recommend that you keep a salad strong but simple, controlling the impulse to cram every single good thing to eat into the salad bowl at once. But even if you lose control, you can't go too far wrong with fresh salads.

Good salads directly reflect the seasons since they rely on the availability of fruits and vegetables at their prime. In fall and winter, salads can serve as the raw, crunchy, and refreshing accompaniment to soups and main dishes. Middle Eastern Carrot Salad is a welcome sidekick for Yogurt-Barley Soup or Kolokithopita. Or alternatively, salads themselves may become heavier and more complex – we start adding more cooked vegetables, grains, and beans as the weather turns cold. Consider Miso Broth with Broccoli-Mushroom-Tofu Salad and Spicy Szechuan Noodles.

When spring comes, a quick trip to the garden or produce stand will satisfy a winter's longing for the singular keen flavors of young lettuces, chives, asparagus, peas, and watercress. In summer, as the days become so long and lazy that no one wants to spend much time cooking, salads really shine. A lunch to eat while wearing a bathing suit might be Salat Tangiers with fresh fruit. If you marinate vegetables early in the day to serve later with a chilled soup and a crusty bread, then when the sun is setting out on the patio you can open a chilled bottle of wine and savor the full-blown flavors of summer in a meal of salad. And you'll have plenty of time to chase rabbits out of the garden.

Tossed Green Salad

We are great salad eaters at Moosewood. No matter what the season, the kitchen is hot and the work is vigorous, leaving us at the end of a long work shift with a yen for something clean and crisp. The many tossed salads recommended with our recipes throughout this book are a clear indication of our bias for greens. Our best-tasting salads follow these general rules.

Choosing the Greens

Use a selection of greens for a range of sweetness and pungency, tenderness and crunch. Our favorites include small-leafed romaine, escarole, fresh spinach, buttercrunch lettuce, and ruby and green leaf lettuce.

Preparing the Greens

Wash and dry the lettuce well. Immersing the greens in cold water is a gentler process than directing a harsh stream at the individual leaves. Then, a thorough drying will keep the lettuce from becoming limp and will allow the dressing to coat the salad evenly.

When it comes to drying, ingenuity is everything. We have patted our greens with paper towels and spun them in spinners. We have hung wire or cloth mesh baskets filled with greens over bathtubs and sinks. We have stuffed a pillow case with lettuce and stepped outside to spin it over our heads. We have also lightly wrapped our well-drained greens in a cloth and let them rest, peacefully, in the refrigerator. When the lettuce has dried, tear or cut it into 2- to 3-inch pieces.

Dressing Up the Greens

Toss the greens with some or all of the following: finely shredded red cabbage, grated carrots or beets, green or red pepper rings, tomato wedges, cucumber slices, ripe olives, alfalfa sprouts, marinated navy or garbanzo beans, marinated artichoke hearts, pepperoncini, capers, feta, Parmesan, or cheddar cheese, tofu kan *(see Appendix)*, or hard-boiled eggs, chopped or in wedges.

Finally, find the dressing that suits the salad and the occasion.

Make the salad a complete meal or just an accompaniment, but make it beautiful!

French Rice Salad

Serves 6

Here's a creative way of dealing with leftover rice – the result is a cool and crunchy, multicolored dish. It keeps well, tasting even better the next day, and it's easy to eat when you're on the road. The marinade in this recipe has many other uses as well. Try using it to marinate steamed artichokes or asparagus.

3 cups cooked rice *(see Appendix)*

1 cup diced carrots

1 cup diced green or red bell peppers

1 cup sliced mushrooms (4 ounces)

1 cup green peas, fresh or frozen

1 small celery stalk, finely chopped

2 tablespoons chopped fresh parsley

MARINADE

¼ cup olive oil

¼ cup vegetable oil

¼ to ⅓ cup fresh lemon juice

1 garlic clove, pressed

one or two of these herbs: 1 tablespoon fresh or 1 teaspoon dried tarragon, basil, dill, marjoram

□

tomato wedges and green olives

Place the cooked rice in a large bowl. Steam the carrots, peppers, mushrooms, and peas separately until tender but still firm. Add the steamed vegetables, celery, and parsley to the rice. Whisk the marinade ingredients together. Pour the marinade over the vegetable-rice mixture and toss gently.

Refrigerate until well chilled, stirring occasionally, so the marinade will flavor the rice. When ready to serve, garnish with tomato wedges and green olives.

Other serving options and accompaniments:
- A sprinkle of freshly grated Parmesan or feta cheese on the top
- Add dried currants, toasted pine nuts, or almonds
- A wedge of Brie, fontina, Jarlsberg, or any other good flavorful cheese
- Steamed and marinated vegetables
- Stuff a tomato shell or green pepper half with rice salad and bake it for a wintertime lunch

Salat Tangiers

Serves 4 to 6, more if used as a side dish

A confetti-like Moroccan pastiche of colors and flavors.

1½ cups dry couscous

½ teaspoon salt

pinch of saffron *(optional)*

1¼ cups boiling water

1 cup diced carrots

1 large pepper, diced

1 cup cut green or wax beans

⅓ cup finely chopped sliced red onions

⅓ cup currants

½ cup almonds, toasted and chopped

MARINADE

½ cup vegetable oil

4 tablespoons fresh lemon juice

½ teaspoon salt, or more to taste

¼ teaspoon cinnamon

3 tablespoons orange juice (or apple cider)

4 tablespoons chopped fresh parsley

1 tablespoon fresh spearmint (1 teaspoon dried)

pinch of cayenne

Put the couscous, salt, and saffron, if you're using it, in a large bowl, and stir in the boiling water. Cover and let sit for 10 to 15 minutes, stirring occasionally to fluff.

Meanwhile, steam the carrots, green peppers, and beans separately. As soon as each vegetable is barely tender, add it to the couscous. Stir in the red onions, currants, and almonds.

Whisk together the marinade ingredients, leaving out the mint if you used saffron in the couscous. Toss the couscous and vegetable mixture with the marinade and chill at least an hour to allow the flavors to marry.

Serve with Baba Ganouj *(p. 73)* or Tzatziki *(p. 207)* for a light lunch or with Armenian Lentil Soup *(p. 21)* to create a perfect protein.

Tuscan Potato Salad

Serves 8

The addition of the creamy ricotta cheese and robust Parmesan cheese makes this an unusual potato salad. Substantial enough for a salad-dinner, it's a fine side dish as well.

3 pounds (about 12 cups) peeled, cubed red or new white potatoes

⅔ cup freshly grated Parmesan cheese (2 ounces)

1 cup ricotta cheese (9 ounces)

4 garlic cloves, pressed

½ red onion, very thinly sliced

½ cup olive oil

6 tablespoons cider vinegar

salt and black pepper to taste

□

½ cup chopped fresh parsley

Cook the potatoes in boiling salted water until just tender. Drain the potatoes. While they are still hot, stir in the rest of the ingredients. Tuscan Potato Salad can be served warm but improves with chilling.

Garnish with parsley just before serving.

Tuscan Potato Salad is well complemented by Crème de Crécy *(p. 7)* or Tomato-Garlic Soup *(p. 11)*.

Middle Eastern Carrot Salad

Serves 4 to 6

An easy, light, and refreshing salad, sparkling with lemon and mint. Maple syrup gives it an interesting twist.

4 cups grated carrots

3 tablespoons fresh lemon juice

3 tablespoons vegetable oil

½ teaspoon ground coriander seeds

¼ teaspoon salt

2 teaspoons chopped fresh mint
  (½ teaspoon dried)

1 tablespoon chopped fresh parsley

1 to 2 teaspoons honey, sugar, or maple syrup *(optional)*

Mix all the ingredients together and chill at least one hour before serving.

In the summertime, when we serve our customers on the patio, we frequently offer a colorful Middle Eastern salad plate: a cup of Chilled Spinach-Yogurt Soup *(p. 8)*, a square of Kolokithopita *(p. 140)*, and side dishes of Tzatziki *(p. 207)*, a marinated artichoke half, and Middle Eastern Carrot Salad.

Artichoke Heart and Tomato Salad

Serves 4

Artichoke hearts are one of the few canned foods that we recommend and do use in our kitchen. Here they are combined with fresh, ripe tomatoes in a light marinade.

4 ripe, medium tomatoes

8 canned artichoke hearts (not marinated)

½ cup vegetable oil

⅛ cup wine vinegar or white vinegar

1 garlic clove, pressed

1 tablespoon fresh tarragon (¼ teaspoon dried)

1 tablespoon fresh basil (¼ teaspoon dried)

salt and black pepper to taste

Cut each tomato into 6 wedges and each artichoke heart into halves. Blend the rest of the ingredients, pour over the vegetables, and toss. Chill for 20 minutes.

Serve on a bed of greens with fish or a cheese-filled strudel, such as Kolokithopita *(p. 140)* or Cheese Börek *(p. 138)*. Or fill a pita with Artichoke Heart and Tomato Salad, greens, and grated feta or Parmesan cheese.

Peppers and Capers

Serves 4 to 6

We use Peppers and Capers as an interesting salad served on lettuce, as a sharp and assertive side dish, as a garnish for tossed salad, as a topping for baked fish, and as a stuffing for pita bread with greens and feta or Parmesan cheese.

½ cup vegetable oil

5 or 6 large green and/or red peppers, sliced in long, wide strips

1 tablespoon capers *(see Appendix)*

1 small red onion, thinly sliced

2 tablespoons olive oil

2 tablespoons red wine vinegar

1 garlic clove, pressed or minced

salt to taste

Heat the oil in a large, heavy skillet until quite hot. Fry the pepper strips. It is best to do this in two batches, turning the peppers often for even and thorough cooking. They should be well fried – even a little browning doesn't hurt. Drain the peppers on paper towels to absorb as much excess oil as possible.

Place the fried peppers, red onions, and capers in a bowl and dress them with the olive oil, vinegar, garlic, and salt. Toss well and chill.

Pasta Primavera

Serves 6 to 8

This is one of our favorite pasta salads. Make it in the winter using frozen basil or pesto.

1 pound pasta (shells or short tubes)

☐

2 tablespoons olive oil

3 garlic cloves, minced

3 cups sliced mushrooms (12 ounces)

2 cups asparagus, cut into 1-inch pieces

1 cup green peas

5 medium tomatoes, chopped

☐

**3 tablespoons chopped fresh basil and
1 tablespoon olive oil or 4
tablespoons Pesto Genovese** *(p. 151)*

2 tablespoons fresh lemon juice

**½ cup freshly grated Parmesan cheese
(1½ ounces)**

½ cup chopped fresh parsley

½ cup thinly sliced sun-dried tomatoes
(optional)

salt and black pepper to taste

Cook the pasta al dente *(see p. 145)*. Drain it and rinse with cold water. Sauté the garlic in olive oil for 1 minute. Add the mushrooms and cook on medium heat until just tender. Remove from the heat. Steam the asparagus and peas until tender.

Toss all the vegetables with the pasta. Add the rest of the ingredients and toss well.

Serve at room temperature on lettuce, with extra Parmesan.

Pasta Salad with Broccoli and Cashews

Serves 6 to 8

A popular dish for potlucks or summer luncheons.

1 pound medium pasta shells, whole wheat or white

☐

¼ cup vegetable oil

6 cups broccoli florets and peeled and sliced stems

2 cups sliced mushrooms (8 ounces)

1½ cups chopped fresh parsley

2 cups chopped scallions or ½ cup chopped red onion

☐

¼ to ½ cup white vinegar

1 cup Mayonnaise *(p. 57)*

1 teaspoon Dijon mustard

1 cup toasted, unsalted cashews

Cook the pasta al dente *(see p. 145)*, rinse with cold water, drain, toss with a little oil, and set aside.

Sauté the broccoli in the oil for about 10 minutes or until it starts to become tender. Stir frequently. Add the mushrooms and sauté for 5 minutes more. Stir in the parsley and scallions or onions and sauté for another minute. The broccoli should be bright green, yet easily pierced with a fork.

In a large mixing bowl, whisk together the vinegar, mayonnaise, and mustard. Stir in the sautéed vegetables and the pasta. Just before serving, stir in the cashews.

Serve cold or at room temperature as a summer salad with thick tomato slices sprinkled with fresh basil and a wedge of melon.

Princess Summer-Fall-Winter-Spring Pasta Salads

Pasta salads provide a good opportunity for us at Moosewood to improvise with seasonal vegetables and herbs. Suggestions listed below can be used as a starting point for developing your own innovative salads. Choices of vegetables, dressings, and pasta should take into consideration shape, color, and texture. Pasta shapes that are hollow (penne, rigatoni) or curved (shells, spirals) are good for salads because other ingredients adhere well to them. Color can be contrasting and festive (as in our summer and fall variations) or shades and tones of one color (as in our spring variation). Textures provide added interest: soft pasta, tender yet crisp vegetables, and crunchy toasted nuts.

- *Spring:* Steamed peas or snow peas and 1-inch asparagus pieces, tossed with spinach shells and pastel green Herbed Mayonnaise *(p. 57)*.
- *Summer:* Steamed spears of broccoli and rounds of summer squash tossed with cherry tomatoes, penne (or other tubular pasta), and Vinaigrette Salad Dressing *(p. 50)* with fresh tarragon as the dominant herb.
- *Fall:* Steamed cauliflower florets and julienned red pepper and zucchini, tossed with shells, sun-dried tomatoes *(see Appendix)*, Vegetable Marinade *(p. 56)*, and toasted pine nuts or almonds.
- *Winter:* Steamed carrot sticks and green beans tossed with artichoke hearts, the Aïoli Sauce variation of Mayonnaise *(p. 57)*, and multicolored spiral pasta.

Garnishes for All Seasons:
- freshly grated Parmesan cheese
- chopped parsley and/or chives
- pimiento strips
- black olives

Spicy Szechuan Noodles

Serves 4 to 6

Some years ago, Ashley Miller and Bob Love, both Moosewood cooks, introduced this popular dish to the rest of us. They had discovered it in Chinese cooking classes with Stella Fessler, one of our Ithaca mentors. We've been grateful for it ever since.

Today, similar spicy noodle salads seem to be on the menus of most Asian restaurants and every slightly trendy café, but it is still a favorite with us, and we think you'll be glad to learn how easy it is to make at home.

½ pound whole wheat spaghetti or soba noodles *(see Appendix)*

☐

¼ cup peanut butter (or a mixture of peanut butter and tahini)

¼ cup warm water

3 tablespoons tamari soy sauce

2 tablespoons wine vinegar (preferably rice wine vinegar)

1 tablespoon dark sesame oil *(see Appendix)*

1 teaspoon hot chili oil *(see Appendix)*

2 cups fresh mung bean sprouts

1 cucumber, peeled, cut lengthwise, seeded, and cut into crescent slices

☐

chopped scallions

toasted sesame seeds

Cook the pasta al dente in salted water. Drain it and rinse with cold water. Mix the peanut butter, warm water, soy sauce, vinegar, and oils. Toss the noodles with the bean sprouts, cucumbers, and sauce. Top with chopped scallions and/or toasted sesame seeds, if desired. This dish is most flavorful served at room temperature.

Spicy Szechuan Noodles are attractive served on crisp leaves of romaine. Create an Asian ensemble with Korean Greens *(p. 212)*, Broccoli-Mushroom-Tofu Salad *(p. 47)*, or Asian Asparagus Salad *(p. 48)*.

Goi Ga – Vietnamese Salad

Serves 4 to 6

This is a dish for people who enjoy hot and spicy food. Different elements of the salad are prepared separately and assembled on the serving table. It's a salad that is a meal in itself, a spirited blend of ingredients with added visual appeal.

1 cup cooked rice *(see Appendix)* **per serving**

□

½ small red onion, very thinly sliced

1 medium carrot, cut into thin strips

1 green pepper, cut into thin strips

10 ounces fresh spinach, cleaned, stemmed, and dried

1 small cucumber, peeled, cut in half lengthwise, seeded, and sliced diagonally

other raw vegetables, such as turnips and white radishes, cut into thin strips

some leafy lettuces (buttercrunch, ruby, Boston, curly), torn into bite-size pieces

VIETNAMESE SAUCE

3 tablespoons white vinegar

3 tablespoons Thai or other Asian fish sauce *(see Appendix)* *

2 small dried hot peppers, soaked in ½ cup boiling water until soft and then minced

2 tablespoons fresh lemon juice

□

2 cups unsalted roasted peanuts, coarsely chopped

1 cup mung bean sprouts

Cook the rice, place in a bowl, and set aside. Prepare the vegetables, toss them together in a bowl, and set aside. Mix together the sauce ingredients in a bowl. Put the peanuts and the mung bean sprouts in bowls.

To serve the salad, simply take everything to the table. Pass the bowls. On individual plates each person will pile salad vegetables on rice, pour on some sauce, and top with peanuts and sprouts.

---

* *For a vegetarian version of this sauce, substitute tamari soy sauce for the Asian fish sauce.*

Broccoli-Mushroom-Tofu Salad

Serves 6

A salad of contrasting tastes and textures: crisp-tender broccoli, mushrooms, and smooth tofu in a ginger marinade.

3 cakes of tofu, pressed *(see Appendix)* **and cubed**

1 large bunch broccoli

3 cups sliced mushrooms (12 ounces)

4 scallions, sliced diagonally

MARINADE

3 garlic cloves, pressed

1 tablespoon grated fresh ginger root

3 tablespoons dark sesame oil *(see Appendix)*

6 tablespoons tamari soy sauce

6 tablespoons Chinese rice wine *(see Appendix)* **or dry sherry**

¼ teaspoon ground fennel seeds

⅛ teaspoon cayenne

Press the tofu while preparing the vegetables.

Rinse the broccoli. Discard the woody bottoms of the stems. Cut off the florets on 1-inch stems. Peel the thick lower stalks, cut them into lengthwise strips, and then again, diagonally, into 1-inch pieces. Steam the broccoli until just tender and still bright green. Rinse immediately with cold water (to stop the cooking and preserve crispness) and drain.

Steam the sliced mushrooms briefly, a minute or two. Rinse with cold water and drain. Combine the broccoli, mushrooms, and scallions in a large bowl.

In a small bowl whisk together the marinade ingredients. Pour half the marinade over the vegetables. Pour the rest of the marinade over the cubed tofu in a separate bowl. Allow to marinate for an hour or more, gently turning the vegetables and the tofu several times with a wooden spoon.

Toss everything together just before serving.

This salad goes well with Spicy Szechuan Noodles *(p. 45)* or brown rice tossed with toasted sesame seeds. We often serve it on a bed of salad greens, topped with toasted walnuts or almonds, and garnished with a wedge of cantaloupe.

Asian Asparagus Salad

Serves 4 to 6

When you hear the first spring peepers and the breeze feels gentle, celebrate the end of winter with asparagus prepared in an Asian way that is as elegant in its simplicity as a spring haiku. Sometimes steamed green vegetables lose their color, even when you are careful not to overcook them. Follow our directions for keeping those greens green. Broccoli and green beans are also delicious with this marinade.

1½ pounds fresh asparagus

MARINADE

2 tablespoons tamari soy sauce

1½ teaspoons sugar

1 tablespoon dark sesame oil *(see Appendix)*

1 tablespoon white vinegar

1 tablespoon Chinese rice wine *(see Appendix)* **or dry sherry**

½ teaspoon grated fresh ginger root

½ teaspoon Chinese chili paste *(optional) (see Appendix)*

☐

lightly toasted sesame seeds

Whisk together the marinade ingredients and set aside.

Wash the asparagus and remove the tough ends. Ease the asparagus spears into boiling water to cover. The water will stop boiling with the addition of the asparagus. Keep covered on high heat until the water returns to a rapid boil. Cook one or two minutes longer, until the asparagus are tender but still crisp. Plunge the cooked asparagus immediately into cold water to stop the cooking and set the color. Drain well, place in a shallow bowl, and cover with the marinade. Chill at least 30 minutes, but do not wait longer than 2 hours before serving.

Garnish with a sprinkle of toasted sesame seeds.

This dish is also very good served hot. Just drain the hot, cooked vegetables, toss them with the marinade, garnish, and serve.

Asian Asparagus Salad is well paired with Spicy Szechuan Noodles *(p. 45)*, Spicy Peanut Soup *(p. 15)*, or Fish with Teriyaki Sauce *(p. 175)*.

L.D.'s Creamy Green Dressing

Yields 2 cups

This is one of our most frequently requested and admired recipes – our daily house dressing. L.D. (Linda Dickinson) has been working at Moosewood since 1973 and so has had plenty of time to perfect this recipe.

1 cup vegetable oil

2 tablespoons cider vinegar or fresh lemon juice

1 teaspoon honey or 2 tablespoons apple juice

5 or 6 spinach leaves

2 tablespoons chopped fresh parsley

1 teaspoon fresh basil (¼ teaspoon dried)

1 teaspoon fresh marjoram (¼ teaspoon dried)

½ teaspoon salt

1 garlic clove, pressed

1 cup buttermilk

Blend all of the ingredients, except the buttermilk, for one minute. While the blender is running, slowly pour in the buttermilk. As soon as the dressing thickens, turn off the blender or the dressing will separate and become runny. It should be thick and creamy. Chill at least 30 minutes so the flavors have a chance to meld.

Other herbs can be used to vary this dressing. Dill, tarragon, oregano, a dab of Dijon mustard, and freshly ground black pepper are all possible additions or substitutions. Fresh herbs in season are always our choice when available. Yogurt or sour cream may be substituted for the buttermilk. However, buttermilk makes the most creamy and stable (non-separating) dressing.

Refrigerated and tightly covered, it will stay fresh for up to a week. If the dressing separates, reblend.

Vinaigrette Salad Dressing

Yields 1¼ cups

This dressing will enhance, without upstaging, a wide variety of salads. Create a basic vinaigrette by omitting the herbs or choose just one or two as a more dominant note. This will keep indefinitely if refrigerated.

½ cup vegetable oil

¼ cup olive oil

⅓ cup cider vinegar or red wine vinegar

2 garlic cloves, pressed

¼ teaspoon salt

1 tablespoon Dijon mustard

⅛ teaspoon black pepper

1 tablespoon chopped fresh parsley

2 tablespoons chopped fresh basil, marjoram, dill, chives, tarragon in any combination (2 teaspoons dried)

Whisk together all ingredients.

Yogurt-Tahini Dressing

Yields 2 cups

A quick dressing, popular in Middle Eastern countries, Yogurt-Tahini has its own distinctive tang and fullness.

¾ cup plain yogurt

⅓ cup tahini *(see Appendix)*

3 to 6 tablespoons fresh lemon juice

2 garlic cloves, pressed

½ teaspoon salt

¼ cup milk or water

pinch of ground cumin *(optional)*

1 tablespoon chopped fresh parsley *(optional)*

In a medium bowl, whisk together all ingredients until smoothly blended. If the dressing is thicker than you like, add more milk or water.

This dressing is versatile. It's good with salads, pitas, Tofu Burgers *(p. 134)*, Soyfalafel *(p. 136)*, or dipping vegetables.

Refrigerated and tightly covered, it will keep for up to a week.

Flora's Tart and Tangy Dressing

Yields 2 cups

Flora Marranca has contributed much to the original style of Moosewood's cuisine. This is a vibrant, herb-filled dressing, good for cutting the richness of an Italian meal, yet hearty enough to enhance a chef's salad or Caesar salad.

1 large tomato, chopped, or 1 cup cleaned, chopped spinach

1 large lemon, peeled, seeded, and cut into small pieces

2 garlic cloves, pressed

2 tablespoons tamari soy sauce

1 tablespoon fresh oregano (1 teaspoon dried)

1 tablespoon fresh basil (1 teaspoon dried)

1 cup vegetable oil

½ cup olive oil

salt to taste

Place all the ingredients in a blender or food processor and blend until they are thoroughly combined.

Refrigerated and covered, this will keep for up to ten days

Blue Cheese Dressing

Yields a generous 2½ cups

A lusty dressing for ardent lovers of blue (no matter how you spell it) cheese.

1 garlic clove, minced or pressed	**¼ teaspoon black pepper**
6 ounces blue cheese	**2 tablespoons fresh lemon juice**
1½ cups sour cream	**½ cup milk**
½ teaspoon salt	

Put all the ingredients except a third of the blue cheese in a blender or food processor. Blend to a smooth, creamy consistency. Crumble the remaining blue cheese and stir it into the dressing.

Refrigerated and tightly covered, Blue Cheese Dressing will stay fresh for 4 or 5 days. Try it as a dip, as well as on salads.

Miso-Ginger Dressing

Yields 2½ cups

A very popular and lively non-dairy dressing which has introduced many of our customers to the use of miso as a delicious, nutritious seasoning. Perfect on a fresh spinach salad with grated carrot. Excellent as a marinade for steamed broccoli and tofu.

3 to 4 tablespoons light miso *(see Appendix)*

2 tablespoons grated fresh ginger root

¼ cup cider vinegar or ⅓ cup fresh lemon juice

2 tablespoons dark sesame oil *(see Appendix)*

1 cup vegetable oil

½ cup water

In a blender on low speed, combine 3 tablespoons miso, the ginger, vinegar or lemon juice, and sesame oil. Gradually add the vegetable oil in a thin, steady stream until thoroughly mixed. Then very slowly add the water until the dressing is thick and creamy. Taste. If a richer flavor is preferred, blend in an additional tablespoon of miso.

Miso-Ginger Dressing will keep almost forever stored in the refrigerator. If the dressing separates, reblend.

Avocado Dressing

Yields 3 cups

Avocados lend a tropical flavor to this pastel dressing.

1 large or 2 small ripe avocados, peeled, pitted, and chopped

¼ cup vegetable or olive oil

⅓ cup fresh lemon juice or cider vinegar

pinch of cayenne

salt to taste

1 garlic clove, pressed

½ teaspoon ground cumin *(optional)*

¾ cup water

In a blender or food processor, blend all the ingredients, except the water, until smooth. Slowly add the water, blending, until the dressing has a soft mayonnaise-like consistency. Chill 20 minutes before serving.

Store refrigerated, using a covered container to minimize discoloration. Avocado Dressing will remain fresh for two to three days.

Vegetable Marinade

Yields 1 cup

This unobtrusive marinade highlights the natural flavors of fresh vegetables such as broccoli, green beans, zucchini, cauliflower, carrots, mushrooms, red or green peppers, asparagus, artichokes, tomatoes, and snow or snap peas.

½ cup vegetable oil

½ cup olive oil

5 tablespoons fresh lemon juice

2 garlic cloves, pressed

¾ teaspoon salt

¼ teaspoon ground fennel seed *(optional)*

½ teaspoon dried marjoram *(optional)*

dash of black pepper

1 tablespoon chopped fresh parsley

Whisk all ingredients together.

Steam or parboil the vegetables to be marinated. Drain the vegetables well and pour the marinade over them while they're still hot. Marinate for at least an hour, spooning the marinade over them occasionally.

Leftover marinade will keep indefinitely if refrigerated.

Mayonnaise

Yields 1 generous cup

With a food processor or blender, you can easily prepare a homemade mayonnaise that is dramatically superior to store-bought mayonnaise.

1 egg

5 teaspoons vinegar or fresh lemon juice

½ teaspoon salt

2 teaspoons Dijon mustard

dash of Tabasco sauce or cayenne

1 cup vegetable oil

1 tablespoon hot water

Place the egg, vinegar or lemon juice, and seasonings in a blender or food processor. Turn on the blender and begin adding the oil, drop by drop. Gradually increase the flow of oil to a thin stream. Continue until all of the oil is used or until the mayonnaise is the right consistency. Blend in a tablespoon of hot water to stabilize the mayonnaise.

Mayonnaise will stay fresh refrigerated for up to a week.

Variations

- *Herbed Mayonnaise:* Add chopped scallions or chives and finely chopped fresh basil, tarragon, and/or dill.
- *Aïoli Sauce:* Start by adding one pressed garlic clove. Add more garlic to taste. Aïoli Sauce is delicious on steamed vegetables and chilled fish. Optional: replace half of the vegetable oil with olive oil.
- *Russian Dressing:* Peel a tomato and squeeze out the juice and seeds. Mince the pulp and add to the mayonnaise with chopped scallions and horseradish to taste. The color will be pale, but the taste of each ingredient will be fresh and distinct.

Tofu Green Dressing

Yields 3 cups

Tofu is such a versatile food! This appealing dressing is non-dairy and high in protein.

½ **cake of tofu, blanched and crumbled**
   (see Appendix)

6 fresh spinach leaves

1 scallion, chopped

¼ **green pepper, chopped**

3 tablespoons cider vinegar

1 tablespoon fresh basil (1 teaspoon dried)

¾ **teaspoon salt**

¼ **teaspoon black pepper**

½ **cup water**

1 cup vegetable oil

Place all the ingredients except the oil in a blender or food processor and blend them until liquefied. With the blender or food processor running, slowly drizzle in a steady stream of oil until the dressing thickens.

Refrigerated and covered, Tofu Green Dressing will stay fresh for up to a week.

Tahini-Garlic Dressing

Yields 1½ cups

A robust garlic dressing with a nutty, sesame taste. This strongly-flavored dressing is at its best on a very simple salad of one lettuce, such as romaine or buttercrunch.

½ **cup tahini** *(see Appendix)*

2 **tablespoons vegetable oil**

¼ **cup fresh lemon juice**

½ **cup water**

1 **teaspoon cider vinegar**

2 **teaspoons tamari soy sauce**

1 **or 2 garlic cloves, pressed**

⅛ **teaspoon black pepper**

Place all the ingredients in a blender or food processor and blend thoroughly.

Refrigerated, this dressing will keep indefinitely.

SANDWICHES AND DIPS

Sandwiches and Dips

Eating something tasty between two pieces of bread is an age-old custom and arises from the need for a satisfying meal that can be consumed anywhere and in a short time. We imagine the ancients rubbing a crust of bread with oil and garlic and eating it with cheese during a break from tilling the soil. For most of us, though, this kind of simple and fitting repast has fallen on hard times. Recently sandwiches have become the staple of the fast food phenomenon in our culture, which is synonymous with junk food, and that's too bad.

At Moosewood, we value the quick, portable, and casual qualities of sandwiches, but we think they should be prepared with the same imagination we give to the rest of our cuisine. Sometimes a sandwich is just what we want and all that we want, even when we're not in a hurry, not on the move, and not wearing jeans.

These sandwich recipes and suggestions are consistent with our ideas of a classic sandwich, an easy-going meal. Some, such as the B.L. Tease, Tempeh Reuben, and Nutty Butter Spread, are variations of old standbys. Others are in the tradition of the Dagwood sandwich, glorifying unusual combinations. Many of our salads, dressings, dips, and even main dishes make suitable sandwich fillings.

When we think of making a sandwich using pita bread, we first tip our hat to the Middle East with Hummus with Tahini, Baba Ganouj, and feta cheese for ethnic consistency. But then, considering that pita bread is now very much a part of our crazy-quilt food culture, we like to mix things up a bit with Danish, Jakarta, and California Pitas. In a one-world sandwich, anything goes.

We think pita bread is at its best warmed or toasted. We serve pita sandwiches upright in a bowl, so the pocket bread won't spill its contents. If it's got to be a movable feast, we suggest that you keep the filling and the bread separate until serving time, lest the moist dressing cause the bottom to drop out of your sandwich. We have no useful tips on how to manage to transport a brimful pita from hand to mouth, while in a public place and/or polite company. Just persevere and prop up your dignity with the thought that at least your sandwich didn't come in a styrofoam box.

Tempeh Reuben

Serves 4

Get out the dill pickles! This is a wonderful sandwich.

This is one of our favorite sandwiches at Moosewood. When it is on the lunch menu, the workers have to be chased out of the kitchen to ensure that there will be enough for the customers.

¼ cup vegetable oil

2 cups chopped onions

2 garlic cloves, minced or pressed

8 ounces tempeh *(see Appendix)*, thinly sliced or cubed

2 teaspoons tamari soy sauce

☐

4 slices of bread, preferably rye, toasted

1½ cups Russian Dressing *(p. 57)*

1½ cups sauerkraut, warmed

1½ to 2 cups grated Swiss cheese (5 to 7 ounces)

Sauté the onions and garlic in oil for 2 or 3 minutes until the onions begin to soften. Add the tempeh and continue to sauté on low heat, stirring frequently, for about 20 minutes. While the tempeh is browning, get the remaining ingredients ready. When the tempeh is crisp and lightly browned, add the soy sauce.

Build the sandwiches on the toast by layering the tempeh mixture, Russian Dressing, sauerkraut, and Swiss cheese. Broil the sandwiches until the cheese is melted. Serve piping hot.

Thirteen Pita Sandwiches

Here are some of our most popular pita sandwich fillings. Cut vegetables such as tomatoes and cucumbers into bite-size pieces and shred or tear spinach, iceberg, romaine, and loose leaf lettuces for the greens. We use whole wheat pita bread because we prefer its taste and texture.

- *Antipasto Pita:* Any of the zesty ingredients you would put on an antipasto platter are appropriate here. Try pepperoncini *(see Appendix)*, hard-boiled eggs, chopped sun-dried tomatoes *(see Appendix)*, provolone cheese cubes, cucumbers, green peppers, fresh tomatoes, greens, garbanzo beans, bite-size pieces of marinated vegetables, and Vinaigrette Salad Dressing *(p. 50)*.

- *California Pita:* Cubes of avocado, ripe olives, and Monterey Jack cheese place this pita west of the Sierra Nevadas. Add tomatoes, greens, alfalfa sprouts, cucumbers, and Vinaigrette Salad Dressing *(p. 50)*.

- *Danish Pita:* The Danes have been eating sandwiches for a very long time. Here we fill a pita, instead of topping a slice of bread, with greens, Jarlsberg cheese slices, cucumbers, tomatoes, paper-thin slices of red onion, and Mayonnaise *(p. 57)*.

- *Jakarta Pita:* Marinated Tofu *(p. 210)*, fresh spinach leaves, and grated carrots topped with Spicy Peanut Sauce *(p. 191)* and mung bean or alfalfa sprouts create a Southeast Asia-inspired combo.

- *Pita Refrita:* The promise of Pita Refrita for lunch is a good reason for planning to have Refried Beans left over from dinner. Fill the pita with greens, Refried Beans *(p. 208)*, Hot Sauce *(p. 193)*, and grated cheddar cheese.

- *Pesto Pita:* Pesto Genovese *(p. 151)*, Tofu Pesto *(p. 153)*, and Winter Pesto *(p. 154)* all make delicious sandwich fillings. Add crispy greens and juicy tomato chunks and top with freshly grated Parmesan cheese, if desired.

- *Spinach-Mushroom Pita:* Fresh crispy leaves of spinach, sliced raw mushrooms, grated carrots, and chopped tomatoes with any dressing. The addition of sliced hard-boiled eggs and julienned cheese could make this a Chef's Salad Pita.

- *Garden Vegetable-Feta Pita:* Tangy feta cheese and Yogurt-Tahini Dressing *(p. 51)* together with crunchy green peppers, cucumbers, grated carrots, and tomatoes create a Moosewood standby.
- *Baba Ganouj or Hummus Pita:* Combine greens, tomatoes, and cucumbers with Baba Ganouj *(p. 73)* or Hummus with Tahini *(p. 74)*, two spreads which have been filling pita breads for perhaps millenia. For an update, add some crispy alfalfa sprouts.
- *B.L. Tease:* Grate some smoked Swiss cheese and tofu kan *(see Appendix)* to provide the bacony flavor, and accompany with – what else? – lettuce, tomatoes, and Mayonnaise *(p. 57)*.
- *Pita Kan:* Sliced tofu kan *(see Appendix)*, tomatoes, cucumbers, greens, and Yogurt-Tahini Dressing *(p. 51)* or Miso-Ginger Dressing *(p. 54)*, topped with sauerkraut, make a perky pita.
- *2nd Avenue Pita:* Sliced tofu kan *(see Appendix)*, sauerkraut, sliced tomatoes, and Russian Dressing *(p. 57)*.
- *Dixie Pita:* Line the pita with leafy greens and fill with "Barbecued" Tempeh or Tofu *(p. 117)* and, possibly, a grated mild cheese or tangy cole slaw.

What is Moosewood? A moosewood is a tenacious little maple tree that grows in the understory of moist, shady woodland in Ithaca and elsewhere. It's also the name of a canine character in a book by Hugh Prather.

Blue Max

Serves 4

Thick Blue Cheese Dressing covers lightly sautéed vegetables to create a satisfying hot open-faced sandwich to be eaten with a fork, napkin at the ready.

2 tablespoons vegetable oil
1 medium onion, chopped
1 large carrot, in thin diagonal slices
3 cups chopped white cabbage
salt and pepper to taste
2 cups sliced mushrooms (8 ounces)

1½ teaspoons fresh dill (½ teaspoon dried)

□

4 thick slices of whole wheat bread
Blue Cheese Dressing *(p. 53)*

Sauté the onions in oil for 1 minute on high heat. Add the carrots and cook for 2 minutes, stirring frequently. Add the cabbage, salt, and pepper and cook for 2 more minutes, stirring often. Stir in the mushrooms and dill. Cover, lower the heat to medium, and cook until the vegetables are tender.

Toast the whole wheat bread. On individual plates, ladle the vegetables over toast, top with Blue Cheese Dressing, and serve.

- *White Russian:* Prepare vegetables as for Blue Max except sauté 1 garlic clove, minced, with the onions. When vegetables are tender add 6 ounces cream cheese and stir until the cheese melts. Serve on whole wheat toast and, if feeling indulgent, top with Blue Cheese Dressing or crumbled blue cheese.

Mexican Vegetables on Corn Bread

Serves 4 to 6

This is a filling open-faced sandwich to be eaten with a fork for a casual, hearty lunch. Wash it down with lemonade or a beer.

2 tablespoons vegetable oil

2 cups chopped onions

2 garlic cloves, minced

3 carrots, cut into half-moons

1 medium zucchini, cut into half-moons

1 green pepper, diced

2 cups corn, fresh or frozen

2 cups undrained canned tomatoes, chopped

1 teaspoon ground cumin

1 teaspoon ground coriander

1 tablespoon chopped fresh cilantro *(optional)*

salt and cayenne to taste

additional tomato juice, if needed

□

Corn Bread *(p. 235)*

1 cup sour cream *or* 1 cup grated Monterey Jack or cheddar cheese (3 ounces)

In a large skillet, sauté the onions and garlic in the oil for 5 minutes. Add the carrots, cover the pan, and sauté for another 5 minutes, stirring occasionally. Stir in the remaining vegetables and seasonings and cook on low heat until the vegetables are just tender. The mixture should be saucy; add more tomato juice if necessary.

Serve over hot Corn Bread and top with sour cream or cheese. For a hearty variation, try adding some sautéed tempeh cubes.

Herbed Cream Cheese

Yields 1¼ cups

For breakfast, serve Herbed Cream Cheese on toasted bagels or as a filling for omelettes. For lunch, serve it on toast topped with tomato slices and sprouts. Whipped until it's light and frothy and served with whole grain crackers or crudités, it makes a nice change from that tired old onion dip. Should you have any left over, it can be warmed to use in a cheese strudel filling or in a creamy soup to thicken and enhance the flavor.

8 ounces cream cheese, at room
  temperature

1 tablespoon finely chopped fresh dill
  (1 teaspoon dried)

1 tablespoon finely chopped fresh
  parsley

1 tablespoon finely chopped fresh basil
  (1 teaspoon dried)

2 tablespoons finely chopped fresh
  chives or scallion greens

black pepper to taste

Blend the herbs into the softened cream cheese using a food processor or electric mixer or by hand with a fork. Cover and chill.

Other possible additions:
- Chopped sun-dried tomatoes *(see Appendix)*
- Finely chopped jalapeño peppers
- Hot red pepper sauce
- Pimiento slivers
- Pressed garlic
- Toasted ground nuts
- Fresh tarragon, chervil, or marjoram

Nutty Butter Spread

Yields about 4 cups, enough for 8 generous sandwiches

Nutty Butter is good spread on bread and then topped with slices of fruit. Some of our children and their friends like to dip celery sticks or chunks of apple and pear into it.

⅓ **cup sunflower seeds**

¼ **cup sesame seeds**

½ **cup cashews**

2 cups smooth or chunky peanut butter *(see Appendix)*, **at room temperature**

1 cup tahini *(see Appendix)*

1 teaspoon honey *(optional)*

Lightly toast the sunflower and sesame seeds. Chop the cashews and toast lightly. Thoroughly mix all ingredients. This spread lasts a long time when refrigerated.

Feta-Ricotta Spread

Serves 6 as a sandwich spread, many more as a dip

This is a versatile spread, wonderful on dark rye bread with tomato slices and alfalfa sprouts. Or serve it alongside Hummus with Tahini *(p. 74)* and Baba Ganouj *(p. 73)* with vegetables and pita bread for dipping and you've created a Moosewood special known as Casablanca Combo.

2 cups ricotta cheese (1 pound)	¼ to ½ cup chopped fresh parsley
1½ to 2 cups grated feta cheese (7 to 10 ounces)	1 tablespoon chopped fresh chives or scallions
1 tablespoon olive oil	1 teaspoon fresh dill (¼ teaspoon dried)

Mix all the ingredients together with a fork and chill for 30 minutes so that the flavors mingle. For a creamier consistency, mix all the ingredients in the bowl of a food processor.

Leftover spread may be used in the filling for Cheese Börek *(p.138)* or Kolokithopita *(p. 140)* or in the topping of Zucchini-Feta Casserole *(p. 114)*.

Baba Ganouj

(Middle Eastern Eggplant Purée)

Yields 3 cups; serves 4 to 6 as a sandwich spread and more as a dip

The tantalizing taste and texture of roasted eggplant is eternally appealing.

2 pounds eggplant, preferably thin, small ones if roasting over a flame

6 tablespoons fresh lemon juice

4 tablespoons tahini *(see Appendix)*

1 to 4 garlic cloves, pressed or minced

2 tablespoons finely chopped fresh parsley

salt to taste

☐

chopped scallions

olive oil

Pierce the skins of the eggplants several times with a fork and place them on a baking sheet. Bake the whole eggplants at 400° until they are crinkly on the outside and very soft inside, about 40 minutes to 1 hour, depending on their size. Or, for an authentically smoky flavor, skewer the whole eggplants and roast them directly over a flame until they are well charred on the outside. In either case, when the eggplants are cool enough to handle, scoop out the insides. Purée the eggplant pulp and the remaining ingredients in a food processor until smooth. Or mash the eggplant with a fork until smooth and then stir in the remaining ingredients. Cool to room temperature.

Top with chopped scallions and a little olive oil and serve as a dip for raw vegetables with toasted pita bread on the side. Decorate with cherry tomatoes and Greek olives. Baba Ganouj also makes a good Pita Sandwich *(p. 66)*.

Hummus with Tahini

Serves 6 to 8 as a sandwich spread or enough dip for a party

Hummus is an authentic and appealing staple food of Middle Eastern cuisine. It's a perfect balance: the mild and nutty flavor of garbanzo beans is enhanced by zesty lemon and robust garlic.

3 cups well-cooked garbanzo beans (*see Appendix*)

1 cup garbanzo bean cooking liquid or water

4 to 5 tablespoons fresh lemon juice

½ cup tahini (*see Appendix*)

3 garlic cloves, pressed

1 teaspoon salt

⅛ teaspoon cayenne (*optional*)

¼ cup chopped fresh parsley

Hummus is most easily made in a food processor. However, a blender or even a potato masher may be used if the garbanzo beans are very tender.

If using a food processor, process the garbanzo beans with ½ cup of the bean liquid and the lemon juice. Then add the tahini, garlic, and seasonings, being careful not to overblend. The texture of hummus should be both rough and creamy at the same time. Add as much of the reserved cup of liquid as you need to get the consistency you want. Stir in the chopped parsley.

If using a blender, the hummus should be made in 2 or 3 batches with frequent stops to stir the contents up from the bottom of the blender using as much of the reserved bean liquid or water as needed.

If done by hand, mash the garbanzo beans with a bit of their liquid in a flat-bottomed bowl with a potato masher or large pestle. Add the rest of the ingredients and mix well.

Serve as a dip with raw vegetable sticks or toasted pita bread. Try it in a Pita Sandwich *(p. 66)*. This is also a fine side dish with a Mediterranean menu.

Hummus will keep for several days refrigerated. It freezes very well.

Mediterranean Eggplant Caviar

Serves 4 to 6

Moosewood's Wynelle Stein has vivid memories from her childhood of many chilly, drizzling Philadelphia days made warm and sunny as her mother and grandmother prepared this special dish to conjure up the old country.

2 medium eggplants	**2 tablespoons chopped fresh parsley**
2 peppers (1 red and 1 green is nice)	**2 tablespoons olive oil**
□	**2½ teaspoons cider or wine vinegar**
1 celery stalk, finely chopped	**2 garlic cloves, pressed**
1 large tomato, chopped	**salt and cayenne to taste**
1 tablespoon capers *(see Appendix),* **chopped**	

Preheat oven to 400°. Pierce the skins of the eggplants several times with a fork. Place the whole peppers and the eggplants right on the oven rack and line the bottom of the oven with aluminum foil to catch any juices. Done this way, the eggplants and peppers will roast evenly without being turned.

While the eggplants and peppers are roasting, combine everything else in a large bowl.

When the peppers blister in about 25 minutes, remove them from the oven and cool for 5 minutes. Then peel, seed, and chop the peppers and add them to the bowl. The eggplants will take about 50 minutes. Remove them from the oven, scoop out the pulp, chop it finely, and add it to the bowl. Discard the eggplant skins. Add salt and cayenne to taste.

Marinate the "caviar" in the refrigerator for at least 2 hours before serving, or better yet overnight.

This eggplant salad is great with Greek olives, crackers, crudités, and pita bread and harmonizes well with other Middle Eastern appetizers, such as Hummus with Tahini *(p. 74)*, Feta-Ricotta Spread *(p. 72)*, and Tzatziki *(p. 207)*.

Guacamole

Yields at least 2 cups

It's difficult to improve upon the taste of fresh, ripe avocado. Mixed with a bit of garlic and lemon juice, you've got the makings of a dip, appetizer, or sandwich filling.

2 ripe avocados	**fresh lemon or lime juice to taste**
1 to 3 garlic cloves, pressed	**salt and red pepper to taste**

Slice the avocados in half. Remove the pit and scoop out the avocado flesh with a spoon. If you're using smooth, green-skinned large Florida avocados, which are less rich than the smaller, bumpy, darker-skinned California avocados, you may wish to add a teaspoon of vegetable oil.

In a food processor or a mixing bowl, combine the avocado, garlic, and lemon or lime juice to taste. Stir in salt and red pepper to taste. Serve immediately or chill covered. After chilling, taste again for lemon juice.

Mushroom Pâté

Serves 6

The Vegetarian Epicure by Anna Thomas is one of our favorite cookbooks. Her mushroom pâté inspired us to develop this recipe. Mushroom Pâté can be served as a snack, appetizer, side dish, or picnic fare.

1 tablespoon vegetable oil

⅔ cup chopped scallions

1 celery stalk, chopped

5 cups sliced mushrooms (1 pound, 4 ounces)

½ teaspoon dried basil

¼ teaspoon dried thyme

□

1 cup whole wheat bread crumbs

½ cup walnuts, chopped

¼ cup tahini *(see Appendix)*

2 tablespoons tamari soy sauce

1 cake of tofu, blanched *(see Appendix)* and crumbled

⅛ teaspoon black pepper

⅛ teaspoon cayenne

Sauté the scallions and celery in the oil until the scallion whites are translucent. Add the mushrooms, basil, and thyme and continue to cook on low heat until the mushrooms have softened.

Combine the sautéed vegetables with the rest of the ingredients and blend in a food processor or, in small quantities, in a blender.

Oil a medium loaf pan and line it with waxed paper, allowing several inches of waxed paper to hang over the sides of the pan. Oil the waxed paper. Spoon in the pâté. Fold the waxed paper across the top and bake for about 1½ hours at 400°. The pâté is done when a toothpick inserted in the center comes out clean.

When the pâté is cool, fold back the waxed paper on top. Invert the pâté onto a platter and carefully peel away the paper.

Arrange thin slices of the pâté with greens on a platter and serve with various breads, crackers, dips, and crudités for an opulent display.

MAIN DISHES

Main Dishes

What do vegetarians eat? If you're a vegetarian, perhaps you've had the experience of going to a restaurant and discovering that there was nothing on the menu for you. So you settled for a scoop of instant white rice surrounded by overcooked, naked vegetables. Or maybe you were presented with a mound of cottage cheese seated on iceberg lettuce and surrounded by canned peach halves. The cook's creativity was limited by the assumption that something must be put on the plate where the meatloaf used to be.

And what happened in restaurants was paralleled at home. Some of us at Moosewood have been vegetarians for 20 years now, and we remember when we were troubled by the same question. The most difficult hurdle to overcome as we tried to develop new entrées was finding substitutes for meat. We found some wonderful dishes in the process, such as tofu burgers and quiches, but we also learned that we had to stop thinking in terms of replacing meat.

The rewards began to come when we realized that our new diet was far more varied and interesting than the old one. We discovered a whole world of exciting dishes that are based on vegetables, dairy products, and vegetable proteins such as whole grains, beans, tofu, tempeh, seeds, and nuts. For inspiration, we turned to the elaborate cuisines of other cultures which are created around vegetable and dairy proteins. As a result, some of our recipes are quite traditional, while others are eclectic and rather unorthodox blends of techniques and ingredients.

Successful cooking with vegetables requires high quality ingredients. We use fresh herbs, freshly ground spices, and locally grown organic produce when possible. But in winter when hothouse tomatoes are pale, bland, and rock-hard and fresh peas and corn are simply not available, we use canned or frozen vegetables for satisfying, if somewhat different, results. Some dishes, though, simply must be made with fresh ingredients. Our Summer Pasta Sauce, for example, would be a travesty without lush, ripe tomatoes and fresh, pungent basil.

Time is a consideration in choosing entrées. If you are pressed for time, a pasta dish or Chinese-style sauté is a good choice. But if you have the afternoon free and are glad to be in the kitchen, try hearty, cold-weather dishes such as Mushroom-Tofu-Pecan Stuffed Squash or Winter Vegetable Stew. For special occasions, serve elegant and impressive Spinach Lasagna Béchamel or Sara's Piroshki.

A little advance planning can save time spent in the kitchen. If you are cooking garbanzo beans for Hummus, plan for leftover beans to be used in Moroccan Stew or as salad topping. Cook more brown rice than is needed for one meal. The extra rice can be added to Cabbage Strudel or Zucchini-Feta Casserole.

You may choose to entertain with an ethnic food theme as we do at Moosewood on Sunday evenings. A Greek meal featuring Egg-Lemon Soup with Spinach, Kolokithopita, Tzatziki, and Apricot Baklava is sure to delight your friends. For fans of spicy foods, try an Indian feast of North Indian Stuffed Eggplant or Vegetable Curry with sides of Coconut Rice, Date-Lemon Chutney, and Spinach Raita.

Whether you are entertaining or just having a cozy dinner at home, take an extra moment to garnish the entrée. It doesn't need to be fancy but that sprig of parsley, slice of melon or orange, sprinkling of sesame seeds, or dollop of sour cream can transform the simplest dish.

Buddha's Jewels

~

Serves 4 to 6

Joan Adler is a longtime Moosewood member. In her continuing quest for the new and exotic menu feature, Joan discovered this delicious, healthful dish. Golden tofu dumplings filled with crunchy bits of vegetable and topped with a shimmering, pungent sauce. As an appetizer this recipe will serve 8 to 10 people.

DUMPLINGS

3 cakes of tofu pressed and mashed *(see Appendix)*

2 tablespoons peanut butter *(see Appendix)*

3 tablespoons tamari soy sauce

8 scallions, chopped

1 green pepper, diced

1½ cups chopped mushrooms (6 ounces)

¼ cup chopped fresh parsley

½ cup diced water chestnuts

SAUCE

1½ cups pineapple, orange, and/or apple juice

¼ cup maple syrup, honey, or brown sugar

⅓ to ½ cup cider vinegar

¼ cup tamari soy sauce

1 garlic clove, minced or pressed

2 tablespoons cornstarch dissolved in 2 tablespoons cold water

In a large bowl, mix together all the ingredients for the tofu dumplings. Shape into approximately 2 dozen 2-inch balls and place on an oiled baking sheet. Bake at 375° for 45 minutes, until golden and firm.

Combine all the sauce ingredients except the cornstarch in a stainless steel or enamel saucepan. Bring to a boil. Stir in the dissolved cornstarch and simmer, stirring continuously, until the sauce is clear and thickened.

Pour the sauce over the dumplings and serve immediately.

Serve Buddha's Jewels with rice and steamed vegetables.

Sara's Piroshki

(Potato-cabbage-cheese turnover)

Yields 6 large pastries

Traditional piroshki are bite-sized savory pastries. As developed by Sara Robbins they are large, entrée-sized turnovers, which are always very popular at Moosewood. The ingredients are inexpensive and preparation is not difficult. The pastry is simply a rich pie dough.

PASTRY DOUGH

1½ cups unbleached white flour

¼ teaspoon salt

¼ pound butter

3 to 5 tablespoons ice water

FILLING

2 cups sliced potatoes

3 tablespoons butter

2 cups finely chopped cabbage

1 cup finely chopped onions

1 cup cottage cheese

1 cup grated sharp cheddar cheese
 (3 ounces)

1 egg

½ teaspoon salt

2 tablespoons chopped fresh dill
 (2 teaspoons dried)

2 tablespoons chopped fresh parsley

2 tablespoons chopped fresh chives or
 scallions

¼ teaspoon ground caraway seeds

¼ teaspoon white pepper (or black
 pepper)

□

1 egg, beaten with 1 tablespoon water

sesame seeds or poppy seeds for
 topping *(optional)*

□

1 cup sour cream

Mix the flour and salt thoroughly. Cut in the butter with knives or a pastry cutter until the mixture resembles coarse cornmeal. Using a fork and as few strokes as possible, mix in the ice water until the mixture can be formed into a ball. Chill the dough for 15 minutes.

Boil the potatoes until tender, then drain and mash them in a large bowl. Sauté the cabbage and onions in butter in a covered skillet until tender, about 15 minutes. Add them to the potatoes and stir in all the remaining ingredients.

Preheat the oven to 400°.

Divide the dough into six equal balls. Roll each ball into a thin circle, approximately 6 inches in diameter. Place two or three heaping tablespoons of the filling in the center of each circle, brush the edges with the beaten egg mixture, and fold over to form a half-moon. Press the edges with your fingers or a fork to seal. Carefully lift each piroshki with a spatula and place it on an oiled baking sheet. Brush the top of each pastry with the egg-water mixture and sprinkle with seeds. Bake for 25 to 35 minutes or until golden brown.

Top with sour cream and serve with Sweet and Sour Red Cabbage *(p. 209)* and applesauce.

When we learned Isaac Bashevis Singer was coming to dinner, our resident Yiddish grammarian, Allan Warshawsky, translated the evening's menu into Yiddish. Allan was not originally scheduled to work, but put in a guest appearance in order to wait on the Nobel Prize-winning author.

Burritos

~~~~~

Serves 4 to 6

These savory little packages are a hearty and spicy pairing of a popular, perfect protein combination: beans and corn.

5 cups cooked pinto or kidney beans
  (see Appendix)

□

¼ cup vegetable oil

4 to 5 garlic cloves, minced

4 cups chopped onions

3 medium green peppers, chopped

1½ tablespoons ground cumin

¼ teaspoon cayenne, or to taste
  (optional)

1 tablespoon ground coriander seeds

□

1 cup corn

½ cup chopped black olives

**1⅓ cups grated sharp cheddar cheese
  (4 ounces)**

salt to taste

□

12 wheat tortillas

vegetable oil

□

1 cup grated cheddar cheese (3 ounces)
  (optional)

3 cups Hot Sauce *(p. 193)*

1 cup sour cream

Drain the cooked beans and reserve the liquid.

Sauté the garlic and onions in oil for several minutes until the onions are translucent. Add the peppers and all of the spices and continue to sauté until the peppers are tender, stirring occasionally. Cover the vegetables, remove them from the heat, and set them aside.

Mash the beans with a potato masher or wooden pestle and add enough reserved bean liquid to obtain the consistency of stiff mashed potatoes. Mix the mashed beans, sautéed vegetables, corn, olives, and cheese. Salt to taste.

Preheat the oven to 400°.

Place each tortilla flat on the counter. Spoon ½ to ¾ cup of the bean mixture onto the half of the tortilla closest to you. Roll the tortillas from the bottom up, putting pressure on the filling so that it will be evenly distributed and will reach the open edges of the rolled tortilla. Place the burritos, rolled edge down, in an oiled baking pan. Brush them with oil, cover with a damp cotton cloth, and bake, tightly covered with foil, for 15 minutes. Uncover the pan, remove the cloth, and serve immediately, or sprinkle the burritos with the additional grated cheese if desired, and bake about 5 minutes more.

Serve the burritos on heated plates. Top with Hot Sauce and sour cream.

Our whole television crew enjoyed eating in your restaurant. It would be a beautiful day in our neighborhood if you would open a Moosewood in Pittsburgh.

— Mr. Rogers
Fred Rogers from Mr. Rogers Neighborhood

Cheese Empanadas

Yields 6 pastries

Crispy with a rich and spicy filling, empanadas are a wonderful hors d'oeuvre or companion piece for a festive meal or party. In fact, Moosewood's Eliana Parra, from Chile, often makes a party out of making empanadas, trooping into the kitchen at midnight with lively salsa music and a genial group of friends and family to form an empanada assembly line that turns out hundreds.

FILLING

9 ounces Monterey Jack cheese, cut in ½-inch cubes

¾ cup finely chopped pepperoncini *(see Appendix)*

3 hard-boiled eggs, chopped

½ cup chopped Spanish olives

DOUGH

3 cups unbleached white flour

1 teaspoon salt

6 tablespoons melted butter

½ cup yogurt

cold water

oil for frying

Mix together all the filling ingredients.

Sift the flour and salt. Add the melted butter, the yogurt, and enough water to make a firm dough. Knead the dough on a floured surface until smooth. Pinch off dough to make 6 balls. Roll each one into a 5-inch circle. Place about ½ cup of filling in the center of each circle, wet the edges, fold the dough over into a half-circle, and crimp the edge with the tines of a fork. Store on a lightly floured tray.

Deep fry each pastry until golden in 2 to 3 inches of oil heated to 360°. (or until a small piece of bread sizzles when dropped in the oil). These pastries are at their best when fried, but they may also be brushed with oil and baked in a preheated 375° oven for about 20 to 30 minutes or until the crust is golden.

Serve with Guacamole *(p. 76)* and Refried Beans *(p. 208)*.

Cheese and Almond Stuffed Zucchini

Serves 6

A creamy, rich, very satisfying dish based on an old French provincial recipe.

3 medium zucchini

□

2 tablespoons olive oil or butter

1 cup finely chopped onions

1 teaspoon salt

6 ounces cream cheese, cut into small cubes

1½ cup almonds, finely chopped

½ cup whole grain bread crumbs

2 cups grated Swiss cheese (7 ounces)

½ teaspoon nutmeg, preferably freshly grated

¼ teaspoon ground allspice

Cut the zucchini in half lengthwise and, using a soup spoon, scoop out the insides of the zucchini to leave a fillable outer shell. Save the inner pulp and chop it.

Sauté the onions in the oil until translucent. Add the salt and chopped zucchini pulp and continue to cook on medium heat until the zucchini is soft. Remove from the heat. Stir the cream cheese cubes into the vegetables and cover for several minutes. Meanwhile, in a large bowl mix together the almonds, bread crumbs, grated Swiss cheese, nutmeg, and allspice. When the cream cheese has softened, thoroughly combine all the ingredients.

Fill the zucchini shells and place them in an oiled 9 × 14-inch baking pan. Add water to cover the bottom of the pan about ¼-inch deep. Tightly cover the pan so that the zucchini shells will steam. Bake covered at 350° for 30 minutes. Uncover and bake for another 5 to 10 minutes, until the filling has browned a little.

Serve on a bed of rice with a side of Artichoke Heart and Tomato Salad *(p. 40)*.

Armenian Stuffed Cabbage

Serves 6

Drawing from her Armenian heritage, Laura Branca created this vegetarian version of a classic favorite rich with nuts, aromatic mint, and tangy lemon.

2 cups uncooked brown rice	½ cup chopped fresh parsley
1 tablespoon olive oil	⅓ cup olive oil
2 bay leaves	3 garlic cloves, pressed or minced
½ teaspoon salt	⅓ cup fresh lemon juice
1 tablespoon tomato paste	3 cups canned tomatoes
3½ cups water	salt and black pepper to taste
□	□
1 large green cabbage*	yogurt
1 cup walnuts, finely chopped	chopped fresh parsley
1 cup almonds, finely chopped	
¼ cup chopped fresh spearmint (1 tablespoon dried)	

Sauté the rice in a tablespoon of olive oil, stirring continuously, for 3 to 4 minutes. The rice will begin to smell "nutty," somewhat reminiscent of popcorn. Add the bay leaves, salt, tomato paste, and water and stir until the tomato paste is dissolved. Cover and cook until tender *(see Appendix)*.

Immerse the cored head of cabbage in boiling water. After several minutes, as each leaf begins to separate from the head, gently but nimbly pull it completely off the cabbage and set aside to cool. Continue until there are 12 good leaves to stuff.

Combine the nuts, mint, and parsley in a mixing bowl. When the rice is ready, remove the bay leaves and add the rice to the nuts. Mix in 2 to 3 tablespoons of olive oil, the garlic, and half the lemon juice.

Make a thin sauce by crushing the tomatoes in their juice and then mixing in the salt and pepper, lemon juice, and the remaining olive oil. Thin the sauce with water if necessary. Ladle some of the sauce into a large skillet or soup pot.

Put ⅓ to ½ cup of the rice-nut filling on the thick end of each cabbage leaf. Fold the sides over the mixture and then roll up toward the thin edge of the leaf. Arrange the cabbage rolls on top of the sauce, seam side down. Pour the rest of the sauce over the rolls, cover, and simmer for 30 to 45 minutes. Test the cabbage for tenderness by piercing with a fork.

Top with a dollop of yogurt and more chopped parsley if desired. Serve with steamed, fresh green beans and julienned carrots.

---

* Suzie Tuch, a cousin of Moosewood's Allan Warshawsky, has stuffed many a cabbage leaf in her day and gave us this very useful tip. Freeze a head of cabbage a few days before you intend to make stuffed cabbage. Thaw it the day before and the cabbage leaves will easily peel off the head. Blanch the leaves for a few minutes in boiling water. This is a lot easier than the boil-and-retrieve method of peeling cabbage leaves.

Stuffed Zucchini Bretonne

Serves 4 to 6

Flavorful and aromatic. Don't spare the garlic – if sautéed gently, it gives a pungent accent to the dish. This is one of many recipes developed by Alan Warshawsky.

3 cups cooked and drained navy beans
  (see Appendix)

½ cup liquid from cooking the beans or
  Vegetable Stock *(p. 30)* or water

□

2 tablespoons olive oil

2 cups chopped onions

1 cup diced carrots

2 celery stalks, diced

½ teaspoon salt

pinch of black pepper

1½ teaspoons dried tarragon

1 teaspoon dried dill

2 bay leaves

1 green pepper, diced

□

2 tablespoons butter

3 garlic cloves, minced or pressed

4 ounces cream cheese, cubed

1 teaspoon fresh lemon juice

¼ teaspoon hot red pepper sauce

□

4 medium or 6 small zucchini

□

chopped fresh parsley

Sauté the onions in the olive oil for 5 minutes. Stir in the carrots, celery, salt, pepper, tarragon, dill, and bay leaves and sauté another 5 minutes. Stir in the green peppers and simmer covered until the vegetables are tender. Discard the bay leaves.

Sauté the garlic in the butter, taking care not to burn it. In a blender or food processor, purée 1 cup of the cooked beans with ½ cup liquid.

In a large bowl, gently stir the cream cheese cubes, lemon juice, and red pepper sauce into the sautéed vegetables. Stir in the sautéed garlic and the puréed and whole beans. Taste the filling and adjust the seasonings.

Slice the zucchini in half lengthwise. Carefully scoop out the middle of each zucchini half without breaking the skin. Spoon the filling into each zucchini boat and pack the little boats into a baking pan, propping them against each other and the sides of the pan, so they won't capsize. Add half an inch of water to the bottom of the pan, cover tightly, and bake at 350° for 45 minutes.

Top with chopped parsley and serve with Potage Plaisance *(p. 19)* and French Bread *(p. 225)*.

Today far too many restaurants serve tiny over-decorated portions of exotic food in an atmosphere of expensive pretentiousness. Moosewood remains untouched by this trend. It is famous all through the Finger Lakes region for its inventive combination of fresh local ingredients, generous helpings, and friendly, casual ambiance.

— Alison Lurie
author of *Foreign Affairs*

Eggplant Provençale

Serves 6

Saffron provides the distinctive flavor, color, and ambience in this Mediterranean stuffed eggplant. The pilaf filling could also be used to stuff zucchini, peppers, or tomatoes, or as an accompaniment to fish.

1½ cups uncooked brown rice	1 large red or green pepper, minced
1 tablespoon olive oil	1 tablespoon sherry
generous pinch of saffron	½ teaspoon cayenne *(optional)*
3 cups water	2 medium tomatoes, chopped
1½ teaspoons salt	½ cup dried currants
□	½ cup chopped fresh parsley
2 tablespoons olive oil	¼ teaspoon black pepper
3 medium eggplants	□
¼ cup water	½ cup tomato juice or water
¼ cup sherry	□
□	½ cup toasted, slivered almonds
2 tablespoons olive oil	chopped fresh parsley
3 cups minced onions	

Cook the rice *(see Appendix)*, sautéing it in olive oil and crumbling the saffron into the pan before adding the water and salt.

Brush a large baking pan with olive oil. Leaving the stems on, slice the eggplants in half lengthwise and place them in the pan, cut side down. Add ¼ cup water and ¼ cup sherry. Cover tightly with aluminum foil and bake at 375° until tender, about 45 minutes.

Meanwhile, sauté the onions in 2 tablespoons olive oil for 10 minutes. Add the peppers, 1 tablespoon sherry, and the cayenne. Sauté covered for 5 minutes. Stir in the tomatoes, currants, parsley, and pepper. Simmer covered a few minutes, until the vegetables begin to release their juices.

Combine the rice and the vegetable mixture.

When the baked eggplants are cool enough to handle, turn them over in the baking pan and gently mash and push to the side the soft middle. Mound the rice pilaf on each eggplant half. Pour ½ cup of tomato juice or water into the baking pan. Cover the pan tightly and return it to the oven to bake about 30 minutes. Serve garnished with slivered almonds and parsley.

One is never bored by the Moosewood menu. It changes with every meal. Where else would one find a menu offering Mexican, Middle Eastern, and Italian food one day and French, American, and Chinese on another? The food is always good, frequently inspired! If vegetarian cooking were always like this, more people would eat vegetarian.

— Mary E. Nygaard
librarian, Tompkins County Library

Japanese Braised Eggplant

Serves 4

Eggplants braised in a Japanese manner in a sweetened sherry sauce are then stuffed with a rich, eclectic filling.

2 medium eggplants	1 teaspoon ground coriander seeds
½ cup dry sherry	1 medium green pepper, diced
⅓ cup tamari soy sauce	4 cups sliced mushrooms (1 pound)
1 tablespoon molasses	3 tablespoons tomato paste
□	salt to taste
¼ cup vegetable oil	□
8 ounces tempeh *(see Appendix)*, cubed	brown rice
2½ cups chopped onions	chopped scallions
2 teaspoons ground fennel seeds	toasted sesame seeds
¼ teaspoon cayenne	

Leaving the stems on, cut the eggplants in half lengthwise. Mix together the sherry, soy sauce, and molasses. Oil a baking pan. Pour the sherry mixture into the pan, place the eggplant halves, cut side down, in the pan, cover it tightly, and bake at 350° for 45 minutes, until tender.

Brown the cubed tempeh, ½ cup of the onions, 1 teaspoon of the fennel, and ¼ teaspoon cayenne in oil for 20 minutes, stirring frequently to avoid burning. In a separate pan, sauté the remaining 2 cups onions, the coriander, and the remaining teaspoon of fennel until the onions are translucent. Add the peppers and the mushrooms and sauté another 15 to 20 minutes, until tender.

With a slotted spoon, lift the tempeh and onions from the oil and stir them into the sautéed vegetables. Stir in the tomato paste and 2 tablespoons of the braising liquid from the eggplant baking pan. Salt the filling to taste.

Turn the eggplant halves over in the baking pan. With a fork or spoon, carefully mash the pulp a little and then push it to the sides making a hollow in each half and taking care not to break the skins. Fill each hollow with one-fourth of the filling. Cover the pan tightly and bake at 350° for 20 minutes, until piping hot.

Serve on a bed of rice, pour some juice from the pan over the eggplant, and sprinkle with chopped scallions and toasted sesame seeds.

To my mind Moosewood can only be described with superlatives. The most careful planning, imagination, and attention to details, as well as attractive presentations, all contribute to extremely tasteful and well-balanced meals. In the many years I have enjoyed Moosewood, I have only observed improvement. Whether it be a Mexican, Italian, French, Chilean, Middle Eastern, Hungarian, or even an American meal, it is unquestionably my favorite restaurant.

— **George A. Everett**
biochemist

North Indian Stuffed Eggplant

Serves 4

If you're a fan of Indian food and would like to prepare something other than a curry, try this creamy yet spicy eggplant dish.

2 medium eggplants	**¼ teaspoon ground cloves**
□	**1 tablespoon minced fresh ginger root**
4 cups cubed potatoes	**2 garlic cloves, minced or pressed**
8 ounces cream cheese, at room temperature	**2 medium carrots, diced**
	1 large green pepper, diced
□	**1 cup green peas, fresh or frozen**
2 tablespoons vegetable oil	**1 tomato, diced** *(optional)*
2 cups chopped onions	**2 tablespoons fresh lemon juice**
2 teaspoons ground cumin	□
1 tablespoon ground coriander	**sesame seeds** *(optional)*
1 teaspoon turmeric	
½ teaspoon hot red pepper (or 2 small fresh hot peppers, minced)	

Leaving the stems on, slice the eggplants in half lengthwise and place cut side down on an oiled baking sheet. Cover and bake at 375° until tender, about 30 to 40 minutes.

While the eggplant is baking, boil the potatoes until tender and then drain. Mash the drained, hot potatoes with the cream cheese in a large bowl. Meanwhile, sauté the onions and the dried spices in oil for 1 minute, then add the ginger and garlic and continue to sauté until the onions are translucent. Add the carrots and cook 5 minutes. Add the peppers and peas and cook until just tender. Stir in the tomatoes and lemon juice. Combine the sautéed vegetables and the potato-cream cheese mixture.

Turn baked eggplant halves over in the baking pan. With a fork or spoon mash the pulp a little, taking care not to break the skin. Push aside some of the pulp, making a hollow in each half. Mound a quarter of the filling on each half.

Sprinkle the top with sesame seeds, if desired, and bake covered at 375° for 15 minutes, then uncovered for an additional 15 to 20 minutes.

Serve with Raita *(p. 217)* and perhaps Peach Chutney *(p. 215)*. If you have more filling than needed for the eggplants, try stuffing a green pepper or tomato as well. This is also the perfect leftover to use as a base for Potage St. Cloud *(p. 23)*.

Spirits sometimes run high at Moosewood, especially after a long Ithaca winter. One particularly fine June first evening, the entire kitchen staff was moved to burst into the dining room, wooden spoons waving, to perform a rousing rendition of "June Is Bustin' Out All Over" to the surprise and amusement of the customers.

Hungarian Stuffed Peppers

Serves 4 to 6

This is a sort of Hungarian goulash in a pepper shell, slightly sweet with paprika. We don't know if they've discovered tempeh in Budapest yet, but if they have, it may go something like this....

4 tablespoons vegetable oil

3 garlic cloves, minced or pressed

2 cups chopped onions

8 ounces tempeh *(see Appendix)*, cut in ½-inch cubes

2 tomatoes, chopped

3 medium celery stalks, diced

1 cup diced carrots

1½ cups diced potatoes

2 tablespoons dry red wine

1 tablespoon sweet Hungarian paprika *(see Appendix)*

1 tablespoon dried dill

2 teaspoons salt

½ teaspoon black pepper

½ teaspoon Dijon mustard

☐

6 red or green peppers

¾ to 1 cup tomato juice or water

☐

1 cup sour cream

Sauté the garlic and onions in the oil until the onions begin to soften. Add the tempeh and cook until it begins to brown, stirring often. Add the tomatoes, celery, carrots, potatoes, wine, and seasonings and cook covered on low heat, until the vegetables are tender. It may be necessary to add a small amount of stock or water to prevent the mixture from sticking.

Cut the peppers in half lengthwise and remove the seed. Leave the stems on if you can, because then the pepper halves will hold their shape better during baking. Fill each pepper half with stuffing and place in an oiled baking pan. Add about ½ inch of tomato juice or water to the bottom of the pan. Bake tightly covered at 375° for 40 minutes.

Serve on a bed of rice or noodles. Spoon some of the baking liquid over the stuffed peppers and top with a dollop of sour cream.

Mexican Bean Stuffed Peppers

Serves 4 to 6

A piquant filling for peppers that features the high protein and appealing texture of tempeh.

4 tablespoons vegetable oil

2 cups chopped onions

4 garlic cloves, minced or pressed

8 ounces tempeh* *(see Appendix)*, in ½-inch cubes

3 tomatoes, chopped

2 cups corn

1 teaspoon ground cumin

2 teaspoons ground coriander seeds

3 cups cooked kidney or pinto beans *(see Appendix)*, slightly mashed

½ cup chopped Spanish olives *(optional)*

2 tablespoons tamari soy sauce

salt and black pepper to taste

☐

6 red or green peppers

¾ to 1 cup tomato juice or water

☐

Hot Sauce *(p. 193)*

1 cup sour cream or grated cheddar or Monterey Jack cheese

In a heavy skillet, cook the onions and garlic in the oil until they begin to soften. Add the tempeh and sauté, stirring often, until it is browned. Add the tomatoes, corn, and seasonings. Cook covered until thoroughly heated. Mix in the cooked beans, olives, and soy sauce. Adjust the salt and pepper to taste.

Cut the peppers in half lengthwise and remove the seeds. Leave the stems on if you can, because then the pepper halves will hold their shape better during baking. Fill each pepper half with vegetable-tempeh mixture and place in an oiled pan with ½ inch of tomato juice or water in the bottom. Bake tightly covered at 375° for 30 to 40 minutes.

Serve on a bed of rice topped with Hot Sauce. Garnish with sour cream or grated cheese.

If you have trouble finding tempeh, use an additional cup of cooked beans in its place.

Mexican Corn and Cheese Stuffed Peppers

Serves 4 to 6

Each of these tasty little peppers works as its own casserole covered with a delicious sauce. And how wonderfully the cheese and peppers complement each other, especially south of the border style!

2 tablespoons vegetable oil or butter

1 cup chopped onions

3 garlic cloves, minced or pressed

1½ teaspoons ground cumin

1 teaspoon ground coriander seeds

¼ teaspoon cayenne

1 medium tomato, chopped

2 cups corn, fresh or frozen

salt to taste

□

3 eggs

1 cup grated cheddar cheese (3 ounces)

¼ cup milk or half-and-half

¼ cup chopped Spanish olives

□

6 medium green and/or red peppers

¼ cup tomato juice or water

□

Salsa Cruda *(p.194)* or Hot Sauce *(p.193)*

Sauté the onions, garlic, cumin, coriander, and cayenne in the oil or butter until the onions are translucent. Be careful not to burn the spices. Add the tomatoes, corn, and salt. Simmer until the corn is barely tender.

Lightly beat the eggs in a large bowl. Add the cheese, milk, olives, and sautéed vegetables.

Cut the peppers in half lengthwise and remove the seeds. Leave the stems on if you can, because then the pepper halves will hold their shape better during baking. Stuff the pepper halves with the egg-vegetable mixture and place them in an oiled baking dish. Pour the tomato juice or water into the bottom of the dish. Bake tightly covered at 375° for 30 minutes. Uncover and bake 10 minutes more.

Serve on a bed of rice topped with Hot Sauce or Salsa Cruda.

Mushroom-Tofu-Pecan Stuffed Squash

Serves 6 to 8

This is a festive and hearty dish, appropriate for a holiday dinner. It is a perfect Thanksgiving alternative to turkey, served with steamed Brussels sprouts and cranberry sauce, naturally.

3 or 4 small winter squash (such as acorn or buttercup), halved and seeded

1 cake of tofu, pressed *(see Appendix)* **and cut into small cubes**

3 tablespoons tamari soy sauce

3 tablespoons dry sherry

4 cups small bread cubes

□

2 tablespoons vegetable oil

3 cups chopped onions

3 celery stalks, chopped

4 cups sliced mushrooms (1 pound)

½ teaspoon dried marjoram

¼ teaspoon dried thyme

½ cup Vegetable Stock *(p. 30)* **or water**

1 cup pecans, toasted and chopped

1 tablespoon fresh lemon juice

Place the squash halves, cut side down, in an oiled baking pan. Add about ½ inch of water to the pan and bake at 350° for about 40 minutes, until the squash is just tender. Meanwhile, marinate the tofu in the soy sauce and sherry. Toast the bread cubes on a baking sheet for 5 minutes.

Sauté the onions and celery in 2 tablespoons oil, using a pot large enough for all the remaining ingredients. When the onions are translucent, add the mushrooms, marjoram, thyme, and stock or water. Cook covered for 10 minutes, then add the tofu with its marinade and the bread cubes. Sauté for another 5 minutes. Adjust the seasoning. Remove from the heat. Stir in the pecans and lemon juice.

Mound the filling in the baked squash halves and bake covered at 350° for 20 minutes.

This cold weather dish is nicely accompanied by Scandinavian Apple Soup *(p. 9)* and Squash Rolls *(p. 231)*. It is even more delicious topped with Light and Tangy Orange Sauce *(p. 192)*.

Caserola Milanese

Serves 6

Although cornmeal mush doesn't stir many in America, its Italian cousin, polenta *(see Appendix)* has won the hearts of the cooks and customers at Moosewood. Here it forms the base of a casserole filled with spicy vegetables and topped with mozzarella.

POLENTA

2 cups cornmeal

6 cups water

¼ cup butter

salt to taste

⅛ teaspoon black pepper

¾ cup freshly grated Parmesan cheese
   (2 ounces)

□

3 tablespoons olive oil

3 garlic cloves, minced or pressed

4 cups chopped onions

2 medium carrots, diced

3 celery stalks, diced

⅓ cup fresh basil (3 tablespoons dried)

2 teaspoons dried oregano

1 teaspoon salt

black pepper to taste

3 cups cubed eggplant

1 green pepper, chopped

1½ cups cubed zucchini

1½ cups drained canned tomatoes

3 tablespoons tomato paste

½ cup red wine *(optional)*

½ cup freshly grated Parmesan cheese
   (1½ ounces)

□

3 cups grated mozzarella cheese
   (12 ounces)

Bring the water to a rapid boil. Gradually add the cornmeal in a thin stream, stirring rapidly. While continuing to stir, add the butter, salt, and pepper. Simmer on low heat for about 20 minutes. Stir often, especially at the bottom of the pot, to avoid sticking. When the polenta has thickened, remove it from the heat and stir in ¾ cup of Parmesan. Pour the polenta into a well-buttered 12-inch casserole dish and let it cool for several minutes. Then refrigerate it until you are ready to assemble the casserole.

Sauté the garlic and onions in oil until the onions are translucent. Add the carrots, celery, herbs, and spices, and continue to cook on medium heat for several minutes. When the carrots are bright in color, add the eggplant and continue to sauté for 5 minutes. Stir frequently. Add the peppers and zucchini and cook until tender. Add the tomatoes, tomato paste, and red wine, if desired, and simmer 5 minutes longer. Remove the vegetables from the heat and stir in the ½ cup of Parmesan.

Take the chilled polenta from the refrigerator and spoon on the vegetable sauce. Top with the grated mozzarella. Bake uncovered at 350° for 45 minutes to 1 hour, until the cheese begins to brown at the edges. Allow to rest 15 minutes before serving

If you have too little time to bake the casserole, try serving the vegetables over hot polenta topped with the mozzarella. We prefer the casserole, but when time is of the essence, it pays to be flexible.

Serve with a crisp green salad dressed with L.D.'s Creamy Green Dressing *(p. 49)*.

Musicians on the road, who travel the small club circuit, are generally unable to find good vegetarian meals within their limitations of time and money. With Moosewood just blocks away from my club, I often take entire bands over for dinner after sound check and before the show. Jamaican reggae bands, Texas rockers, and Chicago bluesmen have all raved about the virtues of eating at Moosewood before the show. I've seen and heard it often enough to say with confidence that a meal at Moosewood makes for a better performance.

— John Peterson
cultural instigator, local club owner and producer

Chilaquiles

Serves 4 to 6

This is the perfect dish to prepare with leftover Refried Beans and Hot Sauce or spicy chili. In fact, this dish is such a fine tasting casserole that you may want to make it from scratch, which will be time-consuming at first, but worth consuming in the end!

2 tablespoons vegetable oil

2 cups chopped onions

2 medium green peppers, chopped

□

8 corn tortillas, brushed with oil and baked until crisp, or 1 medium bag of tortilla chips

4 cups Refried Beans *(p. 208)*

⅓ cup chopped Spanish olives *(optional)*

2 cups Hot Sauce *(p. 193)*

1 cup grated sharp cheddar cheese (3 ounces)

Sauté the onions in the oil until they are translucent. Add the peppers and continue to sauté until the peppers soften. Stir occasionally. To assemble the casserole, line the bottom of a well-oiled 12×12-inch casserole dish with broken tortillas or tortilla chips. Then spread on a thick layer of Refried Beans. Cover the bean layer with the sautéed onions and peppers. Sprinkle on the chopped olives, if desired. Ladle on the Hot Sauce. Top with the grated cheddar.

Bake covered at 375° for 30 to 35 minutes, until the cheese is bubbly. Then uncover the casserole and allow it to bake 5 to 10 minutes more until the edges begin to brown.

Serve with Chilled Avocado-Grapefruit Soup *(p. 6)*, Arroz Verde *(p. 198)*, or Guacamole *(p. 76)*.

Corn and Cheese Casserole

Serves 4 to 6

Easy to prepare and easy to like. This humble dish makes a gratifying school night supper *en famille*.

3 eggs	□
3 tablespoons unbleached white flour	**2 tablespoons butter**
½ cup heavy cream or half-and-half	**2 cups diced onions**
1 cup milk	**1 large carrot, grated**
1 tablespoon honey *(optional)*	**1 small green pepper, chopped,**
½ teaspoon salt	**1 cup grated sharp cheddar cheese (3 ounces)**
dash of black pepper	
1 teaspoon dried dill	□
2 tablespoons chopped fresh parsley	**2 cups Salsa Cruda** *(p. 194)* **or Hot Sauce** *(p. 193) (optional)*
2 cups corn, fresh or frozen	

Combine the eggs and flour in a blender. Add the cream, milk, honey, salt, pepper, dill, parsley, and half of the corn and blend. If you do not have a blender, whisk together all the above ingredients except the corn.

Preheat the oven to 350°

Sauté the onions in the butter until translucent. Add the carrots and peppers. Sauté until tender, about 5 minutes. Stir in the remaining corn and then the blended ingredients and the cheddar cheese.

Pour into a buttered 9 × 13-inch baking pan and bake uncovered about 35 minutes, until golden. Test the custard by inserting a knife in the center. If it comes out clean, the casserole is ready.

Serve in squares, topped with Hot Sauce or Salsa Cruda if desired.

Country Style Moussaka

Serves 6

When you have the time for preparing a special dinner, this hearty Greek casserole makes an impressive main course.

SAUCE

3 tablespoons olive oil

2 cups chopped onions, about 2 medium onions

2 garlic cloves, minced or pressed

4 or 5 large tomatoes, chopped

1 large green pepper, chopped

1½ teaspoon fresh dill (½ teaspoon dried)

¼ teaspoon cinnamon

3 tablespoons chopped fresh parsley

salt and black pepper to taste

□

1 large eggplant, sliced in ½-inch thick circles

olive oil for sautéing

1 large zucchini, sliced in ½-inch thick circles

□

CUSTARD

⅓ cup butter

⅓ cup unbleached white flour

2 cups milk, heated

2 egg yolks, beaten

pinch of nutmeg, preferably freshly grated

□

1 cup grated feta cheese (5 ounces)

¾ cup bread crumbs

freshly grated Parmesan cheese

fresh chopped parsley

To make the tomato sauce, sauté the onions and garlic in the olive oil until the onions are translucent. Add the remaining ingredients and simmer uncovered for about 30 minutes.

Place the eggplant slices on an oiled baking sheet, salt lightly, cover with aluminum foil, and bake at 375° until tender, about ½ hour. Sauté the zucchini slices, in enough oil to cover the bottom of the pan or skillet, until they are just tender.

Next make the custard. Heat the milk. In a separate saucepan, melt the butter on medium heat. Stir in the flour and cook for 3 minutes, whisking so that it will not scorch. Gradually pour in the hot milk, whisking it into a smooth, thick sauce. Remove from the heat and allow to cool about 10 minutes. Whisk in the egg yolks and nutmeg.

Now assemble the moussaka. Oil a deep baking dish at least 9 × 13 × 2½-inches. Spread half the sauce on the bottom and layer the eggplant slices, then half of the feta cheese and half of the bread crumbs. Add the rest of the sauce, the zucchini slices, the remaining feta cheese and bread crumbs. Top all of this with the custard and a sprinkling of Parmesan cheese and parsley.

Bake uncovered at 375° for 45 minutes to 1 hour or until bubbly and golden. Allow the casserole to sit for 15 minutes at room temperature before serving.

Serve with Egg-Lemon Soup with Spinach *(p. 22)* and a crisp green salad.

I have enjoyed over 3,000 meals at Moosewood over the past 12 years. Need I say more?

— **Tim Teitelbaum**
associate professor of computer science, Cornell University
(Our most regular, regular customer)

Mushroom-Leek Frittata

Serves 6

Less exacting than a soufflé but lighter in texture than a casserole. This baked frittata is a nice brunch alternative to omelettes or crêpes. At Moosewood our customers often enjoy this for lunch with one of our soups.

1½ cups whole wheat bread cubes

3 tablespoons butter

3 tablespoons olive oil

2 medium garlic cloves, minced or pressed

1 cup chopped leeks *(see Appendix)*

3 cups sliced mushrooms (12 ounces)

1 tablespoon fresh dill or marjoram (1 teaspoon dried)

salt and black pepper to taste

□

4 ounces cream cheese, in ½-inch cubes

1¼ cups grated sharp cheddar cheese (4 ounces)

4 eggs

1¼ cups milk

Toast the bread cubes on a tray in a 375° oven. Meanwhile, lightly sauté the garlic in 2 tablespoons each of the butter and the olive oil until the garlic is golden. When the bread cubes are crispy, remove them from the oven, toss with the garlic butter, and set aside.

Next, sauté the leeks in the remaining 1 tablespoon each of butter and oil for a minute or two. Add the mushrooms, herbs, salt, and pepper and continue to cook, stirring occasionally. Cover the pan to retain the juices. The vegetables are ready when they are just tender.

Preheat the oven to 375°.

Butter a 9×9-inch pan. Layer ingredients as follows: first the bread cubes, next the cream cheese, then the vegetables, and finally the grated cheddar cheese. Beat together the eggs and milk with some salt and pepper and pour this over the other ingredients in the pan. Bake until the frittata is puffy and golden, about 30 minutes. Serve immediately.

Other vegetable combinations work equally well in this dish. Try broccoli and onions, asparagus and scallions, or anything that appeals to you. The cheddar may be replaced by a more exotic cheese such as Gruyère or fontina.

Serve with a tangy tomato soup, such as Potage Plaisance *(p. 19)* and a crisp green salad.

Potato Kugel

Serves 4 to 6

David Hirsch's childhood featured holidays at Aunt Clara's in Borough Park, Brooklyn. One of the best parts of his visit was the promise of tasting again this crispy potato dish.

5 medium potatoes (2½ pounds), peeled if desired

2 medium onions

4 eggs

1 teaspoon salt

black pepper to taste

¼ cup matzoh meal *(see Appendix)* or bread crumbs

¼ cup vegetable oil

Coarsely grate the potatoes using the largest side of a hand grater or the large-holed grater blade of a food processor. Remove the potatoes to a colander and squeeze out as much water as possible.

Preheat the oven to 350°.

Grate the onions on the finer side of the grater or with the appropriate processor blade. Beat the eggs in a large bowl. Add the potatoes, onions, salt, pepper, and matzoh meal or bread crumbs. Mix well.

Put the oil in a 12×12-inch or 9×13-inch baking pan and place it in the hot oven for 5 minutes. Pour the hot oil into the batter, stirring just a little, and then pour the batter into the hot pan. This procedure makes the kugel crusty. Bake for 1 hour or until lightly browned.

Potato Kugel is a good side dish for large holiday meals or for supper at home. In either instance serve it (how else?) with sour cream and applesauce.

New World Matzoh Brie

Serves 2

No fancy-schmancy Brie in this classic, simple Jewish breakfast dish. Matzoh Brie (rhymes with fry) is a hearty pancake traditionally eaten during the Passover holiday. Because matzoh is available all year long, you can enjoy this anytime. Our version is updated with cheese for a more substantial entrée.

3 pieces of matzoh *(see Appendix)*

2 tablespoons butter

½ cup chopped onions

2 eggs

⅓ cup milk

1½ ounces cream cheese, cut into ½-inch cubes

1 cup grated cheese – cheddar, Swiss, Monterey Jack, or one of your choice (3 to 4 ounces)

salt and black pepper

Soften the matzohs by holding them under gently running water for a few seconds per side. Set them aside on a plate.

In a heavy skillet, sauté the onions in 1 tablespoon of butter until translucent. In a bowl, beat together the eggs and the milk. Crumble in the softened matzohs, add the cream cheese, and stir.

Pour the matzoh mixture over the onions and cook on low to medium heat until the bottom is dry and golden brown. Using a spatula, remove the pancake to a plate. Melt another tablespoon of butter in the pan, and then flip the pancake over onto the freshly buttered surface to brown the other side.

Sprinkle the pancake with grated cheese, cover, and cook until the cheese has melted and the matzoh begins to crisp on the bottom.

Serve immediately. Some people like this with a drizzle of honey or maple syrup, others with a splash of soy sauce.

Tortino Di Verdure

(*An Italian Vegetable Casserole*)

Serves 4 to 6

Layered vegetables and cheese baked together create a lavish and colorful production, like a lusty Italian opera.

1 medium eggplant	□
1 large potato	3 eggs
1 medium zucchini	1 teaspoon salt
4 fresh tomatoes	black pepper to taste
□	□
1 cup bread crumbs	½ cup olive oil
2 tablespoons chopped fresh basil (2 teaspoons dried)	1½ cups grated mozzarella cheese (6 ounces)
3 tablespoons chopped fresh parsley	1 cup freshly grated Parmesan cheese (2½ ounces)

Slice the eggplant crosswise into ½-inch rounds. Place the eggplant rounds on a lightly oiled baking sheet. Bake covered with foil at 400° until they are tender, about 45 minutes. Slice the potato and boil until just tender. Then drain and set aside. Slice the zucchini into ¼-inch rounds, slice the tomatoes about ½-inch thick, and set aside.

Mix together the bread crumbs, basil, and parsley. In a separate bowl, lightly beat the eggs with the salt and pepper.

Oil a 9 × 13-inch baking pan and coat the bottom and sides of the pan with about a quarter of the bread crumb mixture.

To layer the casserole, begin with all the eggplant slices. Drizzle 2 tablespoons of olive oil over them and sprinkle on a quarter of the bread crumbs and a quarter of the mozzarella and Parmesan cheeses. Pour a quarter of the beaten eggs on top of the cheese. Next layer all the potato slices. Repeat a layer of oil, crumbs, cheeses, and eggs. Layer all the zucchini, followed by oil, crumbs, cheeses, and eggs. Finally, layer the tomato slices topped with the remaining oil, crumbs, cheeses, and eggs.

Bake covered at 375° for 45 minutes. Allow the casserole to sit for about 10 minutes before serving.

Zucchini-Feta Casserole

Serves 4 to 6

One of our favorites, a dish that exemplifies the good flavors of Balkan cuisine: tangy feta cheese, nutty bulgur, and herbed zucchini. We add a few tastes foreign to the Balkans, too: tamari and cheddar cheese.

¾ cup bulgur (see Appendix)	□
¾ cup boiling water	2 eggs
	1 cup grated feta cheese (5 ounces)
□	1 cup cottage cheese
2½ tablespoons vegetable oil	
2 cups sliced onions	□
4 garlic cloves, minced or pressed	½ to 1 cup chopped fresh parsley
6 cups thinly sliced zucchini rounds	2 tablespoons tomato paste
½ teaspoon dried oregano	1 tablespoon tamari soy sauce
½ teaspoon dried basil	□
½ teaspoon dried marjoram	1 cup grated cheddar cheese (3 ounces)
⅛ teaspoon black pepper	2 medium tomatoes, thinly sliced
	1½ tablespoons sesame seeds (optional)

Place the bulgur in a bowl and pour the boiling water over it. Cover and set it aside until it has absorbed the water and become soft and chewable.

Sauté the onions and garlic in the oil until the onions are just translucent. Add the zucchini, dried herbs, and black pepper and continue to sauté on medium to low heat until the zucchini is tender, but not falling apart.

In a bowl, lightly beat the eggs. Mix in the feta and cottage cheese. Add the chopped parsley, tomato paste, and soy sauce to the bulgur and mix well.

Assemble the casserole in an oiled 9×9-inch casserole dish. Layer first the bulgur mixture, next the sautéed vegetables, and then the feta mixture. Top the casserole with grated cheddar cheese, tomato slices, and a light sprinkling of sesame seeds.

Bake covered at 350° for 45 minutes. For crustier cheese, uncover the casserole for the final 15 minutes of baking. This casserole can be more easily served after it sits for 5 or 10 minutes.

Serve this with a tossed salad and Flora's Tart and Tangy Dressing (p. 52).

Szechuan Sauté

Serves 4 to 6

This is a basic Asian sauté with the additional zing of orange juice. The anise and Szechuan peppercorns add an authentic spicy flavor.

2 cakes of tofu, pressed *(see Appendix)* **and cubed**

SAUCE

⅓ **cup tamari soy sauce**

½ **cup dry sherry**

½ **cup orange juice**

½ **teaspoon ground anise or fennel seeds**

½ **teaspoon Szechuan peppercorns, roasted and ground** *(see Appendix)*

1 tablespoon grated fresh ginger root

1 teaspoon dark sesame oil *(see Appendix)*

□

2 tablespoons cornstarch, dissolved in ½ **cup cold water**

□

¼ **cup vegetable oil**

1 tablespoon grated fresh ginger root

1 pound snow peas, stemmed or 1 large bunch broccoli, cut into florets and stem pieces

1 cup toasted peanuts

hot chili oil *(see Appendix)*, *(optional)*

□

2 scallions, chopped

Combine all the sauce ingredients except the cornstarch. Pour the sauce over the pressed and cubed tofu and allow it to marinate at least 15 minutes. Drain the marinated tofu, reserving the sauce. Stir the dissolved cornstarch into the sauce.

Heat the oil in a wok or large skillet. Add the grated ginger and stir for a minute. Add the snow peas and stir-fry them for just a minute. If you're using broccoli, stir-fry it until crisp, but tender, about 5 minutes. Stir in the marinated tofu. Slowly pour the sauce into the wok, stirring and simmering gently until it thickens, about 5 minutes. Stir in the peanuts. Sprinkle the sauté with a few drops of chili oil for a hotter dish. Serve immediately.

Serve on rice, garnished with chopped scallions.

Garden Vegetable and Tempeh Sauté

Serves 4 to 6

A nice introduction to tempeh, which is a staple of Indonesian cuisine. This sauté is a perfect selection for late summer when zucchini, peppers, and tomatoes are plentiful.

8 ounces tempeh *(see Appendix)*, **cut into ½-inch cubes**

½ cup burgundy or dry red wine

¼ cup tamari soy sauce

□

3 tablespoons vegetable oil

2 cups chopped onions

3 garlic cloves, minced or pressed

4 cups sliced zucchini (half-moons are nice)

1 medium red or green pepper, chopped (red preferred)

4 medium tomatoes, chopped, or 3 cups canned tomatoes, drained and chopped

1 tablespoon fresh dill (¾ teaspoon dried)

3 tablespoons chopped fresh parsley

salt and black pepper to taste

□

chopped scallions

Mix together the wine and soy sauce, pour it over the tempeh cubes, and allow it to marinate while preparing the vegetables.

In a wok or a large skillet or saucepan, sauté the onions and garlic in the oil until translucent. Drain the tempeh, reserving any remaining marinade. Add the tempeh to the onions and garlic and cook on medium heat for 5 to 10 minutes or until the tempeh starts to brown. The tempeh should be stirred frequently to avoid sticking. Add the zucchini slices, salt lightly, and cover the pot. Cook for another 5 minutes, then add the peppers and sauté 5 minutes more. Add the tomatoes and seasonings. Taste. Add the reserved marinade, to taste, being careful that the sauté doesn't become too salty. Cook until the tomatoes begin to break down into a sauce, about 10 minutes.

Serve on rice and garnish with chopped scallions.

"Barbecued" Tempeh or Tofu

Serves 4 to 6

Not the classic BBQ, but spicy and delicious in its own right.

1 pound tempeh, cubed, or 3 cakes of tofu, pressed *(see Appendix)* **and cubed**

☐

3 tablespoons vegetable oil

1 cup finely chopped onions

2 large garlic cloves, minced or pressed

1 teaspoon ground fennel seeds

1 teaspoon chili powder

1 teaspoon ground coriander

1 teaspoon ground cumin

⅛ teaspoon cayenne

1 green or red bell pepper, chopped

SAUCE

2 tablespoons tamari soy sauce

2 tablespoons fresh lemon juice

3 tablespoons molasses or brown sugar

2 tablespoons cider vinegar

1 tablespoon prepared mustard

6 tablespoons tomato paste (7-ounce can)

1 cup water

4 to 5 dashes Tabasco or other hot red pepper sauce

For tempeh:

Sauté the onions, garlic, and spices until the onions begin to soften. Add the peppers and tempeh and continue sautéing until the peppers brighten and the tempeh browns. Transfer this mixture to a shallow baking pan.

Whisk together the sauce ingredients and pour them over the vegetable-tempeh mixture. Bake covered at 350° for ½ hour and uncovered for another ½ hour, stirring frequently throughout.

For tofu:

Sauté the vegetables and spices. Whisk together the sauce ingredients. Combine the sautéed vegetables and the sauce and pour over the tofu cubes in a shallow baking pan. Bake as directed for tempeh, stirring very gently to avoid breaking the tofu cubes.

Serve on rice with a side dish of coleslaw or Italian Greens *(p. 213)*. Or pack it into a pita to make a Dixie Pita Sandwich *(p. 67)*.

"Mapo" Tofu

Serves 4 to 6

Inspired by the cuisine of Szechuan, this spicy dish is substantial and full of flavor. Our meatless variation of this classic has become a favorite at the restaurant among our "hot" food lovers.

2 cakes of tofu

SAUCE

¼ cup tamari soy sauce

¼ cup dry sherry

2 tablespoons white or cider vinegar

1½ tablespoons grated fresh ginger root

3 tablespoons tomato paste

1 cup water

1 tablespoon dark sesame oil *(see Appendix)*

1 to 2 tablespoons chili paste with garlic *(see Appendix)* **or 3 garlic cloves, pressed, and cayenne to taste**

¼ cup vegetable oil

2 cups thinly sliced onions

1 large bunch broccoli, cut into 3-inch spears

4 cups sliced mushrooms (1 pound)

2 tablespoons cornstarch dissolved in 2 tablespoons cold water

☐

toasted walnuts

3 scallions, diagonally sliced

Press the tofu *(see Appendix)* and then cut it into 1-inch cubes and set aside. Whisk together the sauce ingredients and set aside.

Heat the oil in a wok on medium to high heat. Sauté the onions for 3 to 4 minutes, stirring often. Then add the broccoli and sauté for an additional 4 minutes. Next add the mushrooms and cook for about 3 minutes, still stirring often. Pour in the sauce and add the tofu. Lower the heat, cover, and simmer until the tofu is thoroughly heated. Finally, add the dissolved cornstarch and bring back to a simmer, stirring occasionally until the sauce thickens.

Serve on rice, garnished with walnuts and scallions.

Sweet and Sour Vegetables and Tofu

Serves 4 to 6

Sweet-and-sour combinations are always a favorite at Moosewood, and this particular one features tender-crisp vegetables with a zesty sauce.

2 cakes of tofu, pressed *(see Appendix)* **and cubed**

SAUCE

1½ teaspoons grated fresh ginger root

4 tablespoons brown sugar or honey

6 tablespoons white vinegar

3 tablespoons tamari soy sauce

¼ cup tomato paste or catsup

☐

3 tablespoons vegetable oil

3 cups thinly sliced onions

1 tablespoon grated fresh ginger root

2 medium carrots, diagonally sliced

½ pound string beans, whole, if small, or cut into 3-inch pieces

1 large red or green pepper, in long slices

4 cups sliced mushrooms (1 pound)

4 cups zucchini rounds

¾ cup fresh or canned pineapple, in chunks *(optional)*

1 tablespoon cornstarch dissolved in ½ cup cold Vegetable Stock *(p. 30),* **pineapple juice, or water**

☐

hot chili oil *(optional)*

2 scallions, chopped

Stir together the sauce ingredients and set aside, and prepare the tofu and vegetables before you begin to stir-fry.

Heat the oil in a wok or a pot large enough for all the ingredients. Stir-fry the onions and ginger. When the onions are translucent, add the carrots and continue cooking for 3 to 4 minutes before adding the beans (2 more minutes), the pepper (2 more minutes), and then the mushrooms and zucchini.

Turn down the heat, cover the wok or pot, and cook, stirring once or twice, until the vegetables are tender but still crisp. Stir in the pineapple, tofu, sauce, and dissolved cornstarch and bring to a boil. Simmer, stirring gently, for 3 or 4 minutes. If a hot and spicy dish is desired, add a few dashes of hot chili oil.

Serve at once over rice or noodles. Top with sliced scallions.

Vegetable Ragoût

Serves 4 to 6

A crusty loaf of French bread is de rigueur along with a hearty burgundy, a wedge of Brie, and Edith Piaf. Or, for the peasant in you, serve over noodles with sour cream and Rachmaninoff.

2 tablespoons vegetable oil	*SAUCE*
2 garlic cloves, minced or pressed	2 tablespoons tamari soy sauce
2 cups chopped onions	½ teaspoon salt
2 medium carrots, sliced in ½-inch pieces	1 cup Vegetable Stock *(p. 30)* or water
4 medium celery stalks, chopped	3 tablespoons tomato paste
1½ cups cut green beans	1 teaspoon Dijon mustard
2 bay leaves	1 tablespoon vinegar
pinch of dried thyme	1 tablespoon molasses
1½ cups dry red wine	pinch of black pepper
1½ cups sliced zucchini	1 teaspoon dried basil *(optional)*
4 cups sliced mushrooms (1 pound)	2 medium potatoes, cut in chunks

Heat the oil in a heavy stew pot or kettle (not aluminum or cast iron because tomato and wine react chemically with these metals). Sauté the garlic, onions, carrots, celery, and green beans for 3 to 4 minutes. Add the bay leaves, thyme, and red wine and boil, uncovered, for 3 minutes. Reduce heat, cover, and simmer for 5 minutes. Add the zucchini and mushrooms. Combine the sauce ingredients and then stir the sauce into the vegetables. Simmer approximately 30 minutes, until the vegetables are tender and the flavors well blended.

While the vegetables are stewing, cook the potatoes separately in salted, boiling water until they are tender. Drain and add them to the ragoût a few minutes before serving.

Moroccan Stew

Serves 4 to 6

The exotic fragrance of this dish as it's cooking is almost reason enough to make it. This vegetable stew makes a substantial meal, especially when served with hard-boiled eggs, almonds, and couscous or pita bread, which is how we always serve it at the restaurant.

⅓ cup olive oil

3 cups coarsely chopped onions

2 garlic cloves, minced or pressed

1 teaspoon ground cumin

1 teaspoon turmeric

½ teaspoon cinnamon

¼ to 1 teaspoon cayenne

½ teaspoon paprika

☐

1 cup sliced carrots

4 cups cubed sweet potatoes or butternut squash

3 cups cubed eggplant

1 green pepper, sliced in strips

4 cups sliced zucchini or summer squash

2 large tomatoes, chopped

1½ cups cooked garbanzo beans *(see Appendix)*, liquid reserved

pinch of saffron

¾ cup dried currants or ½ cup raisins

☐

¼ cup chopped fresh parsley

In a stew pot, heat the olive oil and sauté the onions for 2 or 3 minutes. Add the garlic and spices, stirring continuously. Add the vegetables in the order given above, so that the starchier vegetables will cook the longest. Sauté after the addition of each vegetable until its color deepens. Stir in the garbanzo beans, the saffron, and the currants or raisins. There should be some liquid at the bottom of the pot from the cooking vegetables. However, if the stew is dry, add ½ cup of tomato juice, liquid from the garbanzo beans, or water.

Cover the stew and simmer on low heat until all the vegetables are tender. Add the chopped parsley just before serving.

West African Groundnut Stew

Serves 4 to 6

The recipe for this stew came from Sierra Leone, Africa and then underwent a few changes in the Moosewood kitchen. To be authentic, the dish would use palm oil, tomato paste, and fewer vegetables, but with all due respect, we prefer our version.

2 sweet potatoes, peeled and cubed	4 cups peeled and cubed eggplant
□	¼ to ½ cup Vegetable Stock *(p. 30)* or water
2 tablespoons vegetable oil	1 cup chopped zucchini or yellow summer squash
3 garlic cloves, minced or pressed	2 green peppers, coarsely chopped
3 tablespoons grated fresh ginger root	□
2 tablespoons ground coriander	2 cups tomato juice
½ teaspoon cayenne (or to taste)	½ cup peanut butter *(see Appendix)*
4 cups chopped onions	
2 tomatoes, chopped	

Steam or boil the sweet potato cubes until just tender.

Meanwhile, sauté the garlic, ginger, and spices in oil for one minute. Add the onions and cook until they begin to soften. Add the tomatoes, eggplant, and a small amount of vegetable stock or water and simmer for 10 minutes. Add the zucchini and peppers and continue to simmer until all of the vegetables are tender, about 20 minutes.

Drain the sweet potatoes and add them to the stew along with the tomato juice and peanut butter. Stir well. Simmer on very low heat for 5 to 10 minutes, stirring occasionally to prevent sticking.

Serve on rice, couscous, or millet. At Moosewood we garnish this stew with hard-boiled egg halves and pineapple and banana slices.

Winter Vegetable Stew

Serves 6 to 8

A nutty, warming, stew based on root vegetables enriched with miso and tahini.

2 cakes of tofu, pressed *(see Appendix)*
   and cubed

□

3 tablespoons vegetable or peanut oil

2 cups chopped onions

3 garlic cloves, minced or pressed

¼ teaspoon cayenne

3 cups quartered mushrooms
   (12 ounces)

3 cups Vegetable Stock *(p. 30)* **or water**

2 cups cubed sweet potatoes

2 cups chopped carrots

1 cup peeled, cubed parsnips

2 cups peeled, cubed turnips

□

¼ cup miso *(see Appendix)*

⅔ cup tahini *(see Appendix)*

¼ cup peanut butter *(see Appendix)*

4 teaspoons tamari soy sauce

2 tablespoons cider vinegar

salt to taste

1 tablespoon kuzu *(see Appendix)* **or**
   cornstarch dissolved in 1 tablespoon
   water *(optional)*

□

¼ cup chopped fresh parsley

½ cup chopped scallions

Prepare the tofu.

Heat the oil in a large stew pot. Sauté the onions, garlic, and cayenne until the onions are translucent. Add the mushrooms and continue to sauté for 5 minutes more, stirring occasionally. Add the stock or water, cover, and bring to a boil. Add the remaining vegetables and simmer for 15 minutes. Add the tofu and continue simmering for another 5 minutes, until the vegetables are tender.

Ladle 1 cup of hot broth into a mixing bowl. Add the miso and mash it until it dissolves. Stir in the tahini and peanut butter and mix until smooth. Add the soy sauce and vinegar. Pour this mixture into the pot of simmering vegetables, stirring gently. Adjust the seasonings with more soy sauce or salt to taste. For a thicker sauce, stir in the kuzu or cornstarch dissolved in water.

Serve on rice or couscous. Garnish with chopped parsley and scallions.

Mixed Vegetable Curry

Serves 4 to 6

Cinnamon, cardamom, turmeric, cumin... the beginning of curry. Traditionally, curries are served with a variety of condiments and side dishes. See our suggestions at the end of the recipe.

2 tablespoons vegetable oil

3 tablespoons butter

½ teaspoon black mustard seeds
  (optional)

3 medium garlic cloves, minced or
  pressed

1 teaspoon cinnamon

½ teaspoon ground cardamom

1½ teaspoons ground cumin

1½ teaspoons ground coriander seeds

½ teaspoons ground fennel seeds

1 teaspoon turmeric

2 teaspoons grated fresh ginger root

½ teaspoon cayenne (or more to taste)

1 teaspoon salt

2 cups chopped onions *(optional)*

2 medium carrots, sliced into
  half-moons

3 cups cubed sweet potatoes or white
  potatoes

1 medium head of cauliflower, cut into
  florets

¾ cup water

2 medium tomatoes, chopped

2 cups green peas or 2 medium green
  peppers, chopped

□

2 cups plain yogurt

½ cup cashews, lightly toasted

½ cup raisins or currants

1 banana

Melt the butter and oil in a skillet or wok. Add the mustard seeds and heat until they begin to pop. Add the remaining spices and cook on low heat for a couple of minutes to enhance the flavors of the spices. Be very careful not to burn them. Add the chopped onions and sauté until translucent.

Add the carrots and cook several minutes. Add the potatoes and cook a few minutes more. Add the cauliflower and stir well to coat all the vegetables with the spice mixture. Add the water, cover the pan, and simmer about 20 minutes, stirring occasionally. When the potatoes are tender but not completely cooked, add the tomatoes and peas or green peppers. Simmer covered for 10 to

15 minutes longer. The vegetables should retain their bright color, and if you use sweet potatoes, they will soften and become part of the sauce making it thicker and more interesting.

Serve on plain or Coconut Rice *(p. 200)*. Garnish with yogurt, cashews, raisins or currants, and banana slices. Accompany with Dhall *(p. 216)* and Date-Lemon Chutney *(p. 214)* or Peach Chutney *(p. 215)*.

Moosewood is more than a restaurant; it is an enhancement of our civilization. And, of course, as a gardener, I rush home to try to apply the principles of both restaurant and book to my own produce.
— Peter Hedrick
baroque oboist and Ithaca College professor

Zucchini Ankara

Serves 4 to 6

An unusual Mediterranean-style dish with a bright lemony flavor.

¼ cup olive oil

2 cups chopped onions

3 to 4 garlic cloves, minced or pressed

3 zucchini and/or yellow squash, cut into half-moons about ½-inch thick (about 6 cups total)

1 teaspoon dried marjoram

1 cup cooked drained garbanzo beans
(see Appendix)

½ cup sliced, pitted black olives (preferably salty Greek ones)

□

1 tablespoon ground cumin or
   2 teaspoons dried mint

3 to 6 tablespoons fresh lemon juice

salt and black pepper to taste

pinch of cayenne

□

1 cup grated feta cheese (5 ounces)

Sauté the onions and garlic until the onion is translucent. Add the squash and marjoram and cook on medium heat, stirring often, until the squash is just tender. If the squash hasn't released enough liquid to simmer in, add ¼ cup of water. This should be a juicy dish. Add the garbanzos, olives, cumin or mint, lemon juice, and seasonings. Remember that if the feta that will be sprinkled on top later is quite salty, little or no salt will be needed in the vegetables themselves. Continue cooking until everything is thoroughly heated. The squash should not become overly soft.

Adjust the lemon and herbs to taste and ladle the vegetables over the rice or couscous. Top with feta cheese and serve immediately.

Cuban Black Beans and Rice

Serves 6

Oh, Ricky, play Babaloo! Here's a well spiced, wholesome meal of contrasting tastes and textures. Rejoice over leftovers, because black beans taste great the second day and can be made into black bean soup simply by adding more tomatoes and orange juice.

7 cups cooked black beans
(see Appendix)

□

3 tablespoons olive oil or butter
2 garlic cloves, minced or pressed
1 cup chopped onions
1 teaspoon ground cumin
1 teaspoon ground coriander seeds
1 teaspoon paprika
1 cup chopped carrots

□

1 medium green pepper, chopped
salt and black pepper to taste
¼ cup chopped fresh parsley
1 cup tomato juice or orange juice
2 medium tomatoes, chopped
6 cups cooked brown rice
(see Appendix)
2 cups Hot Sauce *(p. 193)*
1 cup sour cream

Drain the cooked beans and reserve the liquid.

In a large skillet or sturdy saucepan, sauté the onions, garlic, and spices in the oil or butter until the onions are translucent. Add the carrots and sauté for 3 or 4 minutes. Add the green peppers and sauté for 5 minutes more. Add salt, black pepper, parsley, juice, and tomatoes and simmer until the vegetables are tender.

Combine the drained black beans with the vegetable mixture. Purée 2 to 3 cups of the bean-vegetable mixture in the blender with enough reserved liquid (or stock or water) to make a smooth purée. Stir the purée into the beans and simmer for 10 minutes. Taste for salt.

Serve the beans on hot rice and top with Hot Sauce and a dollop of sour cream.

Creole Beans and Rice

Serves 6

Our version of a New Orleans classic. Traditionally prepared on Mondays, when the washing could be done while the beans simmered away on a back burner.

3 cups dried kidney beans
½ teaspoon cayenne
⅛ teaspoon ground allspice
SALSA
3 scallions, diced
1 cucumber, peeled, seeded, and diced
2 tomatoes, diced
¾ cup chopped fresh parsley
¼ cup vegetable oil
3½ tablespoons cider vinegar
salt to taste
Tabasco or other hot pepper sauce to taste
  □
3 tablespoons vegetable oil
3 cups chopped onions
6 garlic cloves, minced or pressed

3 medium celery stalks, diced
1 cup diced carrots
2 to 3 green peppers, chopped
⅓ cup tomato paste
¼ cup red wine
1 teaspoon apple cider vinegar
1½ teaspoons brown sugar
1 teaspoon Dijon mustard
1¼ teaspoon salt
½ teaspoon dried oregano
⅛ teaspoon cayenne
⅛ teaspoon ground allspice
  □
2½ cups uncooked brown rice
sour cream

Cook the beans *(see Appendix)* with ½ teaspoon cayenne and ⅛ teaspoon ground allspice.

Combine all the salsa ingredients and set aside. After half an hour taste the salsa and add more hot pepper sauce if you'd like it "hotter."

Sauté the onions and garlic in oil on medium heat until the onions are translucent. Add the celery and carrots and continue to cook several minutes longer. Stir occasionally. Add the green pepper and sauté until all the vegetables are just tender. Whisk together the tomato paste, red wine, vinegar, brown sugar, mustard, herbs, and spices. Add this to the sautéed vegetables. In a large pot combine the drained beans and the sautéed vegetable mixture and stir them until thoroughly mixed. Simmer covered for 30 minutes, stirring frequently.

Cook the rice *(see Appendix)*.

When both the beans and the rice are ready, prepare each plate individually with a layer of rice and then beans, topped with a spoonful or two of salsa. Finish with a dollop of sour cream, and get ready to warm your innards.

Moosewood Restaurant is nationally renowned for its recipes, which only partly reflect its style. What many do not know is that the restaurant also provides an important role model for other worker-owned and worker-managed enterprises. Besides providing an excellent example of how we can feed ourselves well, the collective also provides an example of how we can treat each other well.

— Kirby Edmonds
human relations consultant

Habas Verdes Con Queso

(Lima Beans with Cheese)

~

Serves 4 to 6

This spicy, creamy lima bean and vegetable casserole also makes an excellent dip for chips and vegetable sticks.

6 cups cooked lima beans *(see Appendix)*	**2 teaspoons hot chili powder**
8 ounces cream cheese	**½ teaspoon dry mustard**
□	**1 teaspoon ground cumin**
2 tablespoons vegetable oil	**1 teaspoon Spanish paprika**
2 cups chopped onions	**salt to taste**
2 large garlic cloves, minced or pressed	□
3 green and/or red bell peppers, chopped	**tortilla chips**
2 medium carrots, diced	**tomato wedges**
2 cups chopped fresh tomatoes or drained canned tomatoes	**chopped fresh parsley**

In a large bowl add the cream cheese to the hot, drained lima beans and mix well to melt the cream cheese. Cover and set aside.

Sauté the onions and garlic in the oil until the onions are translucent. Add the peppers and carrots and continue to sauté for 5 minutes. Then add the tomatoes and spices, reduce the heat, and simmer about 15 minutes, until the carrots are tender.

Stir the sautéed vegetables into the bean mixture. Pour the mixture into a well-oiled casserole dish and bake at 350° for 25 minutes.

Top Habas Verdes Con Queso with parsley and serve with tortilla chips and tomato wedges.

Boston Black-Eyed Peas

Serves 4

Southerners have a special fondness for black-eyed peas. This treatment has a decidedly New England twist, but the distinctive flavor of the black-eyed peas still comes through. Black-eyed peas are traditionally served on New Year's Day to ensure good luck, and we ain't just whistlin' Dixie.

4 cups fresh black-eyed peas (or 2 10-ounce packages frozen)

3 cups water

1 teaspoon salt

☐

1 tablespoon butter or vegetable oil

2 garlic cloves, minced or pressed

1 cup chopped onions

1 cup chopped fresh beet greens, collards, chard, or spinach *(optional)*

¼ cup tamari soy sauce

⅓ cup molasses

1 teaspoon dried mustard or a good quality prepared mustard

Bring the salted water to a boil in a saucepan. Add the black-eyed peas. Cover and return to a boil, then lower the heat and simmer until just tender, about 15 minutes.

Sauté the garlic and onions in the butter or oil until the onions are just translucent. If you choose to add greens, mix them into the onions and continue to sauté until the greens wilt. Mix together the soy sauce, molasses, and mustard and set aside. Drain the black-eyed peas, saving a cup of the liquid.

In the saucepan, stir together the drained peas, the sautéed onion mixture and the molasses-soy sauce. Cover and simmer on very low heat for 10 to 15 minutes, stirring frequently. During this simmer there is some danger of sticking or scorching, so either use a "waffle" *(see Appendix)* or watch closely, adding a little of the pea stock if the sauce becomes too thick.

We like Boston Black-Eyed Peas served with tart coleslaw and Cornbread *(p. 235)* or Steamed Brown Bread *(p. 234)*.

Cheese Tart

Serves 6

If you're a confirmed vegetarian with a nostalgic yearning for the distinctive flavor and aroma of bacon, here's the dish for you! The trick is in the smoked Swiss cheese.

pastry dough for one 10-inch pie
(p. 253)

□

1½ cups grated sharp cheddar cheese, firmly packed (5 ounces)

1 cup grated Jarlsberg, Swiss, or mild Gruyère cheese, firmly packed (4 ounces)

¾ cup grated smoked Swiss cheese (3 ounces)

6 eggs

2½ tablespoons unbleached white flour

½ teaspoon salt

¼ teaspoon black pepper

1 cup milk

1 cup half-and-half

Roll out the dough and line a 10-inch pie pan with it.

Preheat the oven to 375°.

Sprinkle the cheeses evenly into the prepared pie shell. Blend the eggs, flour, salt, and pepper in a blender or food processor or with a whisk. Add the milk and half-and-half and blend thoroughly. Pour this mixture into the pie shell, over the cheese. Bake for about 45 minutes, until a knife inserted in the center comes out clean.

Serve for brunch, lunch, or a light supper with a tomato half brushed with olive oil, sprinkled with basil, and broiled.

Pissaladière

~~~~~~~~

Serves 4 to 6

This Provençale quiche reflects the Mediterranean fondness for basil, tomatoes, and olives.

pastry dough for one 9-inch pie *(p. 253)*

☐

2 tablespoons olive oil

2 cups chopped onions

1 garlic clove, minced or pressed

¼ teaspoon salt

3 tablespoons chopped fresh basil (1 tablespoon dried)

4 eggs, lightly beaten

1 cup milk

¼ teaspoon dry mustard

1 tablespoon unbleached white flour

⅓ cup freshly grated Parmesan cheese (1 ounce)

¾ cup grated mozzarella cheese, packed (4 ounces)

⅓ cup sliced, pitted black olives

☐

1 medium tomato, thinly sliced

Roll out the pastry dough and line a 9-inch pie pan with it.

Sauté the onions and garlic in olive oil until tender and lightly golden. Add the basil and salt.

Preheat the oven to 375°.

Thoroughly mix the eggs, milk, mustard, and flour and set aside. Combine the two cheeses. Sprinkle half of the cheese into the pie shell. Spread the sautéed onions over the cheese. Scatter on the sliced olives. Pour the egg-milk mixture into the pie. Cover with the remaining cheese and arrange the tomato slices attractively on top. Bake 40 to 45 minutes or until the custard is set.

Now, get out your red-checked tablecloth, open a bottle of wine, light the candles, imagine a soft Mediterranean breeze, and....

Tofu Burgers and "Meatballs"

Yields 6 large burgers

Tofu burgers may sound like the early days of '60s vegetarian cooking, when imitation meat was all the rage. But in fact, these burgers are absolutely delicious and are one of our most popular standard lunch items. We know lots of kids who gladly devour tofu burgers and "meatballs."

3 tablespoons vegetable oil

1 large onion, finely chopped

1 large carrot, grated

1 green pepper, finely chopped

1½ teaspoons dried basil

□

2 large eggs*

1 cup bread crumbs

¾ cup walnuts, ground or finely chopped

¼ cup chopped fresh parsley

1 tablespoon Dijon mustard

1½ tablespoons dark sesame oil *(see Appendix)*

3 tablespoons tamari soy sauce

black pepper to taste

□

3 cakes of tofu, pressed *(see Appendix)*

Sauté the vegetables and basil in oil until tender, about 10 minutes. In a large bowl, lightly beat the eggs, then add the bread crumbs, walnuts, and remaining ingredients. Mash the pressed tofu either with a potato masher or your hands and add it to the bowl, along with the sautéed vegetables. Stir well; the mixture should be firm enough to form into patties.

Pat the mixture into 6 large "burgers." Bake on an oiled baking sheet at 375° until golden brown on the outside, but still moist inside, about 30 minutes.

Serve with Russian Dressing *(p. 57)* or ketchup, tomato slices, lettuce, pickles, chips, and sprouts on whole wheat or rye toast.

- *Tofu "Meatballs":* For about 3 dozen balls, add the following ingredients to the basic burger mix: 3 garlic cloves, minced, 1 teaspoon ground fennel seed, ¾ teaspoon dried oregano, and an additional 1½ teaspoons Dijon mustard. Form 1½-inch balls and bake at 350° on an oiled baking sheet for 20 to 30 minutes.

When that urge for a submarine sandwich hits, stuff some pita or Italian bread with lettuce, bermuda onions, and Tofu "Meatballs" doused with tomato sauce. Or use them to top off spaghetti with tomato sauce and grated Parmesan cheese.

For an eggless version, omit the eggs and add the juice of 1 lemon and ¼ cup tahini (see Appendix). Reduce the tamari soy sauce to 2 tablespoons and increase the bread crumbs to 1¼ cups.

I like Moosewood's food because it's fresh and homemade-tasting. I like their chocolate cake. But, my eyes water when I come into the kitchen because of all the onions.

— Aaron Stein Mank, age 7
Moosewood kid, son of Wynelle Stein

Soyfalafel

Yields approximately 36 small balls

Falafel are the hot dogs of the Middle East. Stuffed into pita bread, Soyfalafel is street food, something to eat on the go. When made the traditional way with cooked garbanzo beans, preparation is a long process. Our version, using tofu, is much faster, equally delectable, and lighter and higher in protein.

3 cakes of tofu, pressed *(see Appendix)* and mashed	black pepper to taste
1 cup finely chopped onions	3 garlic cloves, minced
3 tablespoons vegetable oil	½ cup toasted sesame seeds
1 cup bread crumbs	1 tablespoon ground cumin
¼ cup chopped fresh parsley	1 tablespoon turmeric
1½ tablespoons dark sesame oil *(see Appendix)*	4 tablespoons tahini *(see Appendix)*
3 tablespoons tamari soy sauce	4 tablespoons fresh lemon juice
	¼ to ½ teaspoon cayenne

In a large bowl, mix together all the ingredients. Form into 1-inch balls and bake at 350° on an oiled baking sheet for about 30 minutes. The balls should be golden and a little crusty on the outside, but still moist inside.

Serve with Tahini-Garlic Dressing *(p. 59)*. Soyfalafels make excellent appetizers and are also delicious stuffed into toasted pita bread with shredded lettuce, chopped tomatoes, cucumbers, and dressing.

STRUDELS

Golden strudels and individual turnovers made with phyllo dough look professionally finished and impressive. Many home cooks are intimidated by the thought of making a strudel; they expect that it will be difficult, time-consuming, and tedious. But it's not! Please read about it in the Appendix and give it a try. With enough working space and no breezes to dry out the dough, you won't have any trouble. We promise.

Here are five savory strudels representing the many different strudels we serve at Moosewood. Any number of vegetable, cheese, and herb combinations is possible in a strudel. Sometimes we make an onion and cauliflower strudel, using sharp cheese. Another possibility is broccoli-onion-mushroom, using the same cheeses listed in Russian Vegetable Strudel *(p. 142)* and seasoned with marjoram, fresh parsley, and tarragon.

Experiment! The only way you can go wrong is if your mixture is too bland (add some Dijon mustard) or too wet (crack in an egg or two or add bread crumbs or flour.)

Cheese Börek

Serves 6 to 8

Golden phyllo pastry filled with a lush variety of cheeses and herbs.

**1 pound 8 ounces cream cheese, at
room temperature**

1½ cups grated feta cheese (8 ounces)

3 cups cottage cheese

6 eggs, beaten

3 cups chopped fresh parsley

**⅓ cup chopped fresh dill (1 tablespoon
dried)**

□

¼ pound melted butter

½ pound phyllo dough *(see Appendix)*

□

whole fennel seeds for topping *(optional)*

Combine the first six ingredients in a large mixing bowl.

Preheat the oven to 375°.

Assemble the strudel *(see Appendix)*, sprinkling the top with whole fennel seeds.

Bake for about 45 minutes, or until the top layer of phyllo is puffed and golden and the filling is set. Allow to rest ten minutes after removing from the oven.

Slice into squares or triangles and serve with steamed asparagus in Vinaigrette Salad Dressing *(p. 50)* and plump ripe tomato wedges.

Cabbage Strudel

Serves 6

Cabbage has an undeserved dreary reputation. When you serve this delectable strudel, all golden and puffed from the oven, you will quiet fears, renew faith, and warm hearts.

1½ cups cooked brown rice *(see Appendix)*

□

2 tablespoons veetable oil

3 cups chopped onions

7 to 8 cups shredded cabbage

2 teaspoons caraway seeds

2 teaspoons dried dill

1 teaspoon salt

black pepper to taste

8 ounces cream cheese, cubed

½ cup grated Swiss cheese (1¾ ounces)

1 cup grated cheddar cheese (3 ounces)

2 eggs

□

½ pound phyllo dough *(see Appendix)*

¼ pound melted butter

□

caraway seeds for topping *(optional)*

Sauté the onions in oil until translucent. Add the cabbage, caraway seeds, dill, salt, and pepper. Cook covered stirring frequently, until the cabbage softens. Uncover and continue cooking until the cabbage is limp and both the cabbage and onions are beginning to brown. Light browning gives a sweeter, richer flavor. Remove from the heat and drain the excess liquid.

In a large bowl, mix the cooked rice with the cream cheese and the grated cheeses. Add the eggs and sautéed vegetables. Mix well.

Preheat the oven to 350°.

Assemble the strudel *(see Appendix)* and sprinkle the top with caraway seeds.

Bake for about 45 minutes or until golden brown. Allow to rest 10 minutes before slicing.

Serve with pickled beets and applesauce.

Kolokithopita

(A zucchini-feta cheese strudel)

Serves 6

Strudel is a snazzy centerpiece for any meal. This one has the added advantage of using up some of the mountains of zucchini that even the smallest garden seems to produce.

**4 cups grated zucchini, about 2
   medium zucchini**

□

¼ cup olive oil

1½ cups chopped onions

2 garlic cloves, minced or pressed

2 cups grated feta cheese (10 ounces)

2 cups cottage cheese

4 eggs, lightly beaten

3 tablespoons unbleached white flour

1 tablespoon chopped fresh parsley

**1 tablespoon fresh mint
   (1 teaspoon dried)**

**2 tablespoons fresh dill
   (1½ teaspoons dried)**

½ teaspoon black pepper

□

½ pound phyllo dough *(see Appendix)*

¼ pound melted butter

Place the grated zucchini in a colander, salt it lightly, and cover it with a plate that is weighted down with a heavy can. Allow the zucchini to drain for at least 20 minutes.

Sauté the onions and garlic in olive oil until the onions are translucent. Mix the cheeses, eggs, and flour in a large bowl.

Return to the zucchini. Take a handful at a time and squeeze out as much additional juice as possible. Add the zucchini, herbs, and spices to the pan with the onions and sauté gently for 10 minutes. Combine the sautéed vegetables and cheese mixture.

Preheat the oven to 350°.

Assemble the strudel *(see Appendix)*. Bake for 45 minutes or until puffy and golden. Allow to rest 10 minutes before slicing.

Serve Kolokithopita with Tzatziki *(p. 207)*, Middle Eastern Carrot Salad *(p. 39)*, and glossy kalamata olives.

Mushroom, Spinach, and Cheese Torta

Serves 6

An Italian strudel rich with mellow and sharp cheeses.

¼ cup olive oil

2 cups chopped onions

4 garlic cloves, minced or pressed

6 cups sliced fresh mushrooms
(1 pound 8 ounces)

10 ounces fresh spinach

1½ cups ricotta cheese

1½ cups freshly grated Parmesan
cheese (4 ounces)

1 cup sour cream

3 eggs, beaten

½ cup bread crumbs

¼ cup chopped fresh parsley

☐

½ pound phyllo dough *(see Appendix)*

¼ pound melted butter

☐

2 teaspoons sesame seeds for topping
(optional)

Sauté the onions and garlic in olive oil until the onions are translucent. Add the mushrooms and spinach and continue sautéing until the mushrooms have released their juices and the spinach has wilted. Remove from the heat.

In a large bowl, combine the cheeses, sour cream, eggs, bread crumbs, and parsley. Stir in the mushroom mixture. If the vegetables are very juicy, drain some of the excess liquid before adding them to the cheeses.

Preheat the oven to 375°.

Assemble the strudel *(see Appendix)*. Scatter the sesame seeds across the top layer of buttered phyllo. Bake for 50 minutes or until the filling is set and the phyllo is crisp and golden. Allow to rest 10 minutes before slicing.

Accompany with Peppers and Capers *(p. 41)*.

Russian Vegetable Strudel

Serves 8

Even if you have no Russian ancestors, these strong flavors seem to stir memories of a warm, steamy kitchen, safe from the bitter cold winds of the snowy steppes.

1 tablespoon butter

1 tablespoon vegetable oil

2 cups chopped onions

1½ cups thinly sliced carrots

3 cups chopped cabbage

1 teaspoon salt

1½ teaspoons dried dill

1 teaspoon caraway seeds

3 cups sliced mushrooms (12 ounces)

½ teaspoon black pepper

□

8 ounces cream cheese, at room temperature

2 cups cottage cheese

1 cup grated sharp cheddar cheese (3 ounces)

4 eggs

□

½ pound phyllo dough *(see Appendix)*

¼ pound melted butter

In a large skillet or saucepan, sauté the onions in the butter and oil until they are translucent. Add the carrots and sauté for 5 minutes. Add the cabbage to the pan and sauté covered for another 5 minutes. Season with the salt, dill, and caraway seeds and cook for 5 minutes more. Add the mushrooms and black pepper and sauté for a final 5 minutes.

In a large mixing bowl, combine the softened cream cheese with the cottage cheese, grated cheddar, and eggs. Drain the sautéed vegetables and stir them into the cheese mixture.

Preheat the oven to 375°.

Assemble the strudel *(see Appendix)*. Bake for about 40 minutes, until golden brown. Allow the strudel to sit for 10 minutes before cutting.

Serve with cucumbers in Vinaigrette Salad Dressing *(p. 50)* and a baked apple, and sigh for Mother Russia.

MAIN DISHES:
Pastas

Pastas

What would life be without pasta? What other foodstuff is available in so many shapes, sizes, and colors? Or has an affinity for such a diverse range of sauces and seasonings? Or is so quickly prepared and so soothing to eat?

All pasta begins with a dough made of flour and liquid, but from that point the variations are seemingly endless. The flour may be wheat, rice, or other grain; the liquid water, eggs, or vegetable juice. The best pastas are made with durum wheat, a hard wheat, high in gluten. Our favorite brand is DeCecco, imported from Italy. This company produces many different varieties, including the best whole wheat spaghetti we know of. However, there are many fine brands on the market – just check the ingredients to see that they are made with durum (also called semolina) flour. And don't forget about fresh pasta, which cooks in minutes.

In some of the recipes which follow, we have specified a certain variety of pasta. Often we have not. Choose the pasta which you like best. As a general rule, long, thin pasta cuts (spaghetti, linguine, fettucine) are best with a smooth, light sauce, and smaller cuts (shells or ziti) are more suited to a thick, chunky sauce. But you decide. And please notice our discovery about using uncooked lasagna noodles *(p. 156)* – it really does work!

A pound of dried pasta generally serves 5 or 6, and a pound of fresh pasta serves 3 or 4. Cooking times vary according to the thickness of the pasta and whether it is fresh or dried and white or whole wheat. Fresh pasta cooks in just a minute or two, dried pasta usually takes 5 to 10 minutes, and whole wheat pasta may take up to 15 minutes. We prefer pasta cooked al dente, tender but firm.

To cook pasta, use a large pot and at least 1 gallon of water for each pound of dried or 2 pounds of fresh pasta. Bring the water to a rolling boil and add a tablespoon of oil to prevent the pasta from sticking together. Add a tablespoon of salt, and then add the pasta slowly, maintaining a steady boil. Stir frequently and test often for doneness. When cooked to your taste, drain the pasta immediately. If you're using it for a pasta salad, rinse with cold water. Otherwise, toss the drained pasta with a little butter or oil or some sauce and serve immediately. Warming the serving bowl and dinner plates is a gracious touch.

Experiment. Try new varieties and use old favorites in new ways. Add pasta to soups. Use it in casseroles. Fill your breakfast omelette with a leftover bit of spaghetti and sauce. Have fun with pasta – it's easy to cook, inexpensive, versatile, and delicious.

Ramatuelle Pasta Sauce

Serves 4

This exuberant sauce is a seasonal favorite when honest tomatoes and fresh basil are available. The preparation is so speedy that you can put the water on to boil and then stroll out to pick the fattest, ripest tomatoes, still warm from the sun.

3 large garlic cloves, minced	¼ teaspoon black pepper
⅓ cup coarsely chopped onions	☐
1 cup fresh basil leaves, packed	1 pound pasta
5 or 6 large, ripe tomatoes, quartered	☐
½ cup olive oil	½ cup freshly grated Parmesan cheese
salt to taste	

Put the garlic, onions, basil, and tomatoes in a blender or food processor. Add the olive oil, salt, and pepper and blend until smooth. Set aside. This sauce is served at room temperature.

Heat the serving bowl and plates. Cook and drain the pasta. In the serving bowl, toss the hot pasta with some of the sauce. Serve the rest of the sauce and the grated Parmesan cheese at the table.

Fresh Pea and Mushroom Sauce for Pasta

Serves 4

This sauce is delectable with sautéed vegetables and herbs. You can be flexible about the amount of vegetables and herbs, and the garlic is optional. If you are lucky enough to have fresh tarragon or dill, by all means, seize the opportunity!

3 cups milk

6 tablespoons butter

6 tablespoons unbleached white flour

salt to taste

□

3 tablespoons butter

½ cup chopped onions

1 garlic clove, minced *(optional)*

2 cups sliced mushrooms (8 ounces)

1½ cups peas, fresh or frozen

½ cup chopped fresh parsley

2 tablespoons finely chopped fresh basil, tarragon, and/or dill (2 teaspoons dried)

salt and black pepper to taste

□

1 pound spinach fettucine or other pasta

□

½ cup freshly grated Parmesan cheese

Heat the milk on low heat until very warm, but do not bring it to a boil. Meanwhile, in a separate pan melt 6 tablespoons of butter on medium heat. When it's bubbling, whisk in the flour. Cook, whisking constantly, for at least 3 minutes. Gradually pour in the hot milk and continue whisking until the white sauce thickens.

Sauté the onions and garlic in butter until the onions are translucent. Add the mushrooms and continue sautéing on medium heat until they are juicy. Add the peas, half the chopped parsley, and the herbs, making sure there's enough liquid to steam the peas. Add a little water if necessary. Cover tightly and steam 5 minutes or until the peas are just tender. Stir the undrained vegetables into the white sauce and season with salt and pepper.

Serve over hot pasta, with lots of freshly grated Parmesan cheese and garnish with more parsley. This dish is nicely offset by a salad of ruby leaf lettuce and tomatoes with Vinaigrette Salad Dressing *(p. 50)*.

Pasta Verde

Serves 4

A bright green, protein-rich pasta sauce, a fine alternative to tomato sauce. Especially good with fettucine, spaghetti, or egg noodles.

2 tablespoons olive oil

¾ cup chopped onion

1 garlic clove, minced

3 cups coarsely chopped raw spinach

1 cup ricotta cheese (9 ounces)

1 teaspoon fresh lemon juice

1 tablespoon fresh basil (1 teaspoon dried)

½ cup chopped fresh parsley

¼ teaspoon nutmeg, preferably freshly grated

¼ teaspoon black pepper

½ teaspoon salt

☐

1 to 1½ pounds pasta

☐

freshly grated Parmesan cheese

toasted and chopped almonds *(optional)*

chopped fresh tomatoes *(optional)*

Sauté the onions and garlic in the oil until the onions are translucent. Rinse the washed, chopped spinach in a colander and then add it, still damp, to the onions. Cover the pan. When the spinach is wilted and still very bright green, purée the sautéed vegetables with the other sauce ingredients at medium speed in a blender or food processor. If you need to keep the sauce warm until the pasta is ready or if you reheat it later, use a double boiler to prevent curdling.

Cook and drain the pasta.

Toss the sauce with the hot, drained pasta in a warm bowl. Serve immediately, garnished with grated Parmesan cheese and chopped tomatoes or almonds, if desired.

PESTO

Twenty years ago there were very few restaurants that offered dishes featuring pesto. Many of us remember our first intoxicating bite of a then new and mysteriously pungent sauce. As with other delightful, sensual experiences, once you develop a taste, there's no turning back. Which is probably why the people of Genoa, the birthplace of pesto, grow their basil in greenhouses all year long. No need to suffer even one day of unnecessary deprivation.

The Italian word "pesto" translates as "pounded" and refers to the age-old method of preparing a paste by pounding and grinding the ingredients together with a mortar and pestle. At one time or another, most of us at Moosewood have tried this, but even the most persistent romantics among us concede that similar or even superior results can be achieved using a blender or food processor and with far less time and effort. So, giving up the aromatic immediacy of the old method, we recommend the new. Isn't it wonderful that something so fast can be so delicious?

Some of us consider basil our most important garden crop. Two of our members, David Hirsch and Linda Dickinson, have lovely herb and flower gardens. In the summertime they provide our kitchen with fresh herbs, and their flowers grace the tables in the restaurant. Sprigs of fresh basil are often a fragrant and beautiful addition to their bouquets. You might find fragrant bunches of fresh basil at your farmers' market in the summer.

When basil is at its peak you may want to blend up several batches of pesto to freeze. If so, leave out the cheese, which you can add later when you use the sauce. Freeze some of your pesto in an ice cube tray and pop the frozen squares into a plastic bag in the freezer. This is a convenient way to have just the right amount for flavoring soups and stews. Freezing works for all pestos, except Pesto di Nocce *(p. 152)*.

When you serve pesto on pasta use a dollop, not a ladleful. A little goes a long way. Serve each of the following pestos at room temperature on piping hot pasta. Garnish with chopped fresh parsley, chopped tomatoes, and/or extra freshly grated Parmesan cheese. Steamed vegetables or a simple green salad complement pasta with pesto.

Pesto Genovese

Serves 6

This is the classic pesto made with fresh basil. When we say, "Let's have pesto for supper tonight," this is the pesto we're talking about. Its haunting flavor and heady aroma are the essence of summer's ripeness.

2½ cups firmly packed fresh basil leaves, chopped	**½ cup freshly grated Parmesan cheese (1 ounce)**
2 large garlic cloves, pressed	**½ cup olive oil**
½ cup chopped walnuts or almonds or pine nuts	**salt to taste**

Whirl the basil, garlic, nuts, and Parmesan in a blender or food processor until well mixed. Then add the olive oil in a slow, steady stream until a smooth paste is formed.

Drop a dollop of Pesto Genovese on each serving of hot pasta and top with chopped tomatoes and extra grated Parmesan. Try it spread on a slice of bread or in a pita with lettuce and tomatoes.

Pesto Genovese may be kept refrigerated for several weeks in an airtight jar. Cover the sauce with a thin layer of olive oil to prevent it from discoloring. It's reassuring to have a jar of pesto ready and waiting for any time you need an impromptu but exciting meal.

Pesto Di Nocce

Serves 4 to 6

A quick and easy pasta sauce that requires no cooking. Just blend and serve. Pesto di Nocce (di Nocce means "with nuts") is particularly good on spinach pasta.

1½ cups walnuts or hazelnuts, chopped*

1 cup freshly grated Parmesan cheese (2½ ounces)

½ cup milk

1 cup heavy cream

pinch of dry mustard

salt and black pepper to taste

pinch of freshly grated nutmeg

Blend the chopped nuts in a food processor or on the high-speed setting of a blender until they are fairly smooth, but not a paste. Add the grated Parmesan and continue to blend. Pouring in a continuous, gradual stream, add the milk, then the heavy cream. Add the mustard, salt, pepper, and nutmeg and blend briefly.

When you serve Pesto di Nocce, toss some of the sauce with hot pasta and garnish with fresh parsley. Serve the rest of the sauce and extra grated Parmesan separately.

---

* *Hazelnuts will have a finer flavor if skinned. Spread the hazelnuts on a baking sheet and bake at 325° for about 10 minutes. Cool for a few minutes and then rub with a small towel to remove most of the skins.*

Tofu Pesto

Serves 8 to 10 generously

This unconventional pesto is high in protein and is a non-dairy version that is creamy and delicious.

2 medium tomatoes, chopped

6 garlic cloves, pressed

4 cups firmly packed fresh basil leaves, chopped

1 cup olive oil

1½ cakes of tofu, pressed, cubed, and blanched *(see Appendix)*

1 teaspoon salt

1 tablespoon miso *(see Appendix)*

1 tablespoon fresh lemon juice

1½ cups almonds, chopped

This sauce can be made either in a food processor or blender. Purée the tomatoes and garlic until smooth. Add the basil and olive oil and blend. Add all of the remaining ingredients and purée until the sauce is smooth and creamy.

Winter Pesto

Serves 6 to 8

Since fresh basil is not generally available year round, this pesto uses dried basil – a distinct advantage for satisfying cravings for pesto at any season. The flavor is somewhat different from the classic fresh basil Pesto Genovese, but it does taste remarkably good.

4 cups firmly packed fresh spinach (about 5 ounces)

⅓ to ½ cup fresh lemon juice

½ cup olive oil

½ cup vegetable oil

⅓ cup pine nuts or chopped almonds or walnuts

¾ cup coarsely grated Parmesan cheese (2 ounces)

½ cup chopped fresh parsley

⅓ cup dried basil

2 garlic cloves, minced

If you have time, soak the basil in the olive oil ½ hour before starting the recipe.

Wash and drain the spinach. Remove only the large stems. In a blender or food processor, blend half of the spinach with all of the lemon juice and half of the oil. Add the rest of the ingredients and blend until smooth.

Fettucine San Polo

Serves 4 to 6

Ned Asta was served this dish on the terrace of her friend Luna's house in the village of San Polo in the Tuscan hills. Pasta with a smooth spinach sauce is bright and attractive topped with florets of cauliflower.

2 tablespoons butter	**salt and black pepper**
2 cups chopped onions	**pinch of nutmeg, preferably freshly grated**
½ teaspoon thyme	
⅛ teaspoon cayenne	☐
1 bay leaf	**1 medium head of cauliflower, cut in florets**
10 ounces fresh spinach, cleaned and stemmed	**1 pound fettucine or other pasta**
2 tablespoons fresh lemon juice	
☐	☐
⅓ cup butter	**1 cup freshly grated Parmesan cheese (2½ ounces)**
⅓ cup flour	**¼ cup chopped fresh parsley**
2 cups warm milk	

Sauté the onions in the butter in a skillet with the herbs and spices until the onions are translucent. Place the spinach on top of the onions, cover, and steam gently on low heat until the spinach is wilted. Remove from the heat. Discard the bay leaf and stir in the lemon juice.

In a saucepan, melt ⅓ cup of butter on low heat. Stir in the flour and cook for 3 to 4 minutes, taking care not to scorch. Whisk in the warm milk, stirring steadily until the sauce thickens. Remove from the heat.

Purée the spinach-onion mixture in a blender or food processor. Stir the spinach purée into the sauce. Add the salt, pepper, and nutmeg and cook on low heat until the sauce is fully heated.

Steam the cauliflower florets and cook the pasta. Drain both.

Serve the sauce ladled over the pasta. Top with the steamed cauliflower and garnish with freshly grated Parmesan and chopped parsley. This sauce also works well spooned over baked fish.

Spinach Lasagna Béchamel

Serves 6 to 8

Almost an embarrassment of riches. Impressive dinner party fare. Notice our suggestion about using uncooked noodles – it works for all lasagnas!

BÉCHAMEL SAUCE

6 cups milk

1 cup butter

1 cup unbleached white flour

salt and black pepper to taste

⅛ teaspoon nutmeg, preferably freshly grated *(optional)*

□

¼ cup vegetable oil or butter

2 garlic cloves, minced or pressed

2 cups chopped onions

2 pounds spinach, rinsed, stemmed, and chopped

¾ cup chopped fresh parsley

1 pound ricotta cheese

2 eggs

2 cups freshly grated Parmesan cheese (5 ounces)

2 cups grated mozzarella cheese (8 ounces)

1 package lasagna noodles

To prepare the Béchamel sauce, heat the milk until very warm but not boiling. In another pan melt the butter on medium heat. Do not let it brown. Whisk in the flour and cook for 3 to 4 minutes, stirring constantly. Gradually add the hot milk and continue whisking until the sauce thickens.

Sauté the garlic and onions in the oil or butter. When the onions are translucent, stir in the spinach and ½ cup of the parsley. If the spinach is dry, add a little water. When the spinach has wilted, remove it from the heat and set aside.

Mix together the remaining parsley, the ricotta cheese, eggs, and ⅔ cup of the Parmesan cheese.

At this point either cook the lasagna noodles al dente (p. 145), or do as we do, and don't cook them at all. This method has worked for us time and time again. Just layer the raw noodles in the pan as you would if they were cooked. Go on, simplify your life!

Oil a large casserole or lasagna pan and layer the ingredients in the following order. First, 1½ to 2 cups of Béchamel sauce, a third of the noodles, half of the spinach mixture, all of the mozzarella. Next, 1½ to 2 cups of sauce, a third of the noodles, all of the ricotta mixture, the rest of the spinach mixture. Finally, 1½ to 2 cups sauce, the remaining noodles, the rest of the sauce. Sprinkle 1⅓ cups Parmesan on the top.

Bake covered at 350° for 45 minutes and then uncovered for another 10 to 15 minutes. Remove from the oven and allow 10 to 15 minutes for the lasagna to set up before serving.

Serve with a simple salad or a side dish of steamed or marinated vegetables.

American Indian Movement leader Dennis Banks called from sanctuary on the Onondaga Nation to thank us for sponsoring a benefit brunch in his behalf. Sorry he couldn't attend.

Baked Pasta
with Cauliflower and Cheese

Serves 6 to 8

A very sophisticated version of macaroni and cheese, with the same gratifying golden, crusty goodness. We have customers who see this dish on the menu, note that Tony Del Plato is cooking, and then, without even looking at the other choices, order the baked pasta (their mouths watering in anticipation).

BÉCHAMEL SAUCE

½ cup butter

½ cup unbleached white flour

1 quart milk, heated

1½ tablespoons Dijon mustard

pinch of nutmeg, preferably freshly grated

salt and black pepper to taste

□

¼ cup vegetable oil

4 cups chopped onions

3 garlic cloves, minced or pressed

½ cup fresh basil, chopped (2 teaspoons dried)

1 large head of cauliflower, cut in florets

6 ripe tomatoes, chopped or 3 cups canned tomatoes, drained and chopped

3 tablespoons fresh lemon juice

□

1 pound medium pasta shells

□

1 cup freshly grated Parmesan cheese (2½ ounces)

1½ cups shredded mozzarella or mild provolone cheese (6 ounces)

seasoned bread crumbs

To prepare the Béchamel sauce, melt the butter in a heavy sauce pan on medium heat. Sprinkle in the flour, whisking or stirring constantly, until a smooth paste is formed. Add the heated milk slowly, a cup at a time, continuing to whisk until the sauce begins to thicken. Add the mustard, nutmeg, salt, and pepper and let the sauce thicken further on low heat. Remove from heat and cover.

Sauté the onions, garlic, and basil in oil. When the onions are translucent, add the cauliflower and sauté for 5 minutes more. Add the tomatoes and simmer until the cauliflower is tender.

Cook the pasta al dente *(p. 145)* and then drain.

In a large bowl, combine the cooked pasta, the sautéed vegetables, and the lemon juice. Mix in the Béchamel sauce. Put half of the pasta mixture in an oiled baking dish. Sprinkle on half of each of the cheeses. Add the rest of the pasta mixture and then the rest of the cheese. Top with seasoned bread crumbs and bake covered at 375° for about 30 minutes and then uncovered for about 15 minutes or until bubbling and golden on top.

Serve with Italian Greens *(p. 213).*

Five years ago, when I moved my studio out of my house and into town, I included eating at Moosewood as part of the budget. I figure I've eaten there, say, 250 times since then, which must be close to a full day's output for the entire restaurant. That means I may have eaten a whole restaurant by myself.

Frankly, I'm glad I did it in installments, but what I've noticed over the years is that they have lots of steady customers like me. And I have to say they're a healthy, good lookin' bunch of eaters.

— **Tom Parker**
from across the street, author of *In One Day*

Five Easy Pastas

After a long day at work, when you feel tired and uninspired and the thought of stopping at the grocery store makes you groan, but there are probably a few edibles left in the refrigerator, fall back on the ease of a simple, improvised pasta dish. Here are five suggestions for tasty, nourishing meals that can revive your spirits in almost no time. Amounts and proportions are variable and are left to your judgment.

Just cook the pasta while you prepare the other ingredients. Toss the drained pasta with everything else, and it's ready!

#1

linguine or spaghetti

olive oil

garlic cloves, minced and sautéed
    in olive oil

freshly grated Parmesan cheese

chopped fresh parsley

black pepper

#2

any pasta

olive oil

Swiss chard, chopped and steamed
    or sautéed in olive oil

chopped fresh tomatoes

grated smoked Swiss cheese

black pepper

#3

any pasta

butter

red peppers, sautéed or steamed

sliced mushrooms, raw or lightly
    steamed or sautéed

green peas, lightly steamed

freshly grated Parmesan cheese

#4

spaghetti

butter

asparagus, cut into 1-inch pieces and
    steamed

heavy cream

freshly grated Parmesan cheese

black pepper

#5

soba noodles *(see Appendix)*

broccoli florets and sliced stems,
    steamed

sliced water chestnuts

thinly sliced carrots or celery, steamed
    or sautéed

cubes of tofu, blanched *(see Appendix)*

dark sesame oil *(see Appendix)*

tamari soy sauce

grated fresh ginger root

minced garlic cloves

chopped scallions

Use leftover pasta to make a "spaghetti pancake." Just toss the pasta with lightly beaten eggs, pour it into an oiled skillet, and gently fry until lightly browned. Flip it like a pancake and fry the other side. Salt and pepper to taste, sprinkle on some grated cheese, and you've got a quick little feast.

As a Moosewood customer for over 13 years, I have found Moose-wood cooking to be always satisfying, often innovative, and at times, inspiring. Moosewood deserves credit for its fusion of a restaurant business with community politics and flat-out good food.

— Abby Nash
owner and chef, Abby's Restaurant and Catering

Summer Sauce for Pasta

Serves 4

On those hot, lazy, sultry summer days, when, like a character in a Tennessee Williams play, you haven't got the energy to do much more than lie around the house in an old tattered slip, try this quick, uncooked sauce. It's fragrant, refreshing, and light.

6 ripe tomatoes, chopped	**1 teaspoon salt**
2 cups sliced mushrooms (8 ounces)	☐
6 to 8 ounces mozzarella cheese, grated or cut into thin strips	**1 pound spaghetti or linguine**
½ cup chopped fresh basil	☐
2 garlic cloves, minced	**½ cup freshly grated Parmesan cheese (1 ounce)**
½ cup olive oil	

Mix all the sauce ingredients together and let sit at room temperature for an hour or so, for the flavors to mingle.

Cook and drain the pasta. While the pasta is piping hot, serve it in well-warmed bowls, topped with a ladleful of sauce and garnished with Parmesan cheese.

MAIN DISHES: Fish

Fish

Many of us never include fish in our diets. But we are a diverse group and those of us who do, recognize fish as a low-fat, high-protein food. At Moosewood we serve fish on the weekends, and it is an important part of our Sunday ethnic menus. On ethnic nights we explore the cuisines of different cultures and try ideas from our travels and varied backgrounds. So these recipes for fish reflect a global array of possibilities. You'll find them easy to prepare. A few will send you to a specialty shop where you can enjoy searching for the exotic.

We usually use flounder, scrod, sole, bluefish, cod, or haddock, all easily available fresh from Atlantic Coast markets. Allow ¼ to ⅓ pound of filleted fish per person. Fillets should be rinsed before cooking. When fish is to be baked, it should be placed in the baking pan skinned side down. The "skinned side" is the smoother, outer side of the fillet where the scales were. If baked with the skinned side up, the fillets sometimes curl, because the skinned side shrinks. When rolling fillets, the skinned side should be to the inside of the roll.

Baking time is a variable of the thickness of the fillets and the amount and density of the sauce or vegetables covering it. Fish is done when fillets have lost their translucency (and any hint of pinkness) and can be easily flaked with a fork. This is usually between 20 to 30 minutes when baked covered at 350°.

Creamy Fish Chowder

Serves 6 to 8

An American classic that is rich, thick, and chunky. This chowder will warm you up for an evening of Scrabble or Trivial Pursuit.

3 tablespoons butter or vegetable oil

1 cup chopped onions

1 garlic clove, minced or pressed

2 medium carrots, chopped

2 celery stalks, chopped

2 large potatoes, cubed

2 small zucchini, chopped

1 green pepper, chopped

3 cups Vegetable Stock *(p. 30)* or water

1 bay leaf

1½ teaspoons fresh dill (½ teaspoon dried)

½ teaspoon marjoram

salt and pepper to taste

1½ pounds firm, white fish fillets, cut into bite-sized pieces

1 cup half-and-half or milk

□

chopped fresh parsley

lemon wedges

Sauté the onions and garlic in the butter until the onions are translucent. Add the carrots, celery, and potatoes and sauté gently for 5 minutes. Add the zucchini, green pepper, stock, and herbs and simmer until the vegetables are tender, about 15 minutes. Add the salt, pepper, and cubed fish and simmer until the fish is just cooked, about 5 to 10 minutes. Stir in the half-and-half and adjust the seasonings.

Garnish with parsley and lemon wedges and serve with freshly baked Squash Rolls *(p. 231)*.

Creole Fish Stew

Serves 6 to 8

This robust stew from Louisiana is animated by the Tabasco and lemon.

3 tablespoons butter or vegetable oil

1 cup chopped onions

1 garlic clove, minced or pressed

2 medium carrots, chopped

3 celery stalks, chopped

2 large potatoes, cubed

2 small zucchini, chopped

1 green pepper, chopped

1 bay leaf

pinch of thyme

1 cup chopped tomatoes

1 cup tomato juice

3 cups Vegetable Stock *(p. 30)* or water

□

Tabasco or other hot pepper sauce to taste

salt and black pepper to taste

juice of 1 lemon

1½ pounds firm, white fish, cut into bite-sized pieces

½ pound peeled and deveined shrimp

□

chopped fresh parsley

lemon wedges

Sauté the onions and garlic in the butter until the onions are translucent. Add the carrots, celery, and potatoes and sauté gently for 5 minutes. Add the zucchini and green pepper and sauté for 5 minutes. Add the bay leaf, thyme, tomatoes, tomato juice, and stock or water. Simmer 15 to 20 minutes, until the vegetables are tender.

Add hot pepper sauce, salt, and black pepper to taste. Stir in the lemon juice, fish, and shrimp. Simmer about 5 minutes until the fish is just cooked and flakes easily with a fork but does not fall apart.

Serve with chopped fresh parsley, lemon wedges, and hot pepper sauce. Wonderful with warm Corn Bread *(p. 235)*.

Japanese Fish Stew

Serves 8

This is a soothing, humble East Asian soup of fish with carrots, white cabbage, and shiitake mushrooms. Add green snow peas to the clear broth at the last minute and they will have cooked by the time you reach the table.

8 dried shiitake mushrooms *(see Appendix)*

2 cups water

□

¼ cup vegetable oil

1 medium onion, thinly sliced

1 large carrot, julienned

2 celery stalks, diagonally sliced

¼ of a head of white cabbage, thinly sliced

½ teaspoon salt

8 cups Vegetable Stock *(p. 30)*

1½ pounds bluefish or scrod fillets, cut in bite-sized cubes

□

4 tablespoons tamari soy sauce

2 tablespoons dry sherry, Chinese rice wine, or mirin *(see Appendix)*

1 tablespoon dark sesame oil *(see Appendix)*

½ pound snow peas, stems removed

3 scallions, diagonally sliced

Simmer the shiitake mushrooms in the water for 15 minutes. Drain, reserving the cooking liquid. Remove and discard the mushroom stems. Slice and save the mushroom caps.

In a large soup pot, sauté the onions in the oil until translucent. Add the carrots and sauté for a few minutes. Then add the celery, cabbage, and salt and sauté for a few minutes more. Add the vegetable stock and the reserved mushroom liquid and simmer until the vegetables are just tender. Add the fish cubes and the sliced shiitake mushrooms and simmer 5 to 7 minutes.

Combine the soy sauce, the wine or mirin, and the sesame oil and add to the stew when the fish is done. Add the snow peas and scallions and serve immediately.

For a hotter, spicier soup sauté some cayenne pepper with the vegetables and add some white vinegar and freshly grated ginger root.

Tunisian Fish Soup

Serves 6 to 8

Moosewood's Nancy Harville Lazarus, inspired by dreams of North Africa and the fish soup served by our friends at Café des Amis in Ithaca, developed this recipe, a mix of vegetables, spices, and fish.

¼ cup vegetable oil

3 garlic cloves, minced or pressed

2 cups chopped onions

1 carrot, chopped

1 green pepper, chopped

4 cups finely sliced cabbage

1 tablespoon ground coriander

½ teaspoon ground cumin

3 cups finely chopped or crushed
   tomatoes, fresh or canned

1 cup tomato juice

2 cups Vegetable Stock *(p. 30)* or water

⅓ cup fresh lemon juice

1 cup cooked drained garbanzo beans
   (see Appendix)

☐

1½ pounds firm, white fish fillets

Tabasco or other hot pepper sauce to
   taste

salt to taste

☐

1 lemon, cut into wedges

Heat the oil in a large soup pot. Sauté the onions and garlic for 5 minutes. Add the carrrots and sauté another 5 minutes. Add the peppers and the cabbage and stir the vegetables to coat them with oil. Sprinkle in the coriander and cumin and stir again. Cover and cook for 10 minutes.

Add the tomatoes, tomato juice, Vegetable Stock or water, lemon juice, and garbanzo beans. Cover and heat to a simmer. Simmer until the vegetables are tender.

Cut the fish into 1-inch chunks and add it to the simmering soup. Add hot pepper sauce and salt to taste. Simmer gently, just until the fish is white and flaky.

Serve with lemon wedges and toasted pita bread.

Fish à la Grecque

Serves 4 to 6

This is a zesty, light, easily prepared dish. It's one of our favorite ways to bake fish because the flavors of the herbs, lemon, tomato, and feta harmonize remarkably well.

2 pounds fish fillets	**black pepper to taste**
□	**1 tablespoon chopped fresh parsley**
1 medium red onion, thinly sliced in rounds	**¼ cup fresh lemon juice**
	1 tomato, chopped
1 tablespoon fresh dill (1 teaspoon dried)	**½ cup grated feta cheese (2½ ounces)**

Place the fish in an oiled casserole dish. Top the fillets with the onion rounds and sprinkle them with the dill, pepper, parsley, lemon juice, chopped tomato, and feta cheese.

Bake at 350° about 30 minutes, until the fish flakes with a fork.

Serve under an imaginary grape arbor with real rice or Greek Potatoes *(p. 205)*, creamy Tzatziki *(p. 207)*, and a bottle of Retsina.

Fish with Italian Artichoke Sauce

Serves 4 to 6

This herbed sauce, crammed with artichokes, is a lively topping for fish. We often make this recipe without the mushrooms, giving the artichoke hearts our undivided attention.

¼ cup olive oil

2 cups chopped onions

2 garlic cloves, minced or pressed

3 cups thickly sliced mushrooms
   (12 ounces)

1½ teaspoons fresh basil (½ teaspoon
   dried)

1½ teaspoons fresh oregano
   (½ teaspoon dried)

2 tablespoons fresh lemon juice

¼ cup dry white wine

1 teaspoon salt

☐

2 pounds firm, white fish fillets

1 18-ounce can of artichoke hearts,
   drained and halved

Sauté the onions and garlic in the olive oil. After the onions begin to soften, add the mushrooms and herbs. Sauté until the mushrooms begin to brown, then add the lemon juice, wine, and salt. Simmer briskly so that the sauce will thicken a little.

Place the fillets in an oiled baking pan. Arrange the halved artichoke hearts on top of the fish and then top with the sauce. Bake covered at 375° for 15 minutes and then uncovered for a few more minutes, until the fish is flaky but still moist.

Serve on rice and with Armenian Green Beans *(p. 206)* for a cross-cultural touch.

Flounder Rollatini

Serves 4 to 6

Our customers adore these succulent flounder rolls. At the center of each rollatini is a rich nugget of crunchy nuts and melted Parmesan.

½ **cup freshly grated Parmesan cheese (1 ounce)**

½ **cup chopped fresh parsley**

½ **cup chopped, toasted almonds**

1 tablespoon fresh basil (1 teaspoon dried)

☐

2 pounds flounder fillets

☐

3 tablespoons fresh lemon juice

3 tablespoons melted butter

Mix together the Parmesan cheese, parsley, toasted almonds, and basil.

Rinse the flounder. Place each fillet, skinned side up *(p. 165)*, flat on a board. Spoon some filling onto one end of each fillet, and then roll it up. Place the rolled fish into a buttered baking pan. Pour the lemon juice and melted butter over the fish and sprinkle any remaining filling on top. Bake covered at 375° for about 30 minutes, until the fish flakes and the rolls are cooked through.

Serve on rice with steamed asparagus spears.

Flounder Florentine

Serves 4 to 6

Spinach, dill and almonds are the grace notes to the flounder here, one of our most popular dishes.

2 tablespoons vegetable oil or butter

¼ cup finely chopped onions

10 ounces fresh spinach, stemmed and chopped

1 tablespoon fresh dill (1 teaspoon dried)

¼ to ½ cup toasted almonds, finely chopped

1 tablespoon fresh lemon juice

☐

2 pounds flounder fillets

Sauté the onions in the butter or oil until translucent. Add the chopped spinach and the dill and cook covered until the spinach is wilted. Remove from the heat, add the almonds and lemon juice, and allow to cool.

Rinse the flounder. Place each fillet, skinned side up *(p. 165)*, flat on a board. Spoon a small amount of the spinach filling onto each fillet and then roll it up. Place the rolled fish in an oiled baking pan and bake covered at 375° for 20 to 25 minutes, until the fish is tender and flaky.

Flounder Florentine is delicious served with Lemony Rice *(p. 199)* and Artichoke Heart and Tomato Salad *(p. 40)*.

Fish with Teriyaki Sauce

Serves 4 to 6

Savory and slightly sweet, this sauce is highly recommended for grilled or broiled fish.

2 pounds fish fillets

MARINADE

⅓ cup vegetable oil

⅓ cup tamari soy sauce

2 garlic cloves, minced or pressed

1 tablespoon grated fresh ginger root

½ cup mirin* *(see Appendix)*

□

chopped scallions

Combine the marinade ingredients. Rinse the fish fillets and place them in a deep bowl. Pour the marinade over the fish and chill for ½ to 1 hour.

Place the fish with the marinade in an oiled pan. Cover and bake at 350° for about 20 minutes or until the fish flakes easily with a fork. Or grill the fish, basting it occasionally with the leftover marinade.

Garnish the fish with chopped scallions and serve it on rice with steamed broccoli, and paper-thin radish slices freshened in chilled rice vinegar or white vinegar.

---

*If mirin is unavailable, substitute ¼ cup dry sherry, sake or Chinese rice wine, 2 teaspoons sugar, and 4 tablespoons white or rice vinegar or fresh lemon juice.

Fish with Cantonese Black Bean Sauce

Serves 4 to 6

Traditionally this dish is prepared in a bamboo steamer over a wok. The distinctive, pronounced flavor of Chinese fermented black beans is delicious in our oven-baked version, also, and requires only a baking pan.

1½ to 2 pounds fish fillets

1 tablespoon Chinese fermented black beans *(see Appendix)*

½ cup water

1 garlic clove, pressed or minced

2 tablespoons tamari soy sauce

2 teaspoons dark sesame oil *(see Appendix)*

1 tablespoon grated fresh ginger root

2 teaspoons Chinese rice vinegar *(optional)*

2 scallions, diagonally sliced

Soak the fermented black beans in the water for several minutes and then drain.

In a small bowl, mix together all the ingredients, except the scallions, and mash well. Place the rinsed fish fillets in an oiled baking pan. Spread the paste over the fillets, sprinkle with the chopped scallions, and bake covered at 350° for 20 to 30 minutes.

Serve on rice with Asian Asparagus Salad *(p. 48)* or Chinese Greens *(p. 211)* and a wedge of melon.

Ikan Percek*

(Baked Fish, Malay Style)

Serves 6

This dish really depends upon the tamarind for its authentic tart flavor. Tamarind is available in Asian food stores and some specialty groceries.

3 pounds fish fillets

☐

¾ cup minced onions

1 large garlic clove, minced or pressed

2 teaspoons grated fresh ginger root

salt to taste

☐

1 to 1½ teaspoons dried, hot chili peppers

½ cup coconut milk *(see Appendix)*

¼ cup tamarind *(see Appendix)*

Combine the onions, garlic, and fresh ginger. Rub the fillets with salt and half of the onions-garlic-ginger mixture. Place the fish in an oiled baking pan. Cover and chill for 30 minutes.

Combine the rest of the onions-garlic-ginger mixture with the chili peppers, coconut milk, and tamarind. Spread this sauce over the chilled fish and bake uncovered at 400° for 20 minutes or until the fish flakes easily with a fork. Or, grill over charcoal, basting with the coconut milk-spice sauce.

Serve this juicy dish on rice with Spinach Raita *(p. 217)*.

---

* pronounced E-kahn Prr-chek

Fish Thebaudienne

Serves 4 to 6

A West African-style baked fish that was developed by Celeste Tischler for one of our Sunday Ethnic Nights. The unusual blend of sweet potato, cabbage, tomato, and lemon is surprisingly delicious.

2 tablespoons vegetable oil

1 cup chopped onions

1 green pepper, chopped

⅓ cup tomato juice

⅓ cup tomato paste

☐

1 large sweet potato, peeled and sliced into rounds

1 cup shredded cabbage

¼ cup pimiento slices

☐

2 pounds firm fish fillets (the flavor and texture of too delicate a fish would be lost under this sauce)

salt and black pepper to taste

juice of 1 lemon

Brown the onions in 1 tablespoon of oil, then add the chopped pepper. Sauté until tender. Purée the sauté in a food processor or blender with the tomato juice and tomato paste to make a smooth, thick sauce.

Sauté the sweet potato in 1 tablespoon of oil for 5 minutes, then add the cabbage. Cover and cook on low heat. Cook until just tender, then mix in the pimiento, tomato sauce, salt, and pepper.

Place the fish in an oiled baking pan. Sprinkle with salt, black pepper, and lemon juice. Spoon the sweet potato-tomato sauce over the fish. Bake covered at 350° for about 30 minutes.

Serve on rice or couscous with fresh corn on the cob.

Pescado Veracruz

Serves 4 to 6

This lively and aromatic fish dish is from steamy Veracruz. Listen for the horns of a mariachi band when you open the oven.

2 pounds fish fillets

¼ cup fresh lemon juice

□

3 tablespoons olive oil

1 cup chopped onions

1 large garlic clove, minced or pressed

1 tablespoon chili powder

¼ teaspoon ground cloves

¼ teaspoon ground cumin

¼ teaspoon ground coriander

3 cups canned whole tomatoes, drained and roughly chopped

1 tablespoon honey

1 cup pitted black olives, chopped

salt and black pepper to taste

□

chopped fresh parsley

Arrange the fish in an oiled baking dish. Salt it lightly and sprinkle with a few teaspoons of the lemon juice. Chill.

Sauté the onions, garlic, chili powder, ground cloves, cumin, and coriander in the olive oil until the onions are translucent, taking care not to burn the spices. Add the tomatoes, honey, olives, and the remaining lemon juice and simmer for 15 to 20 minutes.

Pour the sauce over the fish, top it with chopped parsley, and bake at 350° until it is tender, 20 to 30 minutes depending on the thickness of the fillets.

Serve with Arroz Verde *(p. 198)* and a chilled salad of steamed cauliflower with red pepper strips and Avocado Dressing *(p. 55)*.

Fish Dijon

Serves 4 to 6

A creamy sauce, fragrant with dill.

4 tablespoons butter	1 to 2 tablespoons Dijon mustard
1 cup minced onions	2 teaspoons fresh lemon juice
1 tablespoon fresh dill (1 teaspoon dried)	salt and black pepper to taste
3 tablespoons unbleached white flour	2 pounds fish fillets
1 cup milk, at room temperature	
½ cup sour cream	

Sauté the onions and dill in the butter until the onions are translucent. Add the flour to the butter and onion mixture and stir rapidly on low heat, taking care not to scorch the flour. Stir in the milk. The sauce should thicken quickly and become smooth after several more minutes of stirring. Remove from the heat and whisk in the sour cream, mustard, lemon juice, and salt and pepper. Whisk smooth. If the sauce will not be served immediately, keep it warm on very low heat or in a double boiler. Add the lemon juice just before serving.

Meanwhile, bake or broil the fish. As soon as the fish is tender and flakes easily, ladle the sauce over it and serve.

Fish Dijon is delicious served on a bed of noodles accompanied by lightly steamed broccoli and chilled orange wedges.

Fish Lucerne

Serves 4 to 6

Seasoned fillets baked with the richness of a Swiss cheese and sour cream topping.

2 pounds fish fillets

¼ cup fresh lemon juice

1 tablespoon chopped fresh dill (1 teaspoon dried)

salt and black pepper

☐

2 tablespoons vegetable oil or butter

2 cups thinly sliced onions

☐

2 eggs

1 cup sour cream

¼ cup freshly grated Parmesan cheese (½ ounce)

⅓ cup grated Swiss cheese (1 ounce)

salt and black pepper to taste

nutmeg, preferably freshly grated

Place the fillets in an oiled baking pan. Sprinkle with lemon juice, dill, salt, and pepper.

Sauté the onions in the oil or butter until just tender.

In a mixing bowl beat the eggs and blend with the sour cream and cheeses and a dash of salt, pepper, and nutmeg. Top the fillets with the sautéed onions and then with the egg and cheese sauce.

Bake uncovered at 350° for about 30 minutes, until the fish is tender and the sauce is set and slightly browned.

Serve with parsley potatoes and a simple green salad.

Fish with French Mushroom Sauce

Serves 6 to 8

The combination of mushrooms, tarragon, and wine gives this sauce a rich and distinctive flavor and fragrance.

3 to 4 tablespoons butter or vegetable oil

2 cups diced onions

1 bay leaf

1 large carrot, diced or julienned

2 celery stalks, chopped

3 cups sliced mushrooms (12 ounces)

1 tablespoon chopped fresh tarragon (1 teaspoon dried)

½ teaspoon salt

¼ cup dry white or red wine

¼ cup fresh lemon juice

☐

½ cup Vegetable Stock *(p. 30)* or water

1 tablespoon tomato paste

2 tablespoons butter

2 tablespoons unbleached white flour

☐

½ cup chopped fresh parsley

☐

3 pounds fish fillets

Sauté the onions and bay leaf in the butter or oil until the onions are translucent. Add the carrots and celery and continue to sauté for a few minutes before adding the mushrooms, tarragon, and salt. Stir in the wine and lemon juice. Bring to a boil, cover, and simmer on low heat until the vegetables are just tender.

In a small pan, combine the stock or water and the tomato paste and gently heat. In a separate pan on medium heat, bring the butter to a bubble, taking care not to burn. Gradually sprinkle the flour into the hot butter while stirring or whisking vigorously. Stir on medium heat for 2 or 3 minutes, and then slowly pour in the warm tomato liquid, stirring until thick and smooth. Stir this thickening sauce into the hot, cooked vegetables. Add the chopped parsley.

Place the fish fillets in an oiled baking pan. Spread the sauce on the fillets. The sauce will be thick, but the fish juices will thin it as it bakes. Bake covered at 350° for 20 to 30 minutes, until the fish is tender.

Serve on rice with a tossed salad.

Fish with Bouillabaisse Sauce

Serves 6 to 8

Classic bouillabaisse is a stew of fish and shellfish. This sauce incorporates the same complex blend of herbs, saffron, wine, and vegetables, but in a simpler and less expensive fashion.

2 tablespoons olive oil	**1 cup Vegetable Stock** *(p. 30)*
1½ cups chopped leeks *(see Appendix)* **or onions**	**1 tablespoon fresh tarragon (1 teaspoon dried)**
2 green peppers, chopped	**2 tablespoons fresh basil (2 teaspoons dried)**
¼ teaspoon dried thyme	**juice of ½ lemon**
2 teaspoons ground fennel seeds	**pinch of cayenne**
1 teaspoon salt	**pinch of saffron**
3 garlic cloves, minced or pressed	**¼ cup chopped fresh parsley**
3 large tomatoes, chopped	□
1 cup undrained canned tomatoes, chopped	**3 pounds fish fillets**
1 tablespoon grated orange rind	□
1 cup dry red wine	**lemon wedges**

Heat the olive oil in a 2-quart sauce pan. Sauté the leeks or onions for 5 minutes. Add the peppers and sauté another 5 minutes. Add the thyme, fennel, salt, garlic, and tomatoes and simmer covered for 10 minutes. Add the remaining ingredients, reserving 2 tablespoons of chopped parsley. Simmer uncovered for 15 minutes.

Place the fish in an oiled baking pan. Pour on the sauce and bake covered at 375° for approximately 20 minutes, until the fish flakes easily with a fork.

Serve on rice or couscous. Garnish with lemon wedges and the remaining chopped parsley.

Fish Basilico

Serves 4

A crispy topping savory with Parmesan cheese, garlic, and basil contrasts with the tender, juicy fish beneath.

½ **lemon, peeled and seeded**

½ **cup olive oil**

2 **large garlic cloves, minced or pressed**

3 **tablespoons fresh basil (1 tablespoon dried)**

2 **cups whole wheat bread crumbs**

⅔ **cup freshly grated Parmesan cheese (2 ounces)**

⅛ **teaspoon black pepper**

2 **pounds fish fillets**

Purée the lemon in a blender with the olive oil. Pour the lemon mixture into a heated skillet, sizzle for a minute or two, and then add the garlic and basil, sautéing until an aroma rises from the pan. Mix in the bread crumbs until they are thoroughly coated with oil. Sauté the bread crumbs, stirring often, until they are dry. Remove the mixture to a bowl and stir in the Parmesan cheese and black pepper.

Place the fish in an oiled baking pan and spoon on the topping. Cover and bake for 20 minutes at 350° or until the fish whitens and flakes easily with a fork.

Serve with Artichoke Heart and Tomato Salad *(p. 40)* or Tuscan Potato Salad *(p. 38)*, or both!

Spicy Caribbean Fish

Serves 4 to 6

Annato seeds give both a warm flavor and a golden hue to this exciting, highly-seasoned dish.

2 pounds fish fillets

MARINADE

⅓ cup fresh lime juice

⅔ cup water

1 teaspoon salt

SAUCE

2 tablespoons vegetable oil

1 teaspoon whole annato (achiote) seeds
   (see Appendix)

⅓ cup chopped onions

⅔ cup chopped scallions

3 garlic cloves, minced or pressed

1 fresh hot pepper, minced
   (or ½ teaspoon cayenne)

3 tomatoes, chopped (or 2 cups canned, drained)

⅓ cup chopped fresh parsley

½ teaspoon dried thyme

salt and black pepper to taste

   □

lime wedges

chopped fresh parsley

Place the fish fillets in a lightly oiled, flat baking pan. Pour the marinade over them, cover, and chill for ½ hour.

Sauté the annato seeds in the oil for a few minutes, stirring constantly and making sure they do not brown. Remove the annato seeds from the reddish-orange oil and then add the onions, scallions, garlic, and hot pepper. Sauté for a minute or two before adding the tomatoes, herbs, and seasonings. Simmer for 5 minutes.

Pour off the marinade and cover the fish with the sauce. Bake at 350° until flaky. This will take about 20 minutes for small or thin fillets and 30 minutes for thicker, larger ones.

Spicy Caribbean Fish is good served on Coconut Rice *(p. 200)* and garnished with lime wedges and parsley. Sweet potatoes or fried plantains are a nice side dish, and don't forget a tall, cool drink.

Malay Fried Noodles with Shrimp

Serves 4 to 6

A meal in itself. Accompany these fried noodles with sharp-tasting cold beer.

THE GARNISHES

¼ cup vegetable oil

2 large garlic cloves, thinly sliced

1 medium onion, thinly sliced lengthwise

2 scallions

a few fresh or dried chili peppers

THE NOODLES

1 pound Chinese wheat noodles or vermicelli or spaghettini

1 tablespoon dark sesame oil *(see Appendix)*

2 garlic cloves, pressed or minced

½ pound shrimp, shelled and deveined

¼ of a small head of white cabbage, shredded

2 cups snow peas, stemmed

½ cup water chestnuts, sliced ¼-inch thick

1 medium cucumber, peeled, cut in half lengthwise, seeded, and sliced

tamari soy sauce to taste

black pepper to taste

☐

lime wedges

First prepare the garnishes. In a wok or heavy skillet, heat the oil until it is very hot and stir-fry *(see Appendix)* the garlic for a few seconds until it is golden. Remove to a paper towel with a slotted spoon. Then stir-fry the onions in two batches until brown. Remove with a slotted spoon to paper towels. Slice the scallions diagonally in 1-inch pieces and set aside. Cut the fresh chili peppers into small circles, or if you're using dried chili peppers, simmer them in a small amount of water for 10 minutes and then chop.

Cook the noodles or pasta in boiling, salted water until just done. Drain and stir in the sesame oil to prevent the noodles from sticking together.

Reheat the oil in the wok. Add the garlic when the oil is very hot. A few seconds later add the shrimp. Stir-fry until the shrimp turn pink. Add the cabbage, snow peas, and water chestnuts and stir-fry for 2 minutes. Finally, add the cucumber slices and the cooked noodles and stir well. Remove from the heat and season to taste with soy sauce and black pepper.

Transfer to a warm platter and sprinkle with the garnishes or put each garnish in its own tiny bowl and pass with the noodles. Decorate with lime wedges if desired.

SAUCES, SIDE DISHES, AND CONDIMENTS

Sauces, Side Dishes, and Condiments

In this chapter you'll find recipes for dishes we couldn't easily categorize. They are sauces, side dishes, and embellishments, special extras to go on top, underneath or side by side with other foods. Most of our salads and many of our sandwich fillings and dips can act as extras also, with some imaginative mixing and matching. In a vegetarian cuisine, dishes can move in and out of the spotlight or can join forces to create a lavish meal out of equally important components.

Foods enhance each other by providing contrast or harmony in taste, color, or texture. A spicy vegetable curry could stand alone, but accompanied by the cool astringency of Spinach Raita, the richness of Dhall, and maybe the tangy sweetness of Peach Chutney, you have created a memorable feast. The fresh bite of Sweet and Sour Red Cabbage offsets a smooth cheesy strudel. Jonathan's Tofu Dumplings make a miso soup sit up and take notice and Italian Greens are welcome with many pastas. Greek Potatoes might be the just-right completion to a lemony fish dish. Mushroom-Tofu-Pecan Stuffed Squash is enhanced by Light and Tangy Orange Sauce.

These dishes provide an embellishment that express your caring and attention and can elevate a modest meal into an artful performance. For a devoted cook, there is satisfaction in planning the interplay of foods to nourish and delight.

Sour Cream-Paprika Sauce

Serves 4 to 6

A mellow and rosy-hued versatile sauce.

2 tablespoons butter or vegetable oil	½ cup chopped fresh parsley
1 cup diced onions	2 tablespoons unbleached white flour
2 garlic cloves, minced or pressed	1 cup Vegetable Stock *(p. 30)*
1 large green pepper, diced	1½ cups sour cream
½ cup chopped fresh or canned tomatoes	1 tablespoon fresh dill (1 teaspoon dried)
1 tablespoon sweet Hungarian paprika *(see Appendix)*	salt and black pepper to taste

Sauté the onions and garlic in the oil or butter. When the onions are translucent, add the green peppers and tomatoes and simmer until the peppers begin to soften. Stir in the paprika, then add the parsley. Sprinkle in the flour and stir until it coats everything. Add the stock, pouring slowly and stirring vigorously with a whisk. Simmer a minute or two. Remove from the heat and stir in the sour cream and dill. Gently reheat.

This sauce is delicious with steamed vegetables and egg noodles, over Hungarian Stuffed Peppers *(p. 100)*, or with fish. Left over, it makes a good base for Creamy Fish Chowder *(p. 167)*, or add it to your favorite stroganoff.

Spicy Peanut Sauce

Serves 4 to 6

Can't get to Java this January? Here's a sauce that will warm you wherever you are in the western world.

2 tablespoons vegetable oil, preferably peanut oil

2 cups chopped onions

1 bay leaf

1 teaspoon cayenne or to taste

1 teaspoon ground coriander seeds

2 to 3 cups Vegetable Stock *(p. 30)*, coconut milk *(see Appendix)*, or water

2 tablespoons fresh lemon juice or white vinegar, or 1 tablespoon tamarind *(see Appendix)*

2 cups peanut butter

salt to taste

1 to 2 tablespoons honey or brown sugar *(optional)*

In a medium saucepan, brown the onions in oil with the bay leaf. Add the cayenne and coriander and sauté for a few minutes, stirring continuously. Add 2 cups of stock, coconut milk, or water and the lemon juice, vinegar, or tamarind. Simmer for 5 minutes. Add the peanut butter and salt, if needed, and simmer for another 15 minutes, stirring frequently to guard against sticking.

Check the seasonings. If you want a sweeter flavor, add the honey or brown sugar. If the sauce becomes too thick, add more liquid while it simmers.

This sauce has a multiplicity of uses. It is delicious over steamed broccoli, rice, and tofu or in Jakarta Pita *(p. 66)*. Leftovers can be cunningly incorporated into West African Groundnut Stew *(p. 122)* or Mushroom-Sesame-Tofu Soup *(p. 17)*.

Light and Tangy Orange Sauce

Yields 2 cups

This golden sauce can be used 101 ways – it's also quick and easy.

2 cups orange juice	1 teaspoon tamari soy sauce
1 tablespoon freshly grated ginger root	4 teaspoons cornstarch, dissolved in 2 tablespoons cold water
1 tablespoon vegetable oil	
pinch of thyme	

In a small saucepan, heat all the ingredients except the dissolved cornstarch. Bring to a boil and then whisk in the cornstarch. Cook for another minute. Serve hot.

Mushroom-Tofu-Pecan Stuffed Squash *(p. 103)* is even more delicious topped with this orange sauce. Light and Tangy Orange Sauce is delightful on sautéed or steamed vegetables and simply baked fish. Try adding a little to Asian sautés and soups for an extra, interesting flavor.

Hot Sauce

Yields about 3½ cups

This is our basic hot sauce. Adjust the hot seasonings to suit your taste and temperament. If you like the distinctive flavor of fresh cilantro, use a little here.

7 fresh tomatoes, chopped, or 3 cups undrained canned tomatoes

3 to 4 garlic cloves, chopped

2 cups coarsely chopped onions

2 medium green peppers, chopped

cayenne to taste*

2 teaspoons ground cumin

2 teaspoons ground coriander

salt to taste

1 to 2 tablespoons chopped fresh cilantro *(optional)*

2 tablespoons tomato paste *(optional)*

Place all the ingredients in a blender or food processor and purée until smooth. Simmer covered on low heat for 1 to 2 hours, stirring occasionally. If you'd like a thicker, darker hot sauce, stir in some tomato paste.

Serve hot, at room temperature, or cold. Hot Sauce can be stored in a jar for weeks in the refrigerator.

---

* *If you'd like to use fresh hot peppers, replace the green peppers and cayenne with 2 to 4 seeded and chopped hot peppers.*

Salsa Cruda

Yields about 3 cups

An uncooked, speedily prepared tomato hot sauce with a clean, fresh taste and many uses. Depending on the amount and kind of peppers or chilies used, the intensity of hotness can range from mildly piquant to volcanic.

3 ripe tomatoes, chopped

¾ cup chopped Spanish olives

¼ to ½ cup minced hot peppers (fresh or canned)

Tabasco or other hot pepper sauce to taste

Combine all the ingredients and refrigerate at least 1 hour to allow the flavors to mingle.

Salsa Cruda is most flavorful at room temperature and should be taken from the refrigerator an hour before serving time. Use Salsa Cruda as a topping for frittatas or as a condiment for any Mexican entrée. Store in the refrigerator up to 1 week.

Skordalia

Yields 3 to 4 cups

From the Greek "skorda" for garlic, Skordalia is a Macedonian sauce that is appropriately served over baked fish or fried zucchini rounds. It also makes a pleasant dip for raw vegetable sticks.

4 medium potatoes, cubed

1½ cups plain yogurt

6 garlic cloves, pressed

½ teaspoon salt

½ cup chopped fresh parsley

3 to 6 tablespoons fresh lemon juice *(optional)*

¼ cup finely chopped almonds, walnuts, or pine nuts *(optional)*

Boil the potatoes in salted water and drain. With a potato-masher, electric mixer, or food processor, blend the yogurt and drained potatoes until smooth. Stir in the garlic, salt, and parsley. Add lemon juice for a more tangy sauce, and almonds for texture and flavor.

Serve Skordalia at room temperature as a dip and hot as a sauce for fish or vegetables.

Stuffed Spiced Artichokes

Serves 6

Because artichokes are only seasonally available here in Ithaca, it's always a treat to see them back in the markets. Stuffed artichokes are an elegant first course or side dish. We're fond of both fillings. Ginger gives a nice kick to the shrimp filling. The pairing of hazelnuts and feta or chèvre cheese is rich and delightful.

3 artichokes	**2 bay leaves**
1 quart water	**3 whole garlic cloves**
2 teaspoons salt	**6 whole peppercorns or ¼ teaspoon black pepper**
4 tablespoons vinegar	
1 tablespoon olive oil	**½ teaspoon fennel seeds** *(optional)*

Prepare the artichokes for cooking by cutting the stem even with the base and by clipping the barbed top of each leaf with kitchen shears. Cut the artichokes in half lengthwise. Place the artichoke halves and all the remaining ingredients in a stainless steel or enamel pan and bring the liquid to a boil. Reduce the heat and simmer until tender, about 20 minutes.

Drain the artichokes and discard the cooking liquid. Remove the feathery choke with a spoon.

Spiced artichokes are delicious eaten hot with melted butter, or they may be cooled and stuffed with one of the following fillings.

FETA-CREAM CHEESE FILLING	**2 tablespoons chopped sweet red pepper**
½ cup crumbled feta cheese or chèvre cheese (3 ounces)	**2 tablespoons chopped scallions**
½ cup cream cheese, at room temperature	**¼ cup hazelnuts, toasted and chopped**
2 teaspoons fresh lemon juice	

With a food processor or by hand, blend the cheeses and lemon juice until light, fluffy, and creamy. Then stir in the remaining ingredients. Stuff the center of each artichoke half with a rounded spoonful of filling.

SPICY SHRIMP FILLING

1½ cups small shrimp, shelled,
    deveined, and cooked

3 tablespoons Mayonnaise *(p. 57)*

3 tablespoons finely chopped red onion

1½ tablespoons horseradish, or to taste

2 tablespoons fresh lime juice

1½ teaspoons freshly grated ginger root

salt to taste

cayenne to taste

Combine the shrimp with the other ingredients and set aside for at least 15 minutes to allow the flavors to marry. Then taste and add more seasonings if necessary. Stuff the center of each artichoke half with a rounded spoonful of filling.

I feel very fortunate to be one of Moosewood Restaurant's suppliers. It allows me to break a rule: mixing pleasure with business. The pleasure of meeting a wide variety of great people whose friendship and mutual respect overflow and are contagious is mixed with the business of selling them quality produce that they appreciate.

— Bruno Bonierbale
Milestone Farm, Genoa, N.Y.

Arroz Verde

Serves 6

Arroz Verde, green rice, complements a wide variety of foods. For a Latin flavor add 1 teaspoon ground cumin seeds. For a Mediterranean touch try 1 tablespoon capers *(see Appendix)* with 1 tablespoon either dill or basil.

2 medium green peppers, chopped	□
½ cup chopped fresh parsley	2 cups uncooked brown rice
1 medium onion, chopped	3 tablespoons vegetable oil
2 garlic cloves	3 cups water
½ cup water	1 teaspoon salt

Purée the vegetables in a blender with ½ cup of water until smooth.

Sauté the rice in the oil for 2 or 3 minutes, stirring to prevent the rice from scorching. Add the vegetable purée and cook for 5 more minutes, stirring often. Add 3 cups of water and the salt and bring to a boil. Reduce the heat, cover, and cook until the liquid is absorbed, 30 to 45 minutes.

Lemony Rice

Serves 6

A rich and tangy rice dish, delicious with simple, baked fish and steamed vegetables.

2 cups uncooked brown rice

2 tablespoons butter

4½ cups water

1½ teaspoons salt

□

4 egg yolks

⅓ cup fresh lemon juice

3 tablespoons chopped fresh parsley

¾ cup freshly grated Parmesan cheese (2 ounces)

Sauté the rice briefly in the butter. Add the water and salt, cover, and bring to a boil. Lower the heat and simmer until done, 30 to 45 minutes.

Beat together the egg yolks, lemon juice, parsley, and half of the Parmesan cheese. Pour this mixture over the hot cooked rice, stirring to coat each grain. Top with the remaining cheese and serve at once.

Coconut Rice

Serves 4 to 6

This fragrant dish is rice dressed up in yellow with a hint of sweetness.

2½ tablespoons vegetable oil	**½ cup unsweetened coconut flakes**
2 cups uncooked brown rice	**4 cups water**
1½ teaspoons turmeric	**½ stick cinnamon**

Sauté the rice, turmeric, and coconut in oil for 2 to 3 minutes. Stir constantly to coat everything with the oil. Add the water and the cinnamon stick. Cover the pot and increase the heat to bring the water to a rapid boil. It is best not to remove the lid while the rice is cooking, so when steam escapes from the pot, that is the signal to reduce the heat and simmer about 40 minutes.

Coconut Rice is especially handsome with curries and is a natural with Spicy Caribbean Fish *(p. 185)* or Fish Thebaudienne *(p. 178)*.

Arancini

(Italian Rice Balls)

Serves 4

This is the way Tony Del Plato's mama, Pina, makes ordinary rice not so ordinary. Arancini are the favorite street food in Italy.

3 cups cooked brown rice *(see Appendix)*

1 cup freshly grated Parmesan cheese (2½ ounces)

4 eggs, lightly beaten

2 tablespoons chopped fresh parsley

salt and black pepper to taste

1 cup bread crumbs

vegetable oil

Mix together the cooked rice, Parmesan cheese, eggs, parsley, seasonings, and ½ cup of bread crumbs. Form the rice balls by hand, using about ½ cup for each one. If the mixture fails to stick together, mash it to break down the rice kernels. Roll each rice ball in bread crumbs to coat it thoroughly.

Heat ½ inch of oil in a heavy skillet. Fry the rice balls, rolling them often so that they will brown evenly. When they are golden brown, crispy, and thoroughly heated, remove them from the skillet and roll them gently on a paper towel to remove excess oil.

Rice balls can also be filled. Form the rice balls around a cube of mozzarella cheese or make an indentation, fill it with tomato sauce, and then pinch it closed and cook as above.

Rice balls are delicious plain or topped with cheese or tomato sauce.

Nori Rolls

Serves 6 to 8 as an appetizer

Roseann Iacovazzi, our resident macrobiotic expert and teacher, showed us how to make nori rolls, those beautiful little seaweed rolls with a mosaic of vegetables in the center. And once you've gathered the more exotic ingredients and have mastered the rolling technique, Nori Rolls will become an easy, but ever so impressive, part of your repertoire, too.

Nori, wasabi, and bamboo rolling mats are all available at Asian food stores and many natural food stores.

4 or 5 sheets of nori *(see Appendix)*

2 cups uncooked brown rice

4 tablespoons rice vinegar *(see Appendix)*

1 teaspoon salt

2 teaspoons sugar

vegetable strips for filling*

wasabi *(see Appendix)*

tamari soy sauce

special equipment: a bamboo rolling mat, called a *sudore*

Cook the rice, using slightly more water than usual. The Japanese traditionally use a short-grained white rice, but we prefer brown rice. Leftover rice that has been reheated may also be used; cold rice will not roll properly.

While the rice is cooking, prepare the other ingredients. Some nori sheets are sold pre-toasted and should indicate this on the package. If yours aren't, toast them by passing each sheet lightly over an open flame. Mix about 1 teaspoon of the wasabi powder with water to form a smooth paste. Cover and set aside for a few minutes to allow the flavor to fully develop. Combine the vinegar, salt, and sugar and heat briefly to dissolve the sugar. Set aside to cool. Place the cooked rice in a large bowl, pour the vinegar mixture over it, and toss, using a wooden spoon or rice paddle, until the rice has cooled to approximately body temperature.

---

* *One or more of the following vegetables, all cut in thin strips: raw cucumber, avocado or scallions; lightly steamed green beans, carrots, red or green peppers; softened shiitake mushrooms (see Appendix). For an attractive filling, choose vegetables of contrasting colors, though you can use just one kind. Small amounts are adequate – 1 carrot, cucumber, or pepper, 6 to 8 green beans, 3 or 4 scallions.*

Place a nori sheet on the bamboo rolling mat. Moisten your hands and spread ¾ to 1 cup of rice evenly over the nori, leaving a 1½-inch strip at the top edge uncovered. About 2 inches up from the bottom, make a horizontal groove across the rice and spread with a thin layer of wasabi. Place vegetable strips on top of the wasabi, in 3 lines, each line extending from edge to edge of the nori sheet. For example, if using avocados, carrots, and scallions, make one horizontal line of each vegetable. If using only one vegetable, still lay down just three lines to avoid creating a fat, unwieldy roll.

Now, pick up the bottom edge of the mat and start rolling toward the top using firm and steady pressure to shape the roll. Some rice may be squeezed out at the sides. This can be corrected later, but do not allow the bare strip of nori at the top to be covered by rice or the roll won't seal properly. Most nori rolls are self-sealing, but if yours is being difficult, moisten the top edge of the nori sheet with a little water. Adjust the shape of the roll by squeezing gently on the mat. Set the nori roll aside. Repeat this procedure with the remaining sheets of nori, varying the fillings for interest.

With a sharp, wet knife trim off the ragged end pieces of the rolls, if necessary, and then cut each roll into 1-inch slices.

Arrange the slices cut side up on a platter and serve with small bowls of tamari soy sauce and additional wasabi for dipping.

Jonathan's Tofu Dumplings

Serves 4

Jonathan Kline worked at Moosewood for many years and then went on to become an Ithaca tofu maker. Tofu Dumplings make a simple miso soup hearty. Use them in any soup or stew as you would other dumplings.

1 cake of tofu, pressed *(see Appendix)*

1 tablespoon light miso *(see Appendix)*

1 tablespoon unbleached white flour

1 teaspoon kuzu *(see Appendix)* **or cornstarch, dissolved in 1 teaspoon cold water**

½ teaspoon dark sesame oil *(see Appendix)*

Mash the pressed tofu. Squeeze out any excess water through a sieve or cheesecloth. Mix the tofu, miso, flour, and dissolved kuzu or cornstarch. Add the sesame oil.

Shape into small balls, about 1½-inches in diameter.

Drop the dumplings into simmering soup or stew and gently simmer for 10 to 15 minutes. Stir occasionally.

Greek Potatoes

Serves 6

We cajoled the owner of the best Greek restaurant in town into giving us the basics of this recipe. Potatoes are baked with a lemon and garlic flavored marinade. The aroma alone is enough to set you dancing!

6 medium potatoes, cubed (3 pounds)

½ cup fresh lemon juice, about 2½ lemons

⅓ cup vegetable oil

1 tablespoon olive oil

2 teaspoons salt

½ teaspoon black pepper

1½ teaspoon dried oregano

2 garlic cloves, minced or pressed

3 cups hot water

□

chopped fresh parsley

Toss together the potatoes, lemon juice, oils, spices, and garlic in a deep, flat pan about 8×12-inches. Add the water. Bake uncovered for about 1½ hours at 475°. Stir every 20 minutes adding more water if necessary to prevent sticking. Be very careful not to burn the potatoes during the last 30 minutes. During the final 15 to 20 minutes, allow the water to evaporate until only the oil is left.

Garnish with fresh parsley and serve.

Greek Potatoes are delicious alone or can be sprinkled with feta cheese and served with Egg-Lemon Soup with Spinach *(p. 22)*, roasted red bell peppers, and a green salad.

Armenian Green Beans

Serves 4 to 6

A simple time-honored family recipe for preparing fresh green beans. Lemon and an assortment of herbs provide a brisk accent.

2 tablespoons vegetable oil or butter

2 cups chopped onions

3 cups green beans, whole or cut in half

4 medium fresh tomatoes, chopped or 1½ cups undrained canned tomatoes, crushed

3 tablespoons fresh lemon juice

⅛ teaspoon dried thyme

¼ teaspoon dried marjoram

¼ teaspoon dried basil

salt and black pepper to taste

Sauté the onions in the oil or butter until translucent. Add the beans and cook about 5 minutes, stirring frequently, until they turn a bright, shiny green. Stir in the tomatoes, lemon juice, herbs, and spices. Lower the heat and simmer, covered, 10 to 15 minutes, until the beans are tender and the flavors have married. Stir occasionally to prevent sticking.

Tzatziki

Serves 4 to 6

Yogurt, cucumber, and mint all cool and refresh the palate.

2 large cucumbers, peeled and grated	**1 tablespoon fresh mint (¾ teaspoon dried)**
2 garlic cloves, pressed or minced	
2 cups plain yogurt	**salt and black pepper to taste**

Lightly salt the grated cucumbers, place in a colander or strainer, and set aside to drain for about half an hour.

In a bowl, combine the drained cucumbers with the rest of the ingredients. Chill for 30 minutes before serving.

Serve with Baba Ganouj *(p. 73)*, Hummus with Tahini *(p. 74)*, and pita bread. Tzatziki is a refreshing side dish with Fish à la Grecque *(p. 171)*.

Refried Beans

Serves 4 to 6 as a side dish

Pinto or kidney beans that are cooked, spiced, mashed, and fried are one of the tastiest side dishes to spark a Mexican meal. They can also be used to fill a Pita Refrita *(p. 66)* or to make Chilaquiles *(p. 106)*.

5 cups cooked and drained pinto or kidney beans *(see Appendix)*	**2 teaspoons ground cumin**
2 to 3 cups reserved bean liquid	**1 teaspoon ground coriander**
3 to 4 tablespoons olive or vegetable oil	**1½ teaspoons salt or 1 tablespoon tamari soy sauce**
2 cups chopped onions	**¼ teaspoon black pepper**
3 garlic cloves, minced or pressed	**½ cup tomato juice or orange juice** *(optional)*

In a sturdy bowl mash the cooked beans with enough of the reserved bean liquid to obtain the consistency of stiff mashed potatoes. Use a potato masher or wooden pestle and a vigorous arm. If you use the bowl of a food processor, be careful not to over-process.

In a heavy iron skillet sauté the onions and garlic in the oil until the onions are translucent. Add the spices and seasonings and sauté 3 or 4 minutes. Add the mashed beans and continue to cook on medium heat for about 15 minutes. Stir constantly, adding the tomato or orange juice, if desired, to enhance the flavors and to help prevent sticking. When the beans are well-mixed and bubbly hot, they are ready to serve. Adjust the salt to taste.

Very good basic Refried Beans can be made without the spices – just use oil, onions, black pepper, and salt or tamari soy sauce with the beans.

Sweet and Sour Red Cabbage

Serves 4 to 6

An attractive and inexpensive side dish. You really don't need much sweetener, because well-cooked cabbage has a wonderful sweetness all its own.

2 tablespoons butter or vegetable oil

¾ cup chopped onions

6 cups thinly sliced red cabbage

¾ cup apple juice or cider

½ teaspoon salt

black pepper to taste

1 tablespoon fresh dill (1 teaspoon dried)

1 teaspoon whole fennel seeds

¼ cup raisins *(optional)*

3 tablespoons cider vinegar (more to taste)

1 tablespoon honey *(optional)*

Sauté the onions in the oil or butter until lightly browned. Add the cabbage and continue to sauté for 5 to 10 minutes. Then add the rest of the ingredients except the honey. Cook on low heat, covered, for about 30 minutes, stirring occasionally. The cabbage will be greatly reduced in volume. Cabbage and onions are sweeter the longer they simmer, so taste first and then add more vinegar and the honey if needed.

We often serve this at the restaurant with its ethnic relatives Piroshki *(p. 84)* or Russian Vegetable Strudel *(p. 142)*. If you serve it with a strudel already filled with flavorful herbs, you might choose to omit the dill and fennel and enjoy a simpler tasting sweet and sour cabbage.

Marinated Tofu

Serves 4 to 6

Tofu flavored with a versatile marinade that's a bit more Chinese than Japanese, but useful in any East Asian cuisine.

2 cakes of tofu, pressed *(see Appendix)* **and cut into ½-inch cubes**

MARINADE

1 tablespoon fresh grated ginger root

2 tablespoons dry sherry, sake, or Chinese rice wine *(see Appendix)*

¼ cup tamari soy sauce

¼ cup water

1 tablespoon dark sesame oil

1 tablespoon rice, white, or cider vinegar

OPTIONAL INGREDIENTS

2 tablespoons minced scallions

½ teaspoon sugar or honey

½ teaspoon Szechuan hot bean paste or Chinese hot chili oil *(see Appendix)*

pinch of cayenne

1 teaspoon toasted sesame seeds

Place the tofu cubes in a strainer. Either pour boiling water over the tofu or dip the strainer into a pot of simmering water for 1 or 2 minutes. Set aside to drain thoroughly.

Whisk together all the marinade ingredients and add any of the optional ingredients that appeal to you. Pour the marinade over the tofu cubes in a large bowl and toss gently with a spatula. Chill at least 20 minutes before serving. A longer marinating time is fine, but we recommend that the tofu be served within a day for the texture to be at its best.

Serve Marinated Tofu as a side dish with any Asian meal or mix it at the last minute into stir-fried vegetables. Marinated Tofu is good as a topping for tossed or grain salads or an addition to Miso Broth *(p. 10)*. Try frying it with leftover rice or noodles. Or stuff it into a pita and top with Spicy Peanut Sauce *(p. 191)*.

Use this marinade also with foods other than tofu. Vegetables marinated in this sauce are good skewered and roasted on a grill. Do the same with firm, oily fish, such as monkfish or bluefish. Or bake fish fillets marinated in this sauce.

Chinese Greens

Serves 4 to 6

This recipe and the two that follow are ways to prepare greens quickly when your garden is overflowing or you want a fast side dish. Use any greens – spinach, beet greens, kale, chard, rapini, cabbage, or bok choy.*

3 tablespoons vegetable oil

1 large garlic clove, minced or pressed

½ teaspoon grated fresh ginger root

6 to 8 cups washed, stemmed, and chopped bulky greens (cabbage, bok choy, or celery cabbage) *or* 12 to 14 cups washed, stemmed, and chopped delicate greens (spinach or beet greens)

¼ cup dry sherry or Chinese rice wine *(see Appendix)*

1 tablespoon vinegar or fresh lemon juice *(optional)*

1 teaspoon sugar or honey *(optional)*

2 tablespoons fish sauce *(see Appendix)* or tamari soy sauce

Heat the oil in a wok and add the garlic and ginger root. Sauté very briefly. Add the greens and toss to coat with oil. Add the sherry or wine, vinegar or lemon juice, honey or sugar, fish sauce, and a splash of water. Continue sautéing. Delicate greens will take about 1 minute. Sauté bulky greens 5 to 10 minutes, or until tender. If you use tamari soy sauce instead of fish sauce, add it just before serving.

---

* Remember that fresh greens "cook down" a lot. It's difficult to give you specific amounts of greens to use because there are so many variables – how bulky or delicate, how tightly packed into a measuring cup – so our suggestions for amounts of greens are a guide only.

Korean Greens

Serves 6

Korean Spinach is what Popeye eats when he is visiting Seoul.

2 pounds fresh spinach, stemmed and coarsely chopped (other greens may be substituted)

3 tablespoons vegetable oil

☐

2 tablespoons dark sesame oil
(see Appendix)

3 tablespoons white vinegar

3 tablespoons tamari soy sauce

a pinch of sugar *(optional)*

1 tablespoon sesame seeds, toasted

Prepare the sauce by mixing together the sesame oil, vinegar, soy sauce, and sugar.

Heat the vegetable oil in a wok or a large skillet. Add the greens and stir-fry until just tender, but not overcooked. Pour off any excess oil or liquid. Toss the greens with the sauce in a serving bowl. Sprinkle the sesame seeds over the greens and serve.

We like this dish best stir-fried, but if you wish to reduce your oil consumption, it may be prepared by cooking the spinach in ½ cup water until limp, draining it, and then proceeding as above.

Try this as a side dish with an Asian-style fish and rice.

Italian Greens

Serves 4 to 6

The Italians traditionally prepare chard this way, and once you have experienced the simplicity and full flavor of this dish, so will you.

¼ cup olive oil	salt to taste
6 large garlic cloves, minced or pressed	
12 to 14 large chard leaves and stalks, coarsely chopped (other greens may be substituted)	

Heat the olive oil in a wok or heavy skillet and sauté the garlic until golden. Remove the garlic with a slotted spoon and reserve. Add the greens and sauté until tender. Add the salt. Just before serving, sprinkle the reserved garlic over the chard.

Serve with Mushroom-Leek Frittata *(p. 110)*, pasta, or any mild-flavored entrée.

Date-Lemon Chutney

Yields 1½ cups

A spicy, sweet-and-sour sidekick for hot curries.

9 ounces pitted dates

3 tablespoons dried, unsweetened coconut

4 tablespoons fresh lemon juice

2 tablespoons grated fresh ginger root

½ teaspoon ground fennel seeds

½ teaspoon ground coriander

¼ cup chopped fresh parsley

½ teaspoon salt

¼ teaspoon cayenne *(optional)*

Chop the dates. Very dry dates should be steeped in boiling water, drained, and then chopped.

Mix all the ingredients in a bowl. If there is time, let the chutney sit for half an hour, allowing the flavors to blend. If the consistency is too thick, moisten with more lemon juice or water. Refrigerated, this chutney will keep for at least two weeks.

Try chutney with North Indian Stuffed Eggplant *(p. 98)*.

Peach Chutney

Serves 6 to 8

Made with fresh, ripe peaches, this is a sweet-tart, spice-scented accessory to a curry dinner.

2 tablespoons vegetable oil	¼ cup honey
1 cup finely chopped onions	¼ teaspoon cinnamon
2 garlic cloves, minced or pressed *(optional)*	⅛ teaspoon nutmeg, preferably freshly grated
10 ripe peaches, peeled, pitted and sliced	⅛ teaspoon ground cardamom
	⅛ teaspoon cayenne
2 to 4 tablespoons cider vinegar, depending on sweetness of peaches	1 teaspoon grated fresh ginger root

In a saucepan, sauté the onions and garlic in the oil until the onions are golden. Add the peaches and vinegar and continue to cook covered, stirring frequently, until the peaches begin to soften. Add the honey and spices and simmer the chutney gently on low heat for 20 to 30 minutes more, until a chunky sauce consistency is reached.

Serve hot, or cool the chutney to room temperature before serving. Refrigerated, chutney will keep for at least two weeks.

Dhall

Serves 4 to 6

A flavorful side dish with any curry or an excellent addition to an array of Indian dishes. Served with rice and yogurt, dhall can be a meal in itself.

1½ cups dried lentils or split peas

4½ cups Vegetable Stock *(p. 30)*
or water

1 teaspoon turmeric

1 teaspoon salt

□

2 tablespoons vegetable oil

2 cups diced onions

1 garlic clove, minced or pressed

½ teaspoon ground cumin

1 teaspoon turmeric

**½ teaspoon black pepper, coarsely
ground**

**¼ teaspoon hot chili pepper flakes or
cayenne or 1 small fresh hot chili
pepper, minced**

1 cup coconut milk *(see Appendix)*

In a large pot, cook the lentils or peas in the stock or water along with the salt and turmeric. Drain, but reserve the liquid.

Sauté the onions, garlic, and the rest of the spices in the oil until the onions are golden brown, stirring continuously.

Mix the drained lentils or peas with the sautéed spices and reheat gently. When hot, stir in the coconut milk. If the dhall is too dry or thick, add some of the reserved liquid.

For a lighter, less sweet version of this dish, substitute 1 cup chopped tomatoes for the coconut milk.

Two Indian Raitas

Serves 6 as a side dish

These raitas are refreshing counterpoints to curries, piquant fish entrées, and spicy grain salads. Roasting the spices enhances the flavor of the raitas and lends an authentic touch.

SPINACH RAITA

¾ teaspoon whole cumin seeds

10 ounces fresh spinach, stemmed, finely chopped, and steamed (about 1 cup when cooked)

3 cups plain yogurt

¼ teaspoon ground coriander

salt and black pepper to taste

Roast the whole cumin seeds in a small, dry cast iron skillet until they begin to smoke. Grind them with a mortar and pestle. If whole cumin seeds are not available you can substitute ¾ teaspoon ground cumin.

Combine the ground cumin with the other ingredients and chill. Serve cold.

CUCUMBER RAITA

1 large cucumber, peeled, seeded, and diced

2 cups plain yogurt

1 tablespoon butter

¾ teaspoon black mustard seeds

¼ teaspoon ground cardamom

salt and cayenne to taste

Combine the diced cucumber and yogurt. In a very small pan, heat the butter and then add the mustard seeds and cardamom. When the mustard seeds start to pop, remove the pan from the heat and add the spices to the yogurt mixture. Add salt and cayenne to taste.

Chill for at least 1 hour before serving.

BREADS

Breads

Most of us grew up in an age of meat-and-potatoes diets and vitamin-enriched processed foods. This era of mass-produced convenience went a long way toward ending household drudgery, and we don't propose to turn back the clock. But something was lacking.

Several of us can remember having the same fifth grade reader which, upon reflection, must have been written just after the depression and was still in use in our schools in the '50s. The story concerned an eccentric family (Papa was an artist!) traveling from Maine to Oregon in search of work. Throughout their long journey people showed them kindness, usually by giving them generous, quirky meals. This was high romance to a ten-year-old who ate hamburgers and canned green beans in the school cafeteria. The first lovingly detailed meal in the book was Boston baked beans and steamed brown bread. We didn't know what steamed brown bread was, but it certainly seemed more glamorous than packaged, commercial white bread with margarine. As adults now, we're still sentimental enough to aspire to that memorable, evocative, appreciative romance with food, which seems to begin with real bread, made by hand.

In our new speeded-up, specialized, technocratic world, we recommend time out for this age-old process. Even if you find opportunity for it only a few times a year, your children will remember baking bread at home. If you don't have kids, make an occasion for yourself because bread-baking is nourishment for the soul.

Ah, the infinite variety of breads – crusty, crunchy, chewy, sour, delicate, sweet, savory, soft, warm, buttery, soothing, sustaining staff of life! You can't run to the market to buy bread like this. You have to make it yourself, and it's really not hard to do.

All quick breads such as cornbread and muffins truly are quick and easy. The fast action of baking soda or baking powder as leavening means that there's no delayed gratification. You simply mix up the ingredients and put them in the oven to bake.

Yeasted breads, in the opinion of this grateful group, are one of the proud discoveries of human civilization. Perhaps someone once let the grain ferment a little bit and tried to make bread from it anyway and then had the genius to realize what that wonderful difference was. Yeasted breads do require more know-how and you can find instructions for the basic procedure in the appendix of this book if you are a wary novice. The actual hands-on time spent preparing a yeasted bread for baking is usually not more than half an hour. The rest of the time the bread is working on its own.

Bread will be a little different every time you make it, depending on differences in flour, temperature, kneading, and the inexplicable. That's why bread-baking retains a pleasurable element of magic and mystery. It's always an adventure.

Whole Wheat Bread

Yields 3 loaves

Some of us make this basic, rich, and moist bread every week for our families with reassuringly consistent good results.

2 tablespoons (or 2 packages) dry yeast
½ cup warm water
□
3 cups milk, scalded *(see Appendix)*
½ cup honey

½ cup melted butter or vegetable oil
1 tablespoon salt
10 to 12 cups whole wheat bread flour

Read about bread making *(see Appendix)*.

Generously butter three 5×9-inch loaf pans.

Proof the yeast in the warm water.

In a large bowl, mix together the scalded milk, honey, melted butter or oil, and salt. When this mixture is lukewarm, stir in the yeast. Add 4½ cups of the flour and beat 300 strokes. Gradually add more flour, stirring well between additions, until the dough is stiff.

Turn the dough out onto a floured board. Knead for 10 minutes, adding more flour as needed to prevent it from sticking. Place the dough in a large oiled bowl, turning it so that all sides are oiled. Cover the bowl with a cloth. Let the dough rise until doubled, about 1½ hours. Punch it down and let it rise again, about 1 hour. Punch down the dough once more, divide it in 3 equal parts, and shape it into three loaves. Place the loaves in the bread pans. Allow the dough to rise a third time, for 30 to 45 minutes, or until almost doubled.

Bake in a preheated oven at 375° for about 40 minutes.

Cracked Wheat Bread

Yields 2 loaves

A crunchy-textured change-of-pace bread with a warm grainy flavor.

½ cup cracked wheat or bulgur

1½ cups water

¼ cup butter

4 teaspoons salt

¼ cup molasses or honey

1 tablespoon (or 1 package) dry yeast

⅓ cup warm water

□

1 cup milk

2 cups whole wheat bread flour

3½ to 4 cups unbleached white flour

Read about bread making *(see Appendix).*

Generously butter two 5×9-inch loaf pans.

In a saucepan, cook the cracked wheat or bulgur in the water about 10 minutes until water is absorbed and the wheat has a gummy cereal consistency. Stir as needed to prevent sticking. Add the butter, salt, and molasses or honey.

Proof the yeast in the warm water.

Place the wheat mixture in a large mixing bowl and add the milk. When this mixture is lukewarm, add the yeast and stir. Add the whole wheat flour and beat well. Stir in white flour until the dough is stiff enough to knead.

On a floured board, knead the dough for 10 to 15 minutes, adding flour as necessary to prevent the dough from sticking. This will remain a very soft dough and should feel slightly tacky. Place the dough in a buttered bowl, turning to coat with butter. Cover and let rise until doubled, about 1½ hours. Cover your hands with flour and punch down. Knead the dough for 1 minute in the bowl and shape into 2 loaves. Place the loaves in the buttered loaf pans. Cover and let rise until doubled, about 30 minutes.

Bake in a preheated oven at 375° for 30 to 35 minutes.

French Bread

Yields 2 long, thin loaves

An accommodating classic that complements any food – and certainly the best possible bread for dunking in hot chocolate.

Traditional ovens in France heat from the top, bottom, and sides. Placing a pan of boiling water on the floor of your oven will help to create a similar baking condition.

1 tablespoon (or 1 package) dry yeast	□
1½ cups lukewarm water	**cornmeal**
1 tablespoon sugar	**1 egg white**
2 teaspoons salt	
3 to 4 cups unbleached white flour (whole wheat flour may be substituted for up to 2 cups)	

Read about bread making *(see Appendix)*.

In a large bowl, dissolve the yeast in the water. Stir sugar and salt into the yeast mixture and then 2 cups of flour. Working the dough with your hands, add more flour until it will absorb no more. Knead the dough on a floured board until it is no longer sticky, but very smooth and elastic. Cover and let rise until doubled, about 1 hour.

Punch down the dough, divide it in half, and form each piece into a long narrow loaf, about 2 inches in diameter. Place the loaves on a buttered baking sheet sprinkled with cornmeal. Cover and let rise again, 30 to 45 minutes.

Lightly beat 1 egg white with 1 tablespoon water. Brush the tops of the loaves with the egg white glaze and bake in a preheated oven at 400° for 40 to 45 minutes. If you prefer a crustier bread, omit the glaze and brush the tops with cold water once before baking and then twice during baking.

Spicy Cornell Bread

Yields 2 loaves

Cornell breads were developed in Ithaca at the Martha Van Rensselaer School of Home Economics at Cornell University in the '40s during the beginnings of modern nutritional science. It was claimed that man could indeed live by (Cornell) bread alone.

Any bread becomes a nutritious Cornell bread with the addition of powdered milk, wheat germ, and soy flour. This particular recipe makes a spicy, dense bread, at its best toasted and buttered.

2 tablespoons (or 2 packages) dry yeast	**3 eggs, beaten**
⅓ cup warm water	**1 tablespoon ground cumin**
☐	**dash of ground cardamom and/or ground coriander seeds**
2 cups milk, scalded *(see Appendix)*	
1 teaspoon salt	**½ cup dry milk**
¼ cup brown sugar	**1 cup soy flour**
¼ cup honey	**1 cup wheat germ**
⅓ cup butter	**3 cups whole wheat flour**
⅓ cup orange juice concentrate	**3 to 4 cups unbleached white flour**

Read about bread making *(see Appendix)*.

Generously butter two 5×9-inch loaf pans.

Proof the yeast in the warm water.

Pour the hot milk over the salt, sugar, honey, and butter. Cool. Add the orange juice concentrate. Add the yeast and the eggs to the milk mixture. Stir in the spices, dry milk, soy flour, and wheat germ. Add the whole wheat flour and blend well. Stir in the white flour, turn out onto a floured surface, and knead 10 to 15 minutes.

Place the dough in a buttered bowl, turning it to coat it with butter on all sides. Cover and leave in a warm spot for 45 minutes to 1 hour, or until it doubles in bulk. Punch down the dough and knead it again for a minute. Cover and let it rise for 30 minutes. Punch the dough down, shape into two loaves, and place them in buttered bread pans. Cover the pans with a towel and let the dough rise until doubled, about 30 minutes.

Bake in a preheated oven at 425° for 10 minutes and then at 350° for 25 to 30 minutes more. Brush the tops of the loaves with melted butter or oil.

Drawing from the cuisines of many cultures, the Moosewood people serve delightful, tasty, and healthy meals. At the same time they provide support, benefit brunches, and energy to causes near to their hearts.

Moosewood is a great example of people working collectively together to the benefit of their patrons, themselves and their community. In a world of change, where constancy and consistency are not always appreciated or possible, Moosewood has been a small oasis helping to sustain us for 14 years. And we appreciate that.

— **Peter Sayet**
partner, Somadhara Bakery and Natural Foods

Potato-Onion-Rye Bread

Yields 2 loaves

This bread smells so good while it's baking that people will line up in the kitchen for the first slices. It keeps very well and makes toast that gives new meaning to "good morning."

2 tablespoons (or 2 packages) dry yeast	1 tablespoon caraway seeds
½ cup warm water	2 cups boiling water
☐	1 cup potato flour *(see Appendix)*
2 cups finely chopped onions	4 to 5 cups unbleached white flour
3 tablespoons molasses	4 cups rye flour
1 tablespoon salt	
3 tablespoons vegetable oil	

Read about bread making *(see Appendix)*.

Oil two 5×9-inch loaf pans.

Proof the yeast in the warm water.

In a large mixing bowl, combine the onions, molasses, salt, oil, and caraway seeds. Pour the boiling water over the mixture and let it cool to between 105° and 115°. Add the yeast, potato flour, and 2 cups of the white flour. Beat 300 strokes. Add the rye flour and enough of the remaining white flour to make a stiff dough.

Knead the dough on a floured surface for 10 to 15 minutes. The rye flour will make the dough sticky, so use more white flour if necessary to keep the dough from sticking to your hands. Place the dough in an oiled bowl, turn it to coat all sides well, cover with a cloth, and let it rise in a warm place until doubled in size, about 1 hour. Punch down the dough and let it rise for another hour. Punch it down again and shape the dough into two loaves. Place them in oiled bread pans for the final 30-minute rising.

Bake in a preheated oven at 375° for 40 to 45 minutes.

This bread is a perfect companion for Hungarian Vegetable Soup *(p. 13)*.

Russian Vegetable Bread

Yields 2 loaves

A rather solid, interesting bread. This bread presents a rare opportunity to create a rosy-hued loaf, so be sure to include some beets.

1 tablespoon (or 1 package) dry yeast

½ cup warm water

□

1½ cups hot water

3 tablespoons molasses

3 tablespoons vegetable oil

1 tablespoon salt

3 tablespoons chopped fresh dill (1½ tablespoons dried)

2 teaspoons caraway seeds

2 cups peeled grated raw vegetables (beets, potatoes, carrots, parsnips)

2 cups whole wheat flour

3 to 4 cups unbleached white flour

2 cups rye flour

Read about bread making *(see Appendix)*.

Oil two 5×9-inch loaf pans.

Proof the yeast in the warm water.

In a large bowl combine 1½ cups of hot water with the molasses, oil, salt, dill, caraway seeds, and grated vegetables. Cool to lukewarm.

Add the yeast to the bowl along with the whole wheat flour and 1 cup of the white flour. Beat the batter for 300 strokes. Add the rye flour and enough of the remaining white flour to make a stiff dough. Turn the dough onto a floured surface and knead it for 10 to 15 minutes.

Place the dough in an oiled bowl, turn it to coat all sides with oil, cover it with a cloth, and allow it to rise for about 1½ hours. Punch down the dough and let it rise again for about 1 hour. Shape the dough into two loaves and place them in oiled bread pans. Cover the loaves and allow them to rise for about 45 minutes.

Bake in a preheated oven at 375° for 35 to 40 minutes.

The availability of root vegetables in fall and winter makes this a natural for serving with cool weather soups and stews.

Cottage Loaf

Yields 1 loaf

This dill-cottage cheese bread is different and delicious. The cottage cheese gives it a smooth, cake-like texture that's very appealing.

1 tablespoon (or 1 package) dry yeast	**2 tablespoons fresh dill (1 tablespoon dried)**
¼ cup warm water	**1 teaspoon salt**
□	**1 egg**
1 cup cottage cheese	**1 cup whole wheat flour**
2 tablespoons honey	**1½ to 2 cups unbleached white flour**
2 tablespoons minced onion	
2 tablespoons melted butter	

Read about bread making *(see Appendix)*.

Oil a 2-quart casserole dish.

Proof the yeast in the warm water.

Heat the cottage cheese to lukewarm. Mix together the cottage cheese, honey, onions, butter, dill, salt, and egg. Stir in the yeast. Stir in the whole wheat flour. Gradually add white flour until the dough is stiff enough to knead.

Knead for a few minutes on a floured surface. The dough will be very sticky, and if it's impossible to knead, add a little more flour. Place the dough in a well-oiled bowl, turn to coat all sides with oil, and cover it with a cloth. Let the dough rise for 1 hour. Punch the dough down, shape it into a round ball, and place it in the oiled casserole dish. Let the dough rise another hour.

Bake in a preheated oven at 350° for about 40 minutes. Brush the top lightly with melted butter or oil just after removing it from the oven.

This bread complements light soups and salads. It goes equally well with Tomato-Garlic Soup *(p. 11)* or sweet Scandinavian Apple Soup *(p. 9)*.

Squash Rolls

Yields about 15 rolls

Special fall and winter dinners deserve these treats. Squash rolls are at their best still warm from baking, but we often double this recipe so we'll have enough rolls to send home with dinner guests and because they're also a chewy, delicious breakfast.

We call them "squash" rolls, but pumpkin or carrot will provide the same color and gentle sweetness. If you use fresh vegetables, boil or bake and then purée them. If you use frozen squash, thaw the squash and squeeze out any excess moisture. Canned carrots should be mashed, but canned pumpkin needs no preparation.

1 tablespoon (or 1 package) dry yeast	**⅓ cup brown sugar**
¼ cup warm water	**½ teaspoon salt**
☐	**⅓ cup melted butter**
⅔ cup milk, scalded *(see Appendix)*	**2 cups whole wheat flour**
1 cup cooked and puréed winter squash, pumpkin, or carrot	**2 to 3 cups unbleached white flour**

Read about bread making *(see Appendix)*.
Generously butter a large baking sheet.
Proof the yeast in the warm water.
Combine the scalded milk, squash, sugar, salt, and melted butter. When this mixture has cooled to lukewarm, add the yeast and whole wheat flour. Beat well. Gradually stir in the unbleached white flour until the dough is stiff enough to knead. Turn onto a lightly floured surface and knead well, adding flour as necessary to prevent sticking. This is a soft, elastic dough and very pleasant to work with.

Place the dough in a large buttered bowl, and turn the dough to coat it with butter. Cover and let rise until doubled, about 1 hour. Punch down. Shape into tangerine-sized rolls and place them on the buttered baking sheet. Cover with a towel and let rise until doubled, about 30 to 45 minutes.

Bake in a preheated oven at 400° for 20 minutes. Brush the tops of the squash rolls with melted butter after removing them from the oven.

Pita Bread

~~~~~~

Yields 1 dozen 8-inch pitas

Fine commercial pita breads can be purchased almost everywhere now, and sometimes they are even locally produced. But they're not quite as good as those you make yourself. Besides, it's fun to see them puff up in the oven.

2 tablespoons (or 2 packages) dry yeast	1 tablespoon salt
½ cup warm water	3 cups whole wheat flour
1 teaspoon honey	5 cups unbleached white flour
□	□
2 cups warm water	cornmeal
⅓ cup olive oil	

Read about bread making *(see Appendix)*.

Proof the yeast in ½ cup warm water with the honey.

In a large bowl combine the proofed yeast, 2 more cups of warm water, the oil, salt, and whole wheat flour and mix well. Stir in 4 cups of the white flour, one cup at a time. Turn the dough out onto a floured board and knead until smooth and elastic, adding more flour as necessary. Place the ball of dough in an oiled mixing bowl and turn to coat the top with oil. Cover and let rise in a warm place until the dough has doubled in size, about 1 to 1½ hours.

Punch the dough down and turn out onto a floured board. Let it rest for 10 to 15 minutes. Cut the dough into 12 equal pieces and shape each piece into a ball. Cover the balls with a cloth and let them sit for 30 minutes.

Preheat the oven to 500°. With a floured rolling pin, roll each ball into a circle about ⅛- to ¼-inch thick and 8 inches in diameter. Sprinkle baking sheets with cornmeal and place the circles on them, taking care that they touch neither the sides of the pans nor each other. Cover and let rest another 30 minutes. Any rounds that will not fit on the sheets should be left on a lightly floured surface and covered with a cloth.

Place the first baking sheet (or two if your oven is large enough) on the bottom of the oven. It is advisable to remove the lowest oven rack to give the pitas room to puff. Bake for 5 minutes without opening the oven, then move the first sheet(s) up to a middle rack and place another sheet on the bottom. Bake another 5 minutes, remove the first sheet from the oven, move the second up, and so forth. After 10 minutes in the oven the pitas should be puffed and just lightly brown. Remove the pitas from the sheets immediately and cover with a cloth. Baking sheets may be reused by brushing off the old cornmeal and dusting with fresh cornmeal.

Pita breads will soften and deflate as they sit. As soon as the pitas cool, wrap them in foil or plastic to prevent them from becoming crisp. You want them to stay soft and pliable. Pitas can be frozen for later use. Reheat frozen pitas in the oven for 10 to 15 minutes.

- *Onion Board Variation:* Sauté 3 cups chopped onions in butter until translucent, add ¼ teaspoon thyme, salt to taste, and let cool. Proceed as for pitas until dividing the dough into balls. Here you may wish to make either 12 individual balls or 3 large ones. Let the dough rest 30 minutes, then roll it out into ½-inch thick rounds, brush the tops with beaten egg, spread on the onion mixture, and sprinkle with poppy or sesame seeds, if desired. Let sit for another 30 minutes, then bake on the oven racks for 25 to 35 minutes at 425°. These savory pitas also freeze well, if you can restrain the household and yourself from eating them all the first day.

Steamed Brown Bread

Yields 2 loaves

Traditionally served with New England suppers, steamed brown bread is also terrific toasted and buttered for breakfast or with cream cheese as a sandwich for lunch.

1 cup yellow cornmeal	1 teaspoon baking powder
1 cup rye flour	1 cup raisins
1 cup whole wheat flour	□
1 teaspoon salt	2 cups buttermilk
1 teaspoon baking soda	¾ cup molasses

Generously butter two 1-pound coffee cans.

Sift the dry ingredients into a large bowl. Stir in the raisins. In a smaller bowl blend the buttermilk and molasses and pour into the dry ingredients, stirring just enough to moisten.

Fill each coffee can about two-thirds full. Cover tightly with aluminum foil. Place the cans on a rack in a deep kettle and pour in enough boiling water to come half way up the sides of the cans. Cover the kettle and boil gently for 3 hours, adding more water as necessary.

Remove the cans from the water and remove the foil. If the loaves do not slide easily from the cans, place the cans in a hot oven (450°) for 5 minutes. The hot oven treatment should cause the bread to shrink away from the sides of the cans and then slip right out. Keep Steamed Brown Bread refrigerated either in its cans or tightly wrapped in foil.

Serve Steamed Brown Bread for supper with Boston Black-eyed Peas *(p. 131)* and applesauce.

Corn Bread

Yields 12 pieces

Fast and delicious.

1½ cups yellow cornmeal

1 cup whole wheat pastry flour

1 cup unbleached white flour

1 tablespoon baking powder

1 teaspoon baking soda

1 teaspoon salt

2 cups buttermilk or plain yogurt

½ cup milk

¼ cup maple syrup or brown sugar

2 eggs, beaten

¼ cup melted butter, cooled

Preheat the oven to 350°.

Generously butter a 9×13-inch baking pan or a 12-inch cast iron skillet.

Sift the dry ingredients into a large bowl. In another bowl, combine the wet ingredients and stir until mixed. Fold the wet ingredients into the dry ingredients. Smooth the batter into the baking pan or skillet and bake for 25 to 30 minutes, or until a knife inserted into the center comes out clean. Allow the corn bread to cool for at least 10 minutes before serving.

Muffins

Yields 1 dozen muffins

It's early morning. You stumble into the kitchen. Your significant other has left a basket of warm muffins on the table. Love triumphs.

1¾ cups whole wheat pastry flour	¾ cup milk
2½ teaspoons baking powder	⅓ cup vegetable oil
¾ teaspoon salt	¼ cup honey or sugar
□	
1 egg	

Preheat the oven to 400°.

Generously butter a 12-cup muffin tin.

In a medium bowl thoroughly mix the dry ingredients. In a smaller bowl lightly beat the egg with the milk, oil, and honey or sugar and add to the dry ingredients all at once, stirring until the batter is just barely mixed. Spoon the batter into the muffin tin. Bake for 20 to 25 minutes or until a toothpick inserted in the center of a muffin comes out clean.

Variations

- *Blueberry Muffins:* Fold 1 cup drained blueberries (fresh, frozen, or canned) into the batter.
- *Cheese Muffins:* Add ¾ cup grated sharp cheddar cheese and omit the honey or sugar.

Pineapple-Cornmeal Muffins

Yields 1 dozen muffins

The tart-sweet flavors of pineapple and raspberry liven up a basic cornmeal muffin.

1 cup whole wheat pastry flour

2 tablespoons sugar

1 tablespoon baking powder

¾ teaspoon salt

¾ cup yellow cornmeal

□

2 eggs

¼ cup vegetable oil or melted butter

½ cup drained, crushed pineapple

1 cup pineapple juice and/or milk

□

2 tablespoons raspberry jam or raspberry butter

Preheat the oven to 425°.

Generously butter a 12-cup muffin tin.

In a medium bowl thoroughly mix the dry ingredients. In a smaller bowl lightly beat the eggs. Stir in the oil or butter, crushed pineapple, and pineapple juice or milk and add to the dry ingredients all at once, stirring until just barely mixed. Spoon the batter into the muffin tin. Put about ½ teaspoon of jam on top of each muffin. Bake for 15 to 20 minutes or until a toothpick inserted in the center of a muffin comes out clean.

Zucchini-Nut Bread

~

Yields 2 loaves

This sweet bread is moist and nutty when oven-fresh. Later try it toasted and spread with cream cheese.

1 cup vegetable oil	1 teaspoon cinnamon
1 cup brown sugar	1 teaspoon salt
3 eggs	1 teaspoon baking powder
1 tablespoon pure vanilla extract	½ teaspoon baking soda
2 cups grated zucchini	□
□	1 cup coarsely chopped walnuts
1½ cups whole wheat pastry flour	1 cup raisins
1½ cups unbleached white flour	

Preheat the oven to 325°.

Oil two 5×9-inch loaf pans.

In a large mixing bowl, combine the oil and brown sugar. Add the eggs, one at a time, beating after each addition. Stir in the vanilla and zucchini.

In a smaller bowl, sift together the flours, cinnamon, salt, baking powder, and soda. Stir the dry ingredients into the oil and egg mixture until just moistened. Fold in the raisins and walnuts.

Spoon the batter into the prepared loaf pans.

Bake for about 1 hour, until a knife inserted into the center comes out clean.

Applesauce-Raisin Bread

Yields 1 loaf

A quintessential tea party loaf. Worth making just for the sweet spicy aroma that fills the kitchen during baking.

1 egg, beaten

1 cup unsweetened applesauce

¼ cup melted butter

½ cup sugar

¼ cup brown sugar

□

2 cups whole wheat pastry flour

2 teaspoons baking powder

¾ teaspoon salt

½ teaspoon baking soda

½ teaspoon cinnamon

1 teaspoon nutmeg

□

½ cup raisins

1 cup coarsely chopped walnuts

Preheat the oven to 350°.

Generously butter a 5×9-inch loaf pan.

Mix together the first five ingredients. Sift together the dry ingredients and stir them into the applesauce mixture until just smooth. Fold in the raisins and nuts.

Pour the batter into the loaf pan. Bake for about 1 hour or until a knife inserted in the center comes out clean.

DESSERTS

Desserts

Many of our desserts at Moosewood are light and fruity or protein-rich or made without sugar, and we value them highly because of these qualities. Yet the appeal of some of our desserts is not that they are healthful but simply that they indulge the senses so lavishly. Many people seem to think that when they give in to these temptations they are being a little wicked.

One of our dessert cooks was jogging through Ithaca's beautiful and hilly streets, trying to burn off the luscious chocolate cake she had enjoyed the night before. She paused to catch her breath at a favorite shady overlook where she noticed this quote from Shakespeare:

> *They say best men are molded out of faults,*
> *And, for the most, become much more the better*
> *For being a little bad...*

She ran on, her step a little springier after reflecting on these words.

The conclusion we have reached is that it is wise to strike a balance, all things measure for measure, and not deny our bodies that which also feeds our souls. Sometimes we must feed our loves as well as our reason. We value chocolate cake not because it's necessary but because it's delightful and our love of the delightful is one of the finest attributes of us mere mortals.

When there is a variety of interesting taste sensations throughout a meal, dessert needn't carry the burden of being the hard-won reward at the end. Desserts are most enjoyable when coordinated with the rest of the meal. A meal with an emphasis on vegetables is nutritionally balanced by a protein-rich sweet such as Italian Pudding or Creamy Rice Pudding. After a heavier meal of pasta, eggs, or cheeses, a light fruity dessert such as Wine-Poached Pears or Tart Lemon Tart may be more pleasing. Meals with strong ethnic or seasonal themes are best finished with a dessert in the same mode. Apricot Baklava complements a meal with a Middle Eastern flavor. After a fall harvest supper, think of Apple and Cheddar Cheese Pie or Fresh Pear Tart. If you've been craving a particularly indulgent dessert such as Mississippi Mud Cake or Fresh Fruit Trifle, use that as the given in your meal plan and serve it with a brothy soup and a green salad.

A few desserts, such as Carob Sauce on ice cream or Grapes in Lemon Yogurt, are nearly instant and can add an easy finishing touch to a meal that was time-consuming to prepare. A dessert like Russian Chocolate Torte is un-apologetically a production number, but it can single-handedly turn any meal into a proud event.

How agreeable to mark festive holidays and special occasions with the splendor of a glorious confection. All cooking and eating need not be merely routine necessity, but rather a daily ritual in celebration of the good things in life.

Wine-Poached Pears

Serves 6

This elegant, light dessert has its origins in classic French and Italian cuisines. It's perfect after a meal of rich pasta. Good pears for poaching should be large and beautifully shaped. Virtually any variety will do, and the pears don't need to be perfectly ripe – in fact, they'll disintegrate a bit as they cook if they're not just a little firm.

6 whole pears, peeled, with stems intact

5 to 6 cups poaching liquid: red wine and fruit juice (pear, apple, apricot, or other) in any proportion

1 orange, sliced

1 cinnamon stick

a few whole cloves

several whole allspice

□

heavy cream, whipped with a little vanilla and maple syrup

Put the pears into a stainless steel pot large enough for an uncrowded single layer of pears. Add enough poaching liquid to cover the pears so that they float and bob around a bit. Add the sliced orange and the spices. Putting the spices into a tea ball or a piece of cheesecloth helps with clean-up later. Simmer on medium heat. Roll the pears over once or twice so that they poach evenly. Poaching time will vary depending on the variety, size, and ripeness of the pears, but will probably not take more than half an hour.

When the pears are tender and rosy-tinted, carefully remove them from the pot. Arrange them upright in a bowl. Add poaching liquid to about 1 inch deep and refrigerate. The remaining poaching liquid may be refrigerated for several weeks for a head start on the next batch. Or to be extra thrifty and efficient, use the leftover liquid to cook a selection of dried fruits for a succulent fruit compote.

Whip the cream with a little pure vanilla extract and sweetening until it's stiff.

Serve each pear on top of a generous scoop of whipped cream and spoon on a little of the poaching liquid. The stiffly whipped cream will hold the pears upright, glistening and proud.

Apricot Baklava

Yields 24 pieces

Sweet and buttery, this traditional pastry of the Middle East is always made with honey and nuts. In our version, the unorthodox apricot custard layer in the middle comes as a welcome surprise.

2 cups dried apricots	**½ cup melted butter**
2 cups apple or apricot juice or water	**1 pound phyllo dough** *(see Appendix)*
4 eggs	□
□	**1 cup honey**
3 cups almonds, toasted and finely chopped	

Simmer the dried apricots in the juice or water for about 1 hour. Remove from the heat and allow to cool. Purée the cooled, cooked apricots with the eggs in a food processor or in two batches in a blender.

Using a pastry brush or a small paint brush, butter a baking sheet. Unroll the phyllo dough. Carefully place two leaves of phyllo on the baking sheet. They should be flat and unwrinkled. Brush the top with butter and sprinkle with chopped almonds. Work quickly or keep the remaining unbuttered phyllo dough covered or it will dry and crack and become difficult to use. Continue this procedure until about half of the phyllo is used. Then spread the apricot purée evenly on the top layer of phyllo. Continue layering phyllo, butter, and almonds, ending with a buttered leaf of phyllo sprinkled with chopped almonds.

Before baking the baklava, score it with a sharp knife, cutting through the top few layers, but not as deep as the custard layer, to form a diamond or rectangular pattern, each piece a serving size, about 3 inches across. Bake at 350° for about 30 minutes, until the top is golden.

When it has cooled about 20 minutes but is still warm, cut it all the way through the scoring and then drizzle the honey evenly over the entire baklava.

Serve with an apéritif or a cup of your favorite coffee or tea.

Store refrigerated and well covered.

Fruit Cobbler

This very simple and quick recipe is about 100 years old. Most cobblers have a biscuit topping, which becomes hard overnight. This topping is more like cake, so it stays moist. The cobbler should be made with soft fruits, such as peaches, berries, nectarines, or plums, which may be fresh, canned, or frozen.

FRUIT FILLING

5 cups soft fruit

¼ cup maple syrup or honey

1 tablespoon fresh lemon juice

½ teaspoon cinnamon

2 tablespoons cornstarch, dissolved in ¼ cup water or fruit juice

BATTER

½ cup melted butter

½ cup maple syrup or honey

3 eggs

½ cup milk

1 teaspoon pure vanilla extract

1½ cups unbleached white flour

1 tablespoon baking powder

☐

freshly whipped cream

Preheat the oven to 350°.

Prepare the fruit. Wash whole berries; wash, pit and slice fresh fruits; drain the juice from canned or defrosted frozen fruit and reserve it to mix with the cornstarch.

Prepare the filling by mixing sliced fruit or whole berries with the maple syrup or honey, lemon juice, cinnamon, and cornstarch mixture. Set aside.

To make the batter, add the maple syrup or honey to the melted butter. Beat in the eggs, milk, and vanilla. Add the dry ingredients and mix until just blended.

Butter a 9×13-inch pan and pour in half the batter. Spoon in the fruit filling and then top with the remaining batter. Bake for 30 to 35 minutes or until the cake is golden brown and springy to the touch.

Italian Pudding

Serves 6

This smooth, rich, high-protein pudding, studded with multicolored jewels of fruit, can be dessert, a satisfying salad for luncheon, or a special breakfast.

¼ cup dried apricots

1 pound ricotta cheese

½ teaspoon pure vanilla extract

¼ to ½ cup raspberry butter or preserves

2 to 3 cups fresh fruit*

¼ cup raisins or dried currants

¼ cup almonds, toasted

□

1 cup heavy cream, whipped

Slice the dried apricots. If you're using unsulfured apricots, soak them in warm water for 20 minutes to plump before slicing.

Using an electric beater or a food processor, whip the ricotta cheese until smooth. Mix in the vanilla and raspberry butter or preserves (make the pudding as sweet as you like by adding more or less). Fold in the fruits and nuts. To insure fluffiness, add the whipped cream not more than two hours before you intend to serve the pudding. Fold in the whipped cream and – voila!

Serve the pudding in a beautiful bowl and decorate the top with more fruit. We also like Italian Pudding piled on melon wedges for brunch.

---

* The fresh fruit for Italian Pudding may be any combination of blueberries, raspberries, strawberries, grapes, sliced peaches, cubed apples, or cantaloupe. It's a matter of availability and personal choice, but we do not recommend using citrus fruits or pineapple because they may curdle the Italian Pudding.

Chocolate Ricotta "Moose"

Serves 6

This is one of our most often requested recipes. It makes a foolproof, almost instant, rich and velvety dessert.

3 ounces unsweetened chocolate, melted

1 pound ricotta cheese

1 teaspoon pure vanilla extract

honey to taste (about ⅓ cup)

1 cup heavy cream, whipped with a little vanilla and maple syrup

fresh fruit or shaved chocolate

Blend the melted chocolate, ricotta cheese, vanilla, and honey in a blender or food processor until very smooth. Pour into dessert cups and chill.

To serve, mound whipped cream on top and garnish with a fresh, ripe strawberry, a few raspberries, an orange or kiwi fruit slice, or shaved chocolate.

Pots De Crème Au Chocolat

Serves 6 to 8

This impressive chocolate custard may seem to belong solely to the province of fancy French restaurants. In fact, this is a very quick and easy dessert to make. You can vary the richness by the proportion of cream you use; made with all cream, it's very rich, indeed, and a small portion satisfies.

2 cups milk, heavy cream, or
  half-and-half

8 ounces sweet chocolate

6 egg yolks

1 teaspoon pure vanilla extract

□

heavy cream, whipped with vanilla
  and sweetening

In a double boiler or (carefully) in a heavy pan, heat the milk and chocolate until the chocolate has melted and the mixture is a smooth uniform color. In a blender, whip the eggs and then pour the hot milk-chocolate into the whirling blender until smooth and thick.

If it doesn't thicken enough, pour the mixture back into the saucepan and cook it on low heat, stirring until thick. If it is cooked too long or too rapidly, it will become slightly curdled. Then another quick whirl in the blender will smooth it.

Add the vanilla and stir. Pour into dessert cups, filling about half full. Chill. Serve with plenty of the freshly whipped cream.

Creamy Rice Pudding

Serves 6 to 8

This superb rice pudding has a number of virtues over its cousins: it uses leftover rice, it bakes in the oven, and it's unusually wholesome and delicious. In fact, this dessert may become so popular in your household that you find yourself cooking rice especially to make rice pudding. It's been known to happen.

3 cups cooked brown rice *(see Appendix)*

2¼ cups half-and-half or milk

5 eggs

1 teaspoon pure vanilla extract

½ teaspoon cinnamon

¼ teaspoon ground nutmeg

½ cup honey or maple syrup

2 tablespoons grated orange peel (the peel of 1 orange)

⅔ cup raisins

2 medium apples, cored and finely chopped *(optional)*

☐

freshly whipped cream

Butter a deep casserole dish and set aside. Preheat the oven to 325°.

In a blender or mixing bowl combine the half-and-half, eggs, vanilla, spices, and honey. In a large bowl thoroughly mix the rice, egg mixture, grated orange peel, raisins, and chopped apples.

Pour the pudding into the casserole dish and bake uncovered for an hour, until the custard is set and the pudding begins to brown lightly at the edges. Stir the pudding thoroughly at 20-minute intervals while it is baking and add a small amount of milk if it becomes too dry.

Serve Creamy Rice Pudding hot from the oven or chill it and serve it cold later. A dollop of fresh whipped cream adds the perfect finishing touch to each serving.

Custards

Serves 8

It's no trouble at all to have some of these smooth and wholesome high-protein treats in the refrigerator for after-school snacks, dessert, or a quick breakfast.

8 eggs

4 cups milk

½ cup honey or maple syrup

2 teaspoons pure vanilla extract

nutmeg, preferably freshly grated

Preheat the oven to 350°.

Blend the first four ingredients together in a blender. Pour into oven-proof dessert cups. Place the cups in a shallow pan and pour boiling water into the pan to a level about half way up the sides of the cups. Sprinkle the tops of the custards with grated nutmeg. Bake for about ½ hour or until the custards are firm and lightly golden. Chill several hours before serving.

Variations

- *Cashew Custard:* Reduce the milk to 3 cups and add 1 cup of cashew butter.
- *Peach Custard:* Reduce the milk to 3 cups. Add about half a fresh peach, peeled and sliced, to each dessert cup, before pouring in the custard.
- *Coconut Custard:* Use coconut milk *(see Appendix)* instead of milk. Before you add any honey or maple syrup, taste – the coconut milk may be sweet enough. Sprinkle grated coconut on top instead of nutmeg.
- *Banana-Coconut Custard:* Make Coconut Custard, adding 2 bananas to the blender.

Pie Crust

This recipe for an easy-to-handle pastry dough which we use for both dinner and dessert pies is from Tom Walls, our resident pastry-maker, who rolls out the tenderest, flaky crusts.

9-INCH SINGLE PIE CRUST

1 cup unbleached white flour (up to ½ cup whole wheat flour may be substituted)

⅓ cup chilled butter

2 tablespoons ice water

½ teaspoon salt (if unsalted butter is used)

10-INCH SINGLE PIE CRUST

1½ cups unbleached white flour (up to ¾ cup whole wheat flour may be substituted)

½ cup chilled butter

3 tablespoons ice water

½ teaspoon salt (if unsalted butter is used)

Sift the flour into a mixing bowl.

Cut the butter into small pieces and sprinkle onto the flour. Working quickly so that the butter will remain cold, use a pastry cutter, two knives, or your fingertips to cut the butter into the flour until the butter pieces are pea-sized.

Sprinkle the ice water over the flour, a little at a time, as you turn the dough with a wooden spoon. As the water is incorporated, a ball of dough will form. Add a little more ice water if the dough fails to come together.

Roll out the dough immediately on a lightly floured board, or chill until firm, 30 to 60 minutes, before rolling.

Southern Nut Pie Eudora

Our dessert chef, Susan Harville, was excited when she heard that one of her favorite writers, Eudora Welty, was coming to Ithaca to give a reading from her work. Susan made this pie to present to Miss Welty as a token of her appreciation. Miss Welty very graciously accepted the pie and said, "...the pleasure you've had from reading my work? Why, surely it couldn't add up to a whole pecan pie!"

Maple syrup, one of our favorite harvests from Ithaca's surrounding hillsides, gives a Northern twist to our version of a Southern classic.

1 unbaked 9-inch pie shell *(p. 253)*	**3 eggs, well beaten**
□	**1 cup maple syrup**
1½ cups pecan or walnut halves	**1 cup heavy cream or half-and-half**
¼ cup melted butter	□
1 teaspoon pure vanilla extract	**apple slices**
2 tablespoons unbleached white flour	**freshly whipped cream or ice cream**
½ teaspoon salt	

Preheat the oven to 375°.

Spread the nuts evenly across the bottom of the unbaked pie shell. Set aside. In a large bowl, mix the melted butter, vanilla, and flour. Add the salt, eggs, maple syrup, and cream and mix thoroughly. Pour the liquid mixture over the nuts in the pie shell. The nuts will float. Push them down into the liquid with the back of a spoon to wet them, so they won't burn during baking.

Bake at 375° for 50 to 60 minutes or until a knife inserted in the center comes out clean. Let the pie cool at least 15 minutes before slicing.

Serve plain or with a few crisp apple slices and a dollop of whipped cream or a scoop of ice cream.

Apple and Cheddar Cheese Pie

Apple pie without cheese is like a kiss without a hug and a squeeze. This apple pie has the cheese right in the pie, with a sweet crumbly streusel topping.

1 unbaked 10-inch pie shell *(p. 253)*

□

8 tart apples, peeled and thinly sliced

¼ cup sugar

¼ cup unbleached white flour

2 tablespoons fresh lemon juice

STREUSEL TOPPING

¼ cup unbleached white flour

½ cup sugar

⅓ cup butter

□

2 cups grated sharp cheddar cheese (6 ounces)

In a large bowl, dust the apple slices with the flour and sugar, then drizzle them with the lemon juice. Give the mixture a few turns with a big spoon.

Preheat the oven to 425°.

Prepare the streusel topping in a food processor or by hand with a pastry cutter. Mix the flour and sugar and cut in the butter until the topping becomes crumbly. If it seems too sticky, add a little more flour.

Fill the pie crust with the apple slices, sprinkle the grated cheese over the apples, and cover the cheese with the streusel. The streusel prevents the cheese from burning. Bake for 30 to 40 minutes, until the pie is bubbling and golden brown.

Fresh Pear Tart

Serves 4 to 6

A lush dessert, fragrant with vanilla, nutmeg, and fresh fruit.

1 unbaked 10-inch pie shell *(p. 253)*	**⅔ cup sugar**
CUSTARD	**3 eggs**
6 tablespoons unbleached white flour	**1 teaspoon pure vanilla or almond extract**
½ teaspoon nutmeg, preferably freshly grated	
3/4 cup butter	**3 medium pears,* peeled**

Sift together the flour and nutmeg. Melt the butter. Remove it from the heat and add the sugar. Whisk in the flour-nutmeg mixture. Stir in the eggs, one at a time, then the extract. At this point the custard should be thick and smooth.

Cut the pears into eighths, lengthwise. Core the slices and arrange them in the pie shell. Cover with the custard. Bake at 350° for 45 to 50 minutes until the custard is firm and golden.

---

*We prefer Anjou pears for this tart.

Tart Lemon Tart

A very tart tart with a cookie crust, this is a refreshing, sophisticated finale for a rich meal, especially welcome on sultry summer evenings. We like to serve this bright lemon tart on a cobalt blue plate.

TART PASTRY	*FILLING*
1⅓ cups unbleached white flour	4 lemons
7 tablespoons butter	5 tablespoons butter
pinch of salt	½ cup sugar
¼ teaspoon pure vanilla extract	5 eggs, well beaten
¼ cup sugar	¼ teaspoon pure vanilla extract
3 to 4 tablespoons ice water	□
	1 lemon, sliced in very thin rounds

Cut the butter into small pieces and work it into the flour with a pastry cutter, two knives, or your finger tips. Mix in the salt, vanilla, and sugar, and then just enough ice water to bind. Press the dough with your fingers into a 9- or 10-inch drop-bottom tart pan. Chill the crust 1 hour or overnight.

Preheat the oven to 425°.

Line the chilled crust with waxed paper and fill with dried beans or rice to prevent the crust from buckling during baking. Bake at 425° for 15 to 20 minutes. Carefully remove the beans and waxed paper.

Lower the oven temperature to 350°.

Mix together the juice of 4 lemons, the butter, and the sugar and heat until the butter melts and the mixture is just warm. Pour the beaten eggs slowly into this mixture in a steady stream, whisking constantly. Continue to stir on low heat until the mixture thickens into a custard. Stir in the vanilla. Pour into the baked crust and bake for 35 to 50 minutes or until the custard sets and the top becomes golden.

Serve chilled and garnished with thinly sliced rounds of lemon.

Speckled Cheese Tart

This tart features a rich cookie-like crust with a creamy chocolate-flecked filling.

CRUST	FILLING
½ cup butter	1½ pounds ricotta cheese
½ cup sugar	½ cup sugar
1 egg	2 eggs
¼ cup sour cream	½ teaspoon pure vanilla extract
½ teaspoon pure vanilla extract	2 ounces sweet or semi-sweet chocolate, grated
2 cups unbleached white flour	
½ teaspoon baking soda	
½ teaspoon salt	

Cream together the butter and sugar. Mix in the egg, sour cream, and vanilla. Sift the flour, soda, and salt into the bowl with the creamed mixture. Form into a soft dough. Refrigerate for an hour.

Preheat the oven to 350°.

Beat the ricotta cheese until smooth. Stir in the sugar, eggs, vanilla, and grated chocolate.

With floured hands, pat the chilled dough into the bottom and sides of a 10-inch pie plate. It will be thin, but will rise during baking. Pour in the filling and bake about 40 minutes, until the filling is set and bounces back when lightly tapped. Cool and then refrigerate for at least 2 hours before serving.

Hazelnut Cheesecake

Americans have only lately begun to appreciate the glories of the hazelnut, so beloved throughout Europe. Once you've tasted Hazelnut Cheesecake, you will have experienced one of the great earthly joys.

CRUST

1 cup graham cracker crumbs

¼ cup sugar

½ cup melted butter

FILLING

2 pounds cream cheese, at room temperature

5 eggs

1½ cups sugar

1 teaspoon finely grated lemon peel

1 cup hazelnuts, toasted and finely ground*

TOPPING

1 cup sour cream

1 tablespoon powdered sugar

1 teaspoon pure vanilla extract

☐

12 whole hazelnuts

Butter the sides of a 9-inch springform pan. Make graham cracker crumbs by rolling the crackers between two sheets of waxed paper with a rolling pin or by grinding them in a blender or food processor. Lightly blend the crumbs, butter, and sugar with a fork and press this mixture into the bottom of the springform pan.

Preheat the oven to 350°.

Using a food processor or an electric beater, whip the cream cheese, and add the eggs one at a time, until the batter is thin and smooth. Add the sugar and whip again until smooth. Add the lemon peel and ground hazelnuts and blend well. Pour the batter onto the crust. Bake for 1 to 1½ hours until golden brown and firm. Allow the cheesecake to cool in the pan for at least one hour.

When the cake is completely cool, remove it from the pan to a serving plate. Combine the sour cream, powdered sugar, and vanilla and spread on top of the cheesecake. Decorate the outer edge of the cake top with the whole hazelnuts.

---

* Hazelnuts will have a finer flavor if skinned. Spread the hazelnuts on a baking sheet and bake at 325° for about 10 minutes. Cool for a few minutes and then rub with a small towel to remove most of the skins.

Jewish Honey Cake

This is the traditional Jewish honey cake or *lekach* eaten at the beginning of a new year to ensure a sweet year. Once you try it, you'll want to have it much more than just once a year.

3 eggs, beaten

1 cup sugar

2 tablespoons vegetable oil

□

3½ cups whole wheat pastry flour

2 teaspoons baking powder

1 teaspoon baking soda

½ teaspoon salt

½ teaspoon ground ginger

½ teaspoon nutmeg

1 teaspoon cinnamon

pinch of ground cloves

□

1 cup honey

1 cup warm, strong, freshly brewed coffee

□

½ cup almonds or walnuts, chopped

□

powdered sugar

Preheat the oven to 325°.

Butter and flour a 5×9-inch loaf pan and set aside.

Beat the eggs and sugar until well mixed. Add the oil, stirring until smooth. Sift together all the dry ingredients and spices and set aside. Dissolve the honey in the coffee. Add the dry ingredients and the coffee mixture alternately to the egg mixture, about half of each at a time. Stir until the batter is smooth. Then add the nuts.

Pour the batter into the loaf pan and bake for 50 to 60 minutes or until a knife inserted in the center comes out clean. Cool for 15 minutes and remove from the pan. Dust with powdered sugar.

This cake keeps very well if tightly wrapped or covered and often tastes even better one or two days later. We like it with a "shmear" of cream cheese or a scoop of ice cream.

Ginger Cakes

Yields 1 cake or 12 muffins

Maureen Vivino was given this old Irish family recipe by Stella Malloy, her grandmother. We like it because it has all the dark spiciness of gingerbread with the bouyant spring of a cake.

½ **cup butter**	**scant ½ teaspoon ground cloves**
½ **cup sugar**	½ **teaspoon ground ginger**
1 egg	½ **teaspoon salt**
1 cup molasses	☐
☐	**1½ teaspoons baking soda**
2½ cups unbleached white flour	**1 cup hot water or hot strong freshly brewed coffee**
1 teaspoon cinnamon	

Butter an 8×8-inch cake pan or a muffin tin and set aside.

Cream together the butter and sugar until smooth. In a large bowl, beat the egg into the molasses and add the creamed mixture. Sift together the dry ingredients, except the baking soda. Fold the dry ingredients into the wet ingredients.

Preheat the oven to 350°.

Dissolve the baking soda in the water or coffee and add it to the batter, beating vigorously for several minutes. Spoon the batter into the cake pan or muffin tin. Bake the cake for 45 minutes to an hour or until a knife inserted in the center comes out clean. Bake muffins about 30 minutes.

Top Ginger Cakes with Lemon Custard Sauce *(p. 276)* for a real treat.

Aunt Minnie's
Fresh Apple Cake

Our Sara Robbins' Aunt Minnie was a renowned Southern cook. This easy-to-make, homey, and moist cake is one reason why.

1½ cups vegetable oil

2 cups brown sugar

3 eggs

□

3 cups sifted flour (half whole wheat pastry flour and half unbleached white flour works well)

1 teaspoon baking soda

1 teaspoon baking powder

¼ teaspoon ground cardamom

1 teaspoon cinnamon

□

2 teaspoons pure vanilla extract

3 tablespoons apple juice, milk, or water

3 cups chopped apples

1 cup chopped nuts (pecans, walnuts, or almonds)

□

3 tablespoons sesame seeds

powdered sugar

Butter a 10-inch bundt pan, two 9-inch round cake pans, or one 9×13-inch sheet pan. Sprinkle the bottom and sides of the pan with the sesame seeds.

Preheat the oven to 350°.

Beat the oil and sugar until creamy. Add the eggs one at a time, beating well after each addition. In a separate bowl, sift together the flour, leavenings, and spices. Add the dry ingredients to the egg mixture along with the apple juice and vanilla, beating with a wooden spoon until the batter is smooth. Fold in the chopped apples and nuts.

Pour the batter into the pan and bake for 30 to 45 minutes, depending upon the size of the pan, until a knife inserted in the center comes out clean.

Sprinkle the top with sifted powdered sugar when the cake is cool.

Spice Cake
with Prunes and Pecans

A rich, dark, nutty cake that will stay moist almost forever. It's particularly good for the holidays, with all its spices and nuts. With this cake you never know... is one slice enough? Are three too many?

1 cup prune purée*	2 teaspoons cinnamon
1 cup vegetable oil	1 teaspoon ground allspice
2 cups sugar	1 teaspoon ground cloves
1 tablespoon pure vanilla extract	1 teaspoon nutmeg
3 eggs, beaten	½ teaspoon salt
1 cup buttermilk	1 teaspoon baking soda
□	□
2 cups flour (a mixture of unbleached white flour and whole wheat pastry flour is good)	1½ cups pecans, chopped

Preheat the oven to 350°.

Butter and flour a 10-inch bundt pan or a 9 × 13-inch baking pan and set aside.

In a large bowl, beat together the oil, sugar, vanilla, eggs, buttermilk, and prune purée. Sift together the flour, spices, salt, and baking soda and stir these into the wet ingredients. Mix well, then fold in the pecans.

Pour the batter into the pan. Bake for 30 to 45 minutes, depending on the size of the pan, until a knife inserted in the center of the cake comes out clean.

If not using commercially prepared prune purée, cook 1½ cups of prunes in about ¾ cup of water until soft. Pit the prunes if necessary and purée them in a blender with any remaining cooking water.

Carrot Applesauce Cake

This cake has the moistness and spice of a fruitcake, but you won't have to wait a month to eat it.

2 cups unbleached white flour (up to
   1 cup whole wheat pastry flour may
   be substituted)

½ cup rolled oats

1½ teaspoons baking powder

1½ teaspoons baking soda

1 tablespoon cinnamon

1 teaspoon nutmeg

1 teaspoon salt

1 cup raisins or dried currants

□

4 eggs

¾ cup vegetable oil

1¼ cups brown sugar, honey and/or
   maple syrup

1 teaspoon pure vanilla extract

1⅔ cups unsweetened appplesauce

3 cups finely grated carrots

□

sesame seeds

powdered sugar *(optional)*

Preheat the oven to 350°.

Oil a 10-inch bundt or tube pan or a 9 × 13-inch baking pan. Sprinkle the sesame seeds on the bottom and partway up the sides of the oiled pan. Set the pan aside.

In a large bowl, mix together the dry ingredients. Whisk the eggs in a separate bowl. Stir in the oil, sweetener(s), vanilla, applesauce, and carrots and mix well. Add the wet ingredients to the dry, stir until just mixed, and pour the batter into the pan.

Bake for 65 to 70 minutes, until a toothpick inserted in the center of the cake comes out clean. When done, allow the cake to sit in the pan for at least 15 minutes. Then invert it onto a plate and dust it lightly with powdered sugar.

Carob Cake

Lightly textured, yet moist and rich, this cake is delicious either unadorned or frosted with your favorite cream cheese frosting.

2 cups unbleached white flour

1 cup carob powder

2 tablespoons instant coffee

1 teaspoon baking soda

1 teaspoon baking powder

□

3 eggs

1¾ cups honey

¾ cup melted butter

1½ teaspoons pure vanilla extract

□

1½ cups ice water

1 cup chopped nuts *(optional)*

Preheat the oven to 350°.

Oil a 9×13-inch baking pan and set aside.

Sift together the dry ingredients. Beat the eggs in a separate bowl. Blend in the honey, melted butter, and vanilla and beat thoroughly. Add the wet ingredients alternately with the ice water to the dry ingredients. Beat until smooth. The batter will be quite thin. Fold in the nuts, if desired.

Pour the batter into the pan and bake 30 to 40 minutes, until a knife inserted in the middle comes out clean.

Perfect Chocolate Cake

Yields a 3-layer 9-inch cake

This cake is a fantasy fulfilled of that perfect, one-cherry-on-the-top cartoon cake served by Minnie Mouse at Pluto's birthday party. We have on occasion doubled this recipe (baking it in 13-inch round cake pans) and satisfied masses of chocolate lovers.

CAKE

1 cup cocoa (unsweetened)

2 cups boiling water

2¾ cups unbleached white flour

2 teaspoons baking soda

½ teaspoon salt

½ teaspoon baking powder

1 cup butter

2½ cups sugar

4 eggs

1½ teaspoons pure vanilla extract

BUTTER CREAM FROSTING

6 ounces unsweetened baking chocolate

1 cup butter

½ cup heavy cream

2½ cups powdered sugar, sifted

FILLING

1 cup heavy cream

¼ cup powdered sugar

1 tablespoon pure vanilla extract

Preheat the oven to 350°.

Butter and flour three 9-inch round cake pans.

Combine the cocoa with 2 cups of boiling water, stirring until smooth. Cool completely. Sift together the dry ingredients. In a large bowl, beat together the butter, sugar, eggs, and vanilla. Add the dry ingredients alternately with the cocoa mixture to the creamed mixture. Do not overmix. Blend just enough to moisten the dry ingredients.

Pour the batter into the cake pans. Bake for 25 to 30 minutes. Cool in the pans for 10 minutes and then remove the cake from the pans to cool completely before frosting.

While the cake is cooling, prepare the frosting. In a medium saucepan, melt the chocolate and butter. Stir in the cream until smooth. Remove the pan from the stove and place it in a large bowl filled with ice. Using a whisk or electric mixer, beat in the powdered sugar until the frosting holds a stiff shape. Chill.

Whip all the filling ingredients together until stiff. Chill.

Construct the cake when all the parts are cool. Spread the filling between the layers and the frosting on the top and sides.

Plan to serve the cake soon after completion or provide a large space in the refrigerator to keep it cool until it is served.

The late novelist John Gardner and his son arrived "en motocyclette" for a lunch date with Ithaca resident novelist Alison Lurie. Gardner, apparently not expecting to be recognized, timidly asked if we would accept his check. Little did he realize that we'd save his spoon as a cherished memento.

Russian Chocolate Torte

Dense and moist with potatoes, crunchy with almonds, frosted with mocha, flavored with rum, oozing with preserves, this is a rich, rich, rich, Russian sweet.

CAKE

1 cup softened butter

2 cups sugar

4 eggs, separated

½ cup heavy cream

1 cup mashed potatoes

1 cup ground almonds

4 ounces unsweetened chocolate, melted

1 teaspoon pure vanilla extract

2 teaspoons rum

☐

1 teaspoon cinnamon

1½ cups unbleached white flour

2 teaspoons baking powder

FROSTING

3 tablespoons butter, softened

1½ cups powdered sugar, sifted

2 tablespoons strong, warm freshly brewed coffee

1 ounce unsweetened chocolate, melted

1 tablespoon strong, dark rum

½ teaspoon pure vanilla extract

FILLING

½ cup raspberry butter or jam or ½ cup stewed dried apricots, puréed

☐

16 whole almonds or ½ cup slivered almonds

Preheat the oven to 325°.

Generously butter and flour a 10-inch springform pan.

Cream together the butter and sugar. Beat in the egg yolks, one at a time, and then add the next four ingredients, beating until smooth. Mix in the vanilla and rum. Sift together the cinnamon, flour, and baking powder and add to the batter, mixing well. Beat the egg whites until stiff, but not dry, and fold them into the batter. Pour the batter into the pan and bake for 1½ hours or until a knife inserted in the center comes out clean. Allow the cake to cool about 15 minutes in the pan, then slide a knife between the sides of the cake and the detachable side of the springform pan. Remove the pan.

While the cake is cooling, prepare the frosting. Cream together the butter and powdered sugar. Add the rest of the ingredients and beat until smooth.

When the cake is cool, carefully slice it in half horizontally and spread the jam or cooked apricots between the layers. Reassemble the cake and spread the frosting on the top and sides. Decorate with almonds, if you wish.

Russian Chocolate Torte is appropriate for high tea or a late night indulgence. If you have a samovar, you're all set. If you serve it as dessert, wait a couple of hours after the meal to offer it with tea or coffee. Whatever the occasion, we suggest serving this torte with a little lace and linen.

When it leaked out that an entourage from the Soviet embassy was on its way to Moosewood, we avoided international incident by changing the ice cream listing on our menu from "White Russian" to "Kahlua and Cream."

Mississippi Mud Cake

This is a very dark, moist, adult chocolate cake. It keeps well and travels well. The recipe is from Sarah Begus, a famous Baltimore hostess.

2 cups unbleached white flour	**5 ounces unsweetened chocolate**
1 teaspoon baking soda	**1 cup butter**
¼ teaspoon salt	**2 cups sugar**
□	□
1¾ cups strong freshly brewed coffee	**2 eggs, lightly beaten**
¼ cup bourbon, brandy, or a coffee, chocolate, or mocha liqueur	**1 teaspoon pure vanilla extract**

Preheat the oven to 275°. (Yes, that really is 275°.)

Generously butter a 10-inch bundt pan and dust it with cocoa.

Sift together the flour, baking soda, and salt. Heat the coffee and liqueur on low heat for about 5 minutes. Add the chocolate and butter and stir until melted. When this mixture is smooth, add the sugar and stir until dissolved. Let the mixture cool for several minutes and then transfer it to a large mixing bowl. Add the flour mixture to the chocolate mixture about a half-cup at a time, beating after each addition until smooth. Then add the eggs and vanilla. Beat for another minute.

Pour the batter into the bundt pan and bake for about 1½ hours, until the cake pulls away from the sides of the pan and springs back when touched in the middle. Remove the cake from the oven and allow it to cool for 10 minutes in the pan. Then invert the cake onto a plate. Remove the bundt pan when the cake is completely cool.

This cake is good plain or with whipped cream. Or brush the surface of the cake with 2 or 3 ounces of semi-sweet chocolate, melted and mixed with 1 or 2 tablespoons of cream or coffee.

Amaretto Cake

If you love the fragrance of almonds, this cake will drive you wild with its heady triple almond whammy – essence, nuts, and liqueur. A cup of capuccino is the perfect partner.

1 pound butter, softened	¾ cup milk
3 cups sugar	1 cup amaretto (almond liqueur)
6 eggs, well beaten	2 teaspoons baking powder, sifted to remove the lumps
2 teaspoons pure almond extract	
4 cups unbleached white flour	2 cups toasted almonds, ground

Preheat the oven to 350°.

Generously butter and flour a 10-inch bundt pan and set aside.

Cream together the butter and sugar. The butter should be soft, but not melted. Add the beaten eggs and almond extract and mix well. Blend in two cups of the flour. Combine the milk and ¼ cup of the amaretto and stir into the batter, mixing well. Add the remaining flour and the baking powder, mixing well. Fold in the ground almonds and pour the batter into the bundt pan. Bake for one hour or until a toothpick tests clean.

Cool the cake in the pan for 15 minutes and then pour the remaining ¾ cup of amaretto over the warm cake. Let the amaretto soak in and then invert the cake onto a plate. Remove the pan from the cake when thoroughly cool.

Our Favorite Pound Cake

Moist, dense, and buttery pound cake is our standard for cake at Moosewood – perfect unadorned, or served with fresh fruit and whipped cream, or frosted, or in a trifle. Once you've mastered the basic cake, try one of our variations and then make up your own.

1 pound butter, softened

3 cups sugar

6 eggs

4 cups unbleached white flour

1 cup milk

2 teaspoons pure vanilla, almond, or lemon extract

2 teaspoons baking powder

Preheat the oven to 350°.

Generously butter and flour a 10-inch bundt pan and set aside.

Cream the butter and sugar. Beat in the eggs. Add two cups of flour and beat well. Mix in the milk and extract. Combine the baking powder and the remaining 2 cups of flour and then add to the batter. Beat well.

Pour the batter into the bundt pan. Bake about 1 hour, until the cake pulls away from the sides of the pan and a knife inserted in the center comes out clean.

When the cake is done, turn it upside down on a plate to cool, leaving the bundt pan on top of the cake for about 20 minutes, so the cake will hold its shape.

Variations

- *Butterscotch Pecan Pound Cake:* Use pure vanilla extract, replace the white sugar with brown sugar, and add 2 cups of toasted pecan halves.
- *Oasis Cake:* Use apricot juice or coconut milk *(see Appendix)* instead of milk and add ½ cup each of shredded coconut, chopped dried apricots, and chopped dates.
- *Cashew or Peanut Cake:* Use pure vanilla extract, replace half of the butter with cashew butter or peanut butter, and add 1 cup of cashews or toasted peanuts.
- *Cherry-Almond Cake:* Use pure almond extract, reduce the milk to ½ cup,

add 1 cup ground toasted almonds with the flour, and at the last minute fold 1½ cups of fresh, pitted whole cherries into the batter. The fruit adds a lot of liquid to the cake during baking, so this batter is stiffer than usual.

- *Whiskey Cake:* Replace all or part of the milk with whiskey. This is good served with Vanilla Custard Sauce *(p. 278)* and peaches.
- *Chocolate Yogurt Pound Cake:* Replace the milk with plain yogurt, reduce the flour to 3½ cups, and add 1 cup cocoa. If you wish, brush melted sweet chocolate on the cooled cake.
- *Marsala Walnut Pound Cake:* Use pure vanilla extract, replace the white sugar with brown sugar, replace the milk with marsala, and add 1 cup chopped toasted walnuts.
- *Layered Pound Cake:* Carefully cut the cooled basic pound cake into 5 layers with a long, serrated bread knife. Spread raspberry butter or conserve between the layers as you rebuild the cake. Frost with chocolate butter cream frosting *(p. 266)*.

Lemon Custard Sauce

Yields 3 cups

A versatile, sweet-tart sauce that can be the finishing touch to ginger cakes or pound cake. Folded into whipped cream, it becomes an instant mousse to serve with fresh berries.

1 cup sugar	□
3 tablespoons cornstarch	4 egg yolks, beaten
⅛ teaspoon nutmeg, preferably freshly grated	4 tablespoons melted butter
pinch of salt	¼ cup lemon juice
2 cups warm water	

In a stainless steel or enamel saucepan (aluminum will give the custard a metallic taste), mix the first four ingredients. Slowly stir in the water. Heat, stirring constantly, on medium-high heat until the sauce thickens.

Whisk a cup of the hot sauce into the beaten egg yolks. Stir the warmed yolk mixture back into the saucepan and cook for one minute more, continuing to stir. Remove from the heat and blend in the butter and lemon juice. Or use the blender method described in Vanilla Custard Sauce *(p. 278)*. Chill.

Carob Sauce

Yields 2 cups

Carob Sauce is a warm and fudgy topping for ice cream or cakes.

½ **cup carob powder**	½ **cup honey**
½ **cup butter, melted**	**1 teaspoon pure vanilla extract**
3 eggs	¼ **cup milk or half-and-half**

If the carob powder is lumpy, whirl it for several seconds in a dry blender. Mix the carob powder and melted butter until they are smooth. Blend the eggs, honey, and vanilla in a food processor or blender on low speed. Slowly pour in the carob-butter mixture. Finally, add milk or half-and-half and blend until the sauce is smooth and the desired consistency is reached.

Taking care not to let it boil, heat the sauce on low heat for about 5 minutes, stirring frequently.

If you make the sauce ahead, keep it refrigerated. Then slowly reheat the sauce in a double boiler before serving it.

Grapes in Lemon Yogurt

Grapes in Lemon Yogurt can be served as a salad, dessert, or snack. It's made in seconds and is cool and refreshing. It's especially welcome after a rich or spicy meal. Serve it in stemmed glasses.

whole seedless white or red grapes

lemon flavored yogurt (1 cup for each pound of grapes)

Stir the yogurt into the grapes – they should be coated with yogurt. Serve immediately or chill.

As a salad this dish is a cool accompaniment to Middle Eastern casseroles and stews, such as Moroccan Stew *(p. 121)*, Kolokithopita *(p. 140)*, or Zucchini-Feta Casserole *(p. 114)*.

Fresh Fruit Trifle

English trifle is traditionally assembled in a large clear glass bowl, so that all the layers can be seen. We prefer to use fresh fruit, rather than the customary jam, but our trifle still conjures up images of Victorian English holidays. This dessert has a place in Italian cuisine also, where it is called Zuppa Inglese (English Soup). The variations are endless.

5 to 6 cups leftover pound cake, broken into slightly larger than bite-sized chunks

1 cup liqueur (brandy, sherry, rum)

2 cups Vanilla Custard Sauce *(p. 278)*

2 cups fresh fruit (peaches, oranges, cherries, berries)

2 cups heavy cream, whipped with ½ teaspoon pure vanilla extract and maple syrup, honey, or powdered sugar to taste

Prepare the fresh fruit. Peel, pit, and slice peaches. Peel, seed, and section oranges. Pit cherries. Gaze fondly upon labor-free berries.

Using a large bowl or individual dessert cups, arrange a layer of pound cake chunks on the bottom. Pour some of the liqueur over the cake and allow it to soak in. Spoon the custard over that and then sprinkle on the fresh fruit. Layer everything again using all the ingredients. Top with whipped cream and decorate with more fruit. Chill.

Suggested combinations:

- Sherry or brandy over vanilla pound cake with peaches or strawberries and Vanilla Custard Sauce.
- Cherry brandy or amaretto over almond or chocolate pound cake with fresh pitted cherries and Vanilla Custard Sauce.
- Rum over lemon or vanilla pound cake with seedless orange sections and Vanilla Custard Sauce.
- Lemon Custard Sauce *(p. 274)* over lemon or vanilla pound cake with blueberries.
- Try raspberries, mangoes or kiwi fruit.
- Try fruit juice instead of liqueur.

Vanilla Custard Sauce

Yields 2½ cups

A homey and versatile dessert sauce that is speedily prepared with our blender method.

2 cups milk	**4 eggs**
¼ cup sugar	**1 teaspoon pure vanilla extract**

In a heavy saucepan, heat the milk and sugar almost to a boil. Break the eggs into a blender. While the eggs whirl, slowly add the hot milk to cook the eggs. Add the vanilla.

Often the custard is ready at this stage, but if it doesn't thicken enough to coat a spoon, pour the mixture back into the pan and cook gently, stirring, until it thickens. If the custard should then overcook and become lumpy, whirl it in the blender once more.

This sauce is so quickly prepared that you'll often want to serve it immediately, warm and fragrant, but it can also be kept, well covered and refrigerated, for several days, and it is equally delicious cold.

Serve with Wine Poached Pears *(p. 245)*, in your favorite Trifle *(p. 277)*, or poured over slices of Our Favorite Pound Cake *(p. 272)* topped with strawberries or peaches.

APPENDIX

Appendix

If you need to know more...

Annato (Achiote Seed): A hard red seed used in Latin American cooking which imparts a subtle flavor and a beautiful yellow-orange coloring to dishes. Best results are obtained by using the oil in which the seeds have been heated. Place 1 tablespoon whole achiote seeds and 3 to 4 tablespoons vegetable oil in a very small pot or skillet. Maintain a medium heat until the oil turns a bright reddish-orange, approximately 3 to 4 minutes. Strain and discard the seeds. Annato is available in stores that carry foods widely used by the Latin American community.

Arrowroot Powder: See Kuzu.

Artichokes: Look for artichokes that are bright green with firm, tightly packed leaves. Artichokes with brown streaks or spots are either old or frost-bitten, but still may be good to eat if the inner parts of the leaves are green and tender.

To prepare: Place the artichoke on its side and cut the stem off evenly so that the artichoke will stand on its base. Cut off ½ to ¾ inch from the top of the cone. Peel away any small leaves at the bottom, and with kitchen scissors trim away the barbed tops on the rest of the leaves. This trimming isn't absolutely necessary because the prickles soften when cooked. Artichokes should be thoroughly washed in running water or soaked in salt water before cooking to draw out any bugs lurking inside.

To cook: Place the artichokes in a deep pot large enough to hold them all standing upright. Add water to a little more than half the height of the artichokes. Salt, a splash of vinegar, whole cloves of garlic, whole fennel seeds, and/or a tablespoon of oil may be added to the pot. Cover, bring to a rapid boil, reduce to a simmer. Cooking takes from 30 to 45 minutes. Check the water level every 10 minutes, adding boiling water when needed. The artichokes are done when their bases are tender when tested with a fork. The leaves should pull off easily, but if they fall off, the artichokes are overdone.

Drain the artichokes upside down. Serve upright on individual plates with a bowl of lemon-butter or other sauce for each person. Remember to provide an empty bowl for the discarded outer leaves and the chokes.

To eat a whole artichoke: Pull off the leaves one at a time, dip the bottom edge of each leaf into the sauce, and then scrape off the fleshy part with your teeth. Discard the rest of the leaf. After you've eaten the outer leaves, you'll come to smaller inner leaves which are very tender. Under the very small leaves is the feathery, inedible choke. With a spoon, gently scrape off the choke, down to the hollowed, firm surface of the most delicious part of the artichoke, the heart. Cut the heart into bite-size pieces, dip into the sauce, and eat.

Artichoke Hearts: The rich, succulent centers of artichokes. Canned artichoke hearts are available in most supermarkets. They are packed in brine or a marinade. When our recipes call for artichoke hearts, use those packed in brine.

Asparagus: Fresh asparagus is available from February until early summer. Look for young green spears that are uniform in size. They should be firm, and the tips should be tightly budded. Avoid asparagus that appears dried or shriveled. Short, thick stalks and long, thin ones may be equally tender. Remove any sand that clings to the stalks by rubbing gently under cool, running water. Remove the tough, white base of each stalk before cooking.

Barley: Barley is a sweet, low-starch grain. The barley seed itself is quite dense, requiring more water and greater cooking time than most grains.

To cook: Bring one cup of barley and 5 to 6 cups of water to a boil. Reduce to a simmer and cook about an hour and fifteen minutes. Drain excess water. One cup of raw barley yields 3¾ cups of cooked barley.

Basil: Basil, either the familiar green or dark purple, is easy to grow. Freshly cut basil keeps in the refrigerator for several days. The whole leaves can be wrapped in plastic and frozen for up to 6 months. Dried basil is different from fresh. Its aroma does not compare and its flavor is diminished and different, but it is still a valuable herb, and we use it frequently in winter.

Beans: Most dried beans and peas must be softened by soaking in water before they are cooked. No soaking is necessary for lentils or for beans cooked in a pressure cooker. When a recipe calls for cooked beans, canned beans may be substituted; drain and rinse them before using.

Cooking beans: Use the chart below for the correct amount of water and cooking time for specific beans. Before soaking, remove any shriveled or discolored beans and check for pebbles.

Variety	Water to Beans Ratio	Cooking Time	Cooked Equivalent of 1 Cup Dried
Black turtle beans	4:1	1½ to 2 hours	2⅓ cups
Red kidney beans	3:1	1½ to 2 hours	2½ cups
Navy pea beans	3:1	1½ to 2 hours	2½ cups
Pinto beans	3:1	1½ to 2 hours	2½ cups
Lentils	3:1	1¾ hour	2 cups
Garbanzo beans	2:1	1½ hours	2½ cups
Lima beans	2:1	1 hour	2½ cups
Split peas	3:1	1 hour	2 cups

Soak the beans by one of these two methods:

1. Add the water to the beans in a saucepan, cover, and soak overnight or for a minimum of 4 hours.

2. Add the water to the beans in a saucepan, cover, and bring to a rapid boil. Remove the pan from the heat and soak for 2 hours.

After the beans have soaked, drain them, add fresh water, and simmer on medium heat until tender. Check the water level occasionally to avoid scorching. Salt just before serving, or the beans will toughen.

Black Mustard Seeds: These seeds are widely used in Indian cooking, particularly in curries. When added to hot oil, they make a popping sound and release their flavor into the oil. Golden mustard seeds may be substituted but their flavor is somewhat stronger. Black mustard seeds are available in Asian markets and will keep indefinitely in the refrigerator.

Bread Crumbs: We call for bread crumbs in several of our recipes. Bread crumbs are easy to make. Just crush cubes of stale or toasted bread with a rolling pin or whirl them in a blender or food processor. Use a hand grater for chunks of stale bread.

Bread making:

Yeast: One tablespoon of dry yeast equals 1 cake of compressed yeast or 1 package of dry yeast. One package of dry yeast will raise as much as 8 cups of flour. For faster rising, as much as 1 package of dry yeast to each 3 cups of flour may be used. This bread will taste "yeastier."

It is important that yeast be fresh. If it isn't fresh and alive, the bread won't rise. Keep yeast refrigerated between bakings. Yeast can also be frozen.

Proofing yeast: To activate dry yeast in preparation for bread making, sprinkle the yeast over warm water. The temperature of the water should be between 100° and 115°, a temperature that feels comfortably warm on the inside of your wrist. Add a little honey or sugar (½ teaspoon) which will nourish the yeast cells as they divide and grow. After about 5 minutes, the yeast should begin to foam. Compressed yeast takes a little longer. If the yeast doesn't foam, it won't raise bread, so start again with new yeast.

Preparing the dough: Add the other liquid ingredients to the proofed yeast and then stir in the flour gradually until the dough is of a consistency that can be kneaded, dry enough that it doesn't stick to your fingers or the bowl.

Gluten: Essential to all yeast breads is the gluten found in wheat flours. Gluten is a protein which makes bread dough strong and elastic. As yeast releases the gases of its respiration, the gluten allows the dough to stretch and form thousands of air-trapping pockets.

Kneading: Kneading the dough distributes the yeast evenly and gives the dough a smooth texture. Knead the dough by pushing the heels of your hands into the dough and then folding it over, occasionally sprinkling more flour on the surface of the dough and the board to prevent sticking. Give the dough a quarter-turn and repeat. Continue repeating this procedure for about 10 minutes. Fully kneaded dough is satiny and should spring back when pressed with a finger. The texture has been described as being as soft and smooth as a baby's bottom, although of course you can't expect this result if you are making cracked wheat bread.

Rising: Place the dough in a large, buttered bowl and brush the top lightly with oil or melted butter to keep a crust from forming. Cover with a cloth and place in a warm, draft-free spot to rise. Rising times will vary from recipe to recipe. But a general rule is that the dough should be allowed to rise until it is doubled in volume which usually takes an hour or two. As a test, make a small indentation in the dough. If the indentation fills back in within a few minutes, allow the dough to continue rising. If the indentation does not disappear, the dough has finished rising.

Now comes one of the most satisfying moments in bread making – punching down the dough. After punching it down, knead the dough until it is smooth. Form the deflated dough into loaves or rolls and allow them to rise until almost full-sized. The second rising will take less time than the first. The final fullness will be achieved during baking.

Baking: Bake the loaves for the full time recommended. To test for doneness, tip a loaf out of its baking pan and lightly tap the bottom of the loaf. If the bread is done, there will be a distinctly hollow sound. If it doesn't sound hollow, turn the bread back into the pan and bake a short time longer.

Brown Rice: See Rice.

Bulgur: A quick-cooking form of wheat widely used in Balkan and Middle Eastern countries. Bulgur is the end result of wheat berries that have been pre-cooked, dried, and cracked. It is available at natural food stores, Middle Eastern groceries, and often in the international or gourmet food sections of supermarkets. It comes in two textures, fine and coarse.

To cook: Place the bulgur in a bowl with an equal amount of boiling water and a dash of salt. Cover and let sit for 20 to 30 minutes. Stir to fluff. If the bulgur is still too chewy, add another ¼ cup of boiling water, cover, and let sit for 10 minutes more. One cup of dry bulgur yields 2½ cups of cooked bulgur.

Bundt Pan: A round, deep, heavy baking pan with a central tube and fluted sides. The standard bundt pan size is 12 cups.

Capers: The small, green, pickled buds of a Mediterranean flowering plant. They come packed in brine and are strongly flavored. Capers are used mainly as a piquant condiment or garnish for soups, stews, sauces, and vegetable dishes. Capers are usually available in the gourmet food sections of supermarkets.

Cardamom: Also spelled cardamon. Cardamom is a sweetly pungent, aromatic spice popular in Indian, Indonesian, Scandinavian, German, and Middle Eastern cooking. Whole and ground cardamom is available in the spice sections of most supermarkets.

Cayenne: Ground, red chili peppers generally used to add "hot" to savory dishes. The name derives from Cayenne Island, capital of French Guiana. Cayennes vary greatly in hotness. The amount of cayenne needed depends upon the intensity of the particular cayenne used and upon personal taste. Some cayenne is harsh if added to foods at the very end of cooking, so when you want added "hot" after tasting, sauté the cayenne briefly in a little oil before adding it to the food.

Chili Oil: A red oil in which chiles have released their flavor. Chili oil is used as a spice in Asian cooking – sparingly! Available at Asian food stores, chili oil is also easily made at home. Just heat 1 cup of peanut or vegetable oil until hot but not smoking. Stir in about 2 dozen small dried red chiles, 3 tablespoons red pepper flakes, or 1 tablespoon cayenne. Cover, cool, and strain.

Chili Paste with Garlic, or Szechuan Chili Paste: A spicy condiment made with chili peppers, salt, and garlic, chili paste is available in Asian food stores. It will keep almost indefinitely when refrigerated.

Chinese Fermented Black Beans: These are preserved black soybeans with a pungent, salty taste, used as a seasoning rather than as a main ingredient. Generally they are either rinsed under running water or soaked for a short time in water to soften them and remove some of their saltiness before being used in cooking. Fermented black beans are sold in Chinese or Asian food stores, usually packed in small plastic bags. They will keep indefinitely in the refrigerator if stored in a tightly sealed container.

Chinese Rice Wine or Shaoxing: A traditional Chinese cooking wine named for its place of origin. Shaoxing, like sake, is made from rice, but is matured much longer and has a smoother taste. Shaoxing is similar to a dry sherry, but cooking sherry, which is sweet, should not be substituted. Available in some liquor stores and most Asian food stores.

Chutney: An East Indian condiment made of cool fruits, hot spices, sweet vegetables, and tart flavorings. Small batches of this sweet-and-sour side dish can be easily made. Or it can be prepared in large batches and canned for use throughout the year. Leftover chutney keeps for at least two weeks if well sealed and refrigerated.

Cilantro: The fresh green leaves of coriander, called cilantro (sometimes Spanish or Chinese parsley), are used in many cuisines, particularly East Indian, Asian, and Central and South American.

Coconut Milk: Coconut milk is richly flavored, slightly sweet, and smooth. It is used in Southeast Asian and Pacific cuisines in sauces, soups, curries, and desserts. Coconut milk can be made from fresh or dried coconut or purchased canned or bottled. Commercial coconut milk varies greatly in sweetness, flavor, and ingredients, so when using it in a recipe, be aware that the results may vary. Coconut milk is available in Asian and natural food stores. The coconut "milk" or "mix" which is intended for use in mixed drinks is very sweet and different and should not be used as a substitute.

To make coconut milk: If using fresh coconut, cut the coconut meat into 1-inch pieces and place equal amounts of coconut and hot water in the blender. Purée at high speed for a couple of minutes. Let steep for 30 minutes. Then pour the purée into a strainer set over a bowl. Press on the pulp to squeeze out as much milk as possible. Squeeze by the handful to extract any remaining milk. Pour the milk through a fine-mesh strainer. One cup of coconut meat combined with one cup of hot water yields about one cup of coconut milk.

If using dried coconut, combine one cup of unsweetened, dried, shredded coconut with 1½ cups of hot tap water. Allow to stand for 5 minutes. Purée for 1 minute and proceed as above. This yields a little more than one cup of coconut milk. Covered and refrigerated, coconut milk will keep for up to 3 days. Frozen it will keep indefinitely.

Coriander: When we call for coriander in this book, we are referring to the dried seeds, a spice. Fresh cilantro, which is very pungent and aromatic and is usually an acquired taste, is very different from dried, ground coriander seeds and cannot be used interchangeably. Coriander imparts a delightful aroma and sweet flavor and is best when freshly ground. Coriander is available in most supermarkets and health and specialty food stores.

Couscous: A staple food of North Africa, couscous is finely milled semolina wheat, essentially tiny pearls of pasta. We use the quick-cooking variety. If you want to use the longer-cooking traditional variety, refer to a good Moroccan cookbook or the package directions. Couscous is available in Middle Eastern, Greek, and natural food stores and in the international foods sections of supermarkets.

To cook: The traditional North African method of cooking couscous is to steam it over a simmering stew or soup. We use both of the following methods to cook couscous. One cup of dry couscous yields about 2½ cups of cooked couscous.

Steeping method: Place equal amounts of dry couscous and boiling water with a little salt and butter or oil in a bowl. Cover and let sit 10 to 15 minutes, stirring frequently to fluff. If it is still a little crunchy, add another ¼ cup of boiling water, stir, cover, and let sit another 5 minutes.

Steaming method: Place the couscous in a fine-meshed sieve or a colander lined with cheesecloth. Rest the sieve on the rim of a deep pot so that the bottom of the sieve is a couple of inches above the pot bottom. Pour several cups of boiling water over the couscous, making sure to dampen all of the grains. Using foil, tightly cover the pot to seal in the steam. After 5 minutes, stir the couscous to fluff. If the couscous is still crunchy, pour in some more boiling water, taking care that the water doesn't reach high enough to touch the sieve. Cover the pot again and check the couscous after 5 minutes. Stir to fluff when the couscous is ready. Place it in a serving bowl and stir in salt to taste and some butter or a little oil.

Use the steaming method to reheat leftover couscous.

Croutons: Croutons are easily made from bread past its peak of freshness. Cube the bread. Spread the cubes on a baking sheet and place in a preheated 350° oven, stirring occasionally, until crispy, about 10 to 15 minutes. Meanwhile melt some butter. Sauté minced or pressed garlic in the butter until it is golden. Add a pinch of herbs, such as thyme, summer savory, oregano, or marjoram. Toss the bread cubes and garlic-butter well in a bowl. Serve croutons warm or at room temperature. Croutons will keep up to 2 weeks in an airtight container.

Cumin: Cumin is strongly aromatic. Its seeds are widely used, whole or ground, in the cooking of Latin America, North Africa, the Middle East, Asia, and Spain. The whole seeds can be roasted briefly in an iron skillet to release flavor and then used whole or ground. Cumin powder is always best freshly ground.

Curry Powder: Curry powders bought in spice shops or Indian food stores vary greatly in flavor, aroma, and "hotness." Standard commercial curry powders bought in supermarkets are fairly consistent, but considered uninteresting by many cooks. Curry powder may also be mixed at home. At Moosewood we use a small coffee grinder to grind whole curry spices. The following is a suggestion for mixing curry powder; experiment to find a combination you find pleasing:

> 2 teaspoons ground cumin
> 2 teaspoons ground coriander
> 2 teaspoons turmeric
> ½ teaspoon ground cinnamon
> ¼ teaspoon ground nutmeg
> ¼ teaspoon ground cayenne pepper
> ¼ teaspoon ground black pepper
> ¼ teaspoon ground cloves
> ¼ teaspoon ground cardamom

Unless you've roasted the spices before grinding, curry powder should be cooked briefly in a little butter or oil to bring out its full flavor before it is added to foods.

Dhall (or Dal): An East Indian side dish usually made of lentils, split peas, or sprouted beans with onions, garlic, and spices.

Dill: Fresh dill is often available in supermarkets throughout the year. Dried dill weed is available in the spice sections of supermarkets and should be used when fresh is not available. Fresh and dried dill should be added at the end of cooking, because its flavor is quickly lost with overcooking. Dill seeds are a spice and not a substitute for the herb.

Egg Whites: To beat egg whites, separate the whites from the yolks by cracking the egg over a bowl and gently breaking in two, keeping the yolk in one half of the shell. Let the white drain off into the bowl by slipping the yolk from one half shell to the other. Reserve the yolk for other cooking purposes. Using either an electric mixer or a whisk, beat the whites at a steady, high speed. The whites will froth and gradually thicken. A pinch of salt or cream of tartar will hurry the process along. The whites are stiff when peaks form that will stand by themselves.

Fennel Seed: Licorice-flavored fennel seeds are similar to anise, but are milder, sweeter-flavored and plumper. Fennel is the distinctive flavor in Italian sausage, and when we use it in lasagna or strudels, that flavor often prompts the remark, "This is vegetarian?" Fennel seeds are used whole or ground.

Fermented Black Beans: See Chinese Fermented Black Beans.

Feta Cheese: A soft, white Greek cheese usually packed in brine. Some brands are very salty. It can be found in cheese shops, Middle Eastern and Greek groceries, and most supermarkets.

Fish Sauce: Fish sauce is an extract of fermented fish which is used as a basic flavoring in the cuisines of Thailand, Vietnam, the Philippines, and China. It has a distinctive flavor and an odor which disappears when the fish sauce is cooked. It is available in Asian food stores.

Garlic: The entire garlic bulb is called a "head" and each section of the bulb is a "clove." When buying garlic, look for heads that feel firm and have good-sized cloves.

Heads of garlic vary greatly in intensity of flavor and size of cloves, so the amount of garlic called for in recipes should be adjusted for those two factors as well as for personal taste. The way garlic is cooked also determines its strength of flavor. Whole garlic cloves simmered in soups or sauces lend a mild fragrance and flavor. The flavor imparted by minced garlic is half as strong as that of pressed garlic. Raw garlic is very strong. Take care when sautéing garlic by itself, because it burns quickly and then becomes bitter. The flavor of dried garlic in all its forms cannot be compared to the real thing, and we never use it.

To peel garlic easily, lay each clove on its side on a chopping board and whack it with the side of a broad bladed knife. The papery skin will slip right off.

To prepare garlic ahead, peel a whole head of garlic and mince it in a food processor or by hand. Stir it into a small amount of vegetable oil and store in a covered jar. It will keep in the refrigerator for months. Use ¼ teaspoon for each garlic clove called for.

Ginger: Fresh ginger is a knobby root with light-brown papery skin which should be firm and unblemished. When cut, the inside should be juicy and yellow with a clear fresh scent and a hot spicy taste. Ginger root is usually prepared by grating on the finest surface of a hand-held grater or by mincing finely. Fresh ginger root is available in the produce sections of many supermarkets and in Asian food stores. It will keep stored in a plastic bag in the refrigerator for about 2 weeks. For longer storage, peel the ginger root and keep it in a jar of sherry in the refrigerator. The ginger-flavored sherry can be used for cooking also. Powdered or dried ginger has a very different flavor and cannot be substituted for fresh.

Hungarian Paprika: See Paprika.

Kuzu and Arrowroot Powder: Kuzu is a starch extracted from the root of the kudzu vine. Arrowroot is a tuber usually imported from the West Indies. Kuzu and arrowroot are light, colorless, flavorless thickeners used in sauces, soups, puddings, and pie fillings. Either can be substituted for cornstarch. When substituting arrowroot for cornstarch, use two-thirds the amount called for, and when using kuzu, one-third the amount called for. Sift kuzu to remove the lumps. Always dissolve these thickeners in a small amount of cold water before adding to sauces. Some people prefer arrowroot because it is the easiest to digest – it has long been used in cooking for infants and invalids. Kuzu and arrowroot make beautiful, translucent, glossy sauces and glazes. Kuzu and arrowroot are available in Asian and natural food stores.

Leeks: A relative of the lily, milder in flavor and strength than onions, leeks have cylindrical white bulbs and long, strap-shaped green leaves. To prepare leeks, cut off the roots and tops, leaving 8 to 10 inches of bulb and lower leaf. The tops of the leek leaves are tough and should be discarded or used in stock. Leeks are grown in sandy soil and should be washed carefully. Slice the leek down the middle almost to the root and, holding it under running water or immersed in a basin of water, pull each layer away from the bulb, rinsing well. Drain or shake dry. Slice or chop according to recipe directions.

Lemon Grass: A citrus-flavored herb used in Southeast Asian cooking. Grind dried lemon grass to a powder before using. Once it's ground, it quickly loses its flavor. Grated lemon peel, substituted in the same quantity, provides piquancy but a different flavor. Lemon grass is available in Asian food stores.

Marjoram: Marjoram is a delicate herb, best added toward the end of cooking. Marjoram is frequently confused with its cousin, oregano, but is sweeter and milder.

Matzoh: Square, unleavened wheat crackers available in the kosher food section of the supermarket. Finely ground matzoh is referred to as matzoh meal and is used in Jewish cooking in place of bread crumbs.

Mirin: A golden, sweet cooking wine made from sake, sweet rice, and rice malt. Mirin's alcohol content evaporates in the cooking process, leaving a subtle and unique sweetness. If mirin is not available, substitute sugar or another sweetener in one-third the amount of mirin called for. Mirin can be found in Asian markets and natural food stores.

Miso: Miso is a fermented soy bean paste which originated in China over 2,000 years ago. It is salty, high-protein, and good for the digestion. It imparts a rich, full flavor to food. It ranges in color from dark brown to lightly golden and has a consistency similar to peanut butter. There are many different kinds of miso, each with its own aroma, flavor, color, and texture. Miso is made by crushing boiled soybeans, adding barley, rice, or wheat, injecting the mass with a culture, and allowing it to mature for a few months to three years. In the United States, the three best known varieties of miso are rice miso, barley miso, and soy miso. Rice miso, also called light miso, is yellow to amber in color and relatively sweet. Barley miso, also called red miso, is darker colored and very savory. Soy miso is usually thickest and strongest in flavor. Within these three varieties there are countless offshoots of flavor from salty to sweet – a miso for every cooking need.

At Moosewood we primarily use a miso called Onozaki, an unpasteurized rice miso made by the Onozaki family on their farm in Japan. It has a full, slightly sweet flavor. We use it in soups, stews, spreads, and salad dressing.

Miso should not be boiled. Boiling destroys the digestion-aiding enzymes created in the fermentation process.

Miso should be stored refrigerated. It is available at some supermarkets and most Asian and natural food stores.

Mustard Seeds: See Black Mustard Seeds.

Nori: Also called laver. Dark green or purplish seaweed sold dried in thin sheets packaged in cellophane or in cans and available in gourmet or Asian food stores. Nori is used to wrap fillings or, crumbled, as a seasoning. The flavor of nori is enhanced if you "toast" it just before use by very briefly passing it over a gas flame until it becomes greenish and crisp. It is best stored tightly wrapped and frozen.

Paprika: We recommend using sweet Hungarian paprika which is made from dried, ground sweet red peppers. To insure retaining the delicate flavor of this spice, avoid scorching. Hot paprika is pungent and fiery and can be used in place of cayenne.

Parsley: When we call for parsley, we're referring to curly parsley, though some people may prefer the stronger-flavored flat-leaf Italian variety. Dried parsley is so faded in flavor and color that we never use it. Bunches of fresh parsley sprigs can be kept for a week in the refrigerator, or place the stem ends in a tumbler of water and enjoy it as an edible bouquet on the kitchen counter.

Peanut Butter: We use unhomogenized peanut butter with no sweeteners, preservatives, or stabilizers and have found that it works best for cooking. Refrigeration preserves freshness and keeps the oil distributed evenly. For easier handling, bring to room temperature before using. If the oil separates, stir the peanut butter. Unhomogenized peanut butter is available in natural food stores and most supermarkets.

Pepperoncini: Small, Italian-style hot, pickled peppers available in jars or cans.

Phyllo Pastry Dough: Also spelled filo. These very thin sheets of dough are used to make flaky, crispy pastries and strudels. Packaged phyllo dough is available refrigerated or frozen in many supermarkets and in Mediterranean or Middle Eastern food stores.

Strudels may be assembled in many different shapes. After using phyllo a few times and becoming familiar with how it works, experiment with different strudel assemblies. Try rolled strudels or individual tartlike strudels.

Strudel assembly: Find a working surface large enough to accommodate the unfolded stack of phyllo leaves and the baking sheet, side by side. Melt a quarter-pound of butter. Using a pastry brush or a small paint brush, butter the baking sheet. Unwrap and unfold the phyllo leaves. Each leaf of phyllo is so light and delicate that it dries out quickly and then crumbles easily, so working quickly with phyllo from a flat pile and out of drafts will prevent wasted leaves.

Basic rectangle: At a corner of the stack of phyllo, count out 6 to 8 leaves and carefully, in one smooth movement, lift them up and lay them flat on the baking sheet. If the baking sheet is smaller than the phyllo, let the edges of the phyllo drape over the sides. Spread the filling over the middle of the leaves, leaving 3-inch edges all around. Brush the edges with butter. For the top, lay down two leaves at a time, buttering the top leaf each time. After 4 or 5 pairs, fold the corners of all the phyllo leaves up over the filling, butter, then neatly fold each side up over the filling and butter. Lay down two more pairs of leaves, buttering the top leaf of each pair. Then tuck the new edges under the strudel, corners first, then sides. Sprinkle the top with fennel, poppy, or sesame seeds and bake as the recipe directs, 45 minutes to an hour, depending upon the thickness of the filling.

Triangles: To make individual serving triangles, brush 2 sheets of phyllo with butter, place one on top of the other, then fold them in half lengthwise. Butter the top surface and then place ½ to ⅔ cup of filling slightly up from the bottom and toward the right edge of the phyllo rectangle. Fold the left corner of the phyllo up and over the filling so that the bottom edge is now aligned with the right side. Next fold the strip straight up and then to the left so that the filled triangle is aligned with the left edge of the phyllo. Continue folding in this manner until the top edge of the phyllo is reached. Brush the finished triangle with butter, sprinkle with appropriate seeds, and set aside on a baking sheet while you assemble more. Bake at 375° for 20 to 25 minutes.

Apply this same technique to making bite-sized appetizers by buttering and cutting each sheet of phyllo into 4 to 6 narrow strips. Place 1 tablespoon of filling at the bottom of each strip and proceed as above. Bake for only 10 to 15 minutes.

Polenta: A staple of Northern Italian cooking, this is a cereal made from cornmeal and water, and often enriched with butter and grated cheese.

Polenta can be used as a substitute for rice with vegetable stews, a base for casseroles, and for polenta pizza dough. It is also good cooked according to the directions below, poured into a buttered baking dish to about 1 inch deep to cool, and then cut into squares and fried.

To cook: For each cup of cornmeal, use 3 cups of water. Use a heavy pot or a "waffle" *(p. 297)* during the simmer to prevent sticking. Bring the water to a boil. Sprinkle in the cornmeal while whisking briskly. Simmer on low heat about 20 minutes, stirring occasionally. Stir in salt and butter and/or cheese to taste.

Potato Flour: A very fine flour made from cooked, dried, and ground potatoes. Potato flour makes a good coating for crispy, deep-fried tofu. It can often be found in the kosher food sections of supermarkets.

Purée: This process is most easily done in a blender or food processor but can also be accomplished with a sieve. When using a blender or food processor, whirl the vegetables, beans, fruit, etc., with a liquid until smooth. If a sieve is used, place the cooked food in the sieve over a bowl or pot and push it through the mesh with the back of a large spoon or potato masher. Mix in the liquid last.

Raita: A refreshing side dish of yogurt and vegetables or fruits, seasoned with spices or herbs. Traditionally served as a cooling accompaniment to spicy curries.

Rice: After years of experience and experimentation, we've found brown rice to be the grain that pleases most of the people most of the time. When cooked correctly, it strikes a near perfect balance between sweetness, lightness, moistness, and heartiness. Many of our customers have been converted to brown or "unpolished" rice once we've shared our cooking method with them.

To cook brown rice: A heavy saucepan or pot with a tight-fitting lid is best for cooking rice, because it retains more moisture and is less apt to scorch the rice. Good rice can be made in a lighter pot with the use of a flame spreader or "waffle" *(p. 297).*

When uncooked rice is sautéed briefly in oil before the water is added, it yields non-gummy, clearly separated grains of cooked rice. Before adding the water, sauté the rice in a little oil for a minute or two, stirring briskly.

We've learned a foolproof way to determine a good water-to-rice ratio from the Southeast Asians. After the rice has been measured into the pot (but before it has been sautéed) push your index finger through the rice to the bottom of the pot and note, or mark with your thumbnail, how far up your finger the rice reaches. Sauté the rice and turn off the heat. Then touch the top of the rice with the tip of your finger and add cool water to the pot until it meets that point on your finger where the rice originally reached. The depth of the water (from the bottom of the pot to the surface of the water) should be double the depth of the rice alone, unless the rice is deeper than one inch. In that case, be sure that you have no more than one inch of water above the level of the rice. We've found this to work in different sized pots with varying amounts of rice.

Add a pinch of salt, if you wish. Cover the pot and bring the rice to a boil. When you see steam escaping from the lid, turn the heat off for 5 minutes and then simmer the rice on very low heat for 25 minutes. Use a "waffle" at this point if your pot is light or if the heat won't go very low. Honor another time-tested Asian practice: resist looking into the rice once it has come to a boil. Rice is always better steamed, and lifting the lid will spoil that.

After the simmer, let the rice stand off the heat for 10 minutes, then stir it well.

Rice Vinegar: There are many varieties of vinegar made from different rice wines – clear, golden, red, or black, and Chinese or Japanese – but all are more delicately flavored than the cider, wine, or white vinegars that we most commonly use.

The red and black varieties are often used by the Chinese as table condiments, while the mellow flavor of the clear and golden types makes them especially suited to marinades and light salad dressings.

For use in recipes in this book, buy a clear or golden variety, either Chinese or Japanese. Avoid brands that contain added sugar, salt, or monosodium glutamate (MSG). Rice vinegar is available in Asian food stores, natural food stores, and many supermarkets.

Rice Wine: See Chinese Rice Wine.

Roux: A mixture of butter or oil and flour used to thicken sauces, soups, and stews. Sprinkle flour into the melted, bubbling butter, whisking constantly to make a smooth paste. Simmer for a few minutes. Slowly pour heated liquid into the roux, whisking or stirring vigorously until it thickens. Using hot liquid speeds up the thickening.

Saffron: This strongly aromatic spice imparts a bright yellow color and a unique flavor. Saffron threads are dried stamens of the saffron crocus of Southern Europe. It takes 70,000 to 80,000 crocus flowers to yield one pound of saffron, making it a very expensive spice. Purchase saffron in strand form instead of powdered to insure its purity. It lasts virtually forever. "Mexican saffron," sold in some Latin American markets, is actually safflower and should not be confused with saffron.

Sake: In Japan "sake" refers to all liquors, but in the United States it refers only to rice wine. Sake is used as a seasoning in cooking and should be added in time to simmer for at least a few minutes. Sake is available in most liquor stores and Asian food stores.

Scalded Milk: Milk that has been heated to just below the boiling point.

Sesame Oil: Thick, amber-colored, and wonderfully aromatic, this oil is made from roasted sesame seeds. We specify "dark" sesame oil so it will not be confused with paler cold-pressed sesame oil. "Dark" sesame oil is used for seasoning, not for cooking. It burns easily and loses its distinctive, nutty flavor when overheated. It is available in bottles and cans in natural and Asian food stores.

Shaoxing: See Chinese Rice Wine.

Shiitake Mushrooms: A distinctively flavored Japanese mushroom, sold fresh or dried. They are expensive – but a very few will richly flavor a dish. To soften the dried mushrooms, submerge in boiling water, cover, and soak for at least an hour. After soaking, cut the caps from the stems, slice caps thinly, and add to sautés, stews, or soups. The soaking liquid is an excellent addition to stocks or sauces. Shiitakes are available at many Asian and natural food stores.

Soba: Widely known as "Japanese pasta," these noodles are made of either 100 percent buckwheat flour (good for those with wheat allergies) or with varying percentages of buckwheat flour and whole wheat flour (or white flour). Soba are brownish-grey, usually flat and thin, and they vary in texture and density. Soba are used traditionally in miso broths but adapt well to chilled, Asian pasta salads. They can be found at Asian food stores and many natural food stores.

Soy Flour: Made from ground soy beans. Used primarily in bread baking to boost the protein content.

Star Anise: A strong-flavored, aromatic spice used in Chinese and Southeast Asian cooking. Star anise comes from brown pods in 8-pointed star-shaped clusters. To use, break off "points" (1 or 2 are usually ample) from the whole cluster and tie in cheesecloth or place in a "spice bob" to simmer in the cooking food. Chinese Five Spice Powder, which is sold in Asian food stores, has star anise as an ingredient and is the only substitute we know for star anise that will give a similar flavor.

Steaming: Steamers are made specifically for this purpose, but you can also use a colander in a tightly-covered pot of water. The water level should always be below the bottom of the steamer basket or colander to avoid sogginess. Bring the water to a boil, add the food to be steamed, and maintain heat at a medium boil. Vegetables can also be gently steamed in a small amount of water, using a heavy pot with a tight lid. If vegetables are being steamed prior to addition to a salad, briefly plunge the cooked vegetables in ice water. This stops their cooking and helps to maintain their bright colors.

Stir-Fry: A method of cooking sliced or diced ingredients quickly over high heat using only a small amount of oil. Vegetables cooked in this manner retain their color, texture, and nutritional value. Stir-frying is best done in a wok *(p. 297)*, but a large heavy skillet may also be used. Because the cooking process is so brief, all ingredients must be prepared in advance. Chop the vegetables, measure seasonings, prepare any sauces needed, and assemble everything in the order in which it will be used, and you are ready to start stir-frying.

Preheat the wok for a few moments and then add the oil, swirling it around to coat the wok's surface. When the oil is hot, add the seasonings, such as ginger, garlic, or chili peppers. Then sprinkle in the vegetables that will take the longest to cook while using a wok shovel (a broad-bladed metal spatula) to toss them and coat them with hot oil. Ingredients should not be added so quickly that the temperature of the wok is lowered. Searing the vegetables in hot oil is essential to seal in natural flavors and juices.

Add any remaining vegetables and continue to toss to ensure that the food is cooked evenly and doesn't burn or stick. When the vegetables reach the point of being crisp-tender, add any sauces or thickeners and cook for just a minute more. Remove from the heat and add a few drops of sesame oil or chili oil for additional flavor, if desired, and serve immediately.

Strudel Assembly: See Phyllo Pastry Dough.

Summer Savory: Summer savory is an herb whose flavor is similar to but milder than thyme, and it is often preferable to thyme for that reason. It is used in stuffings, croutons, stews and soups, and beans and lentils. It is available dried in natural food stores and supermarkets.

Sun-dried Tomatoes: Sun-dried tomatoes, packed in olive oil, add a piquant and concentrated tomato flavor to salads, sandwiches, and pasta dishes. Dice the tomatoes or cut into thin slices. Save the packing oil to enliven salad dressings and marinades. Available in Italian groceries and some supermarkets.

Szechuan Chili Paste: See Chili Paste with Garlic.

Szechuan Peppercorns: Nutty, spicy, small, reddish-brown peppercorns used in Chinese cooking. Briefly toast peppercorns in a hot skillet until they begin to smoke. Remove and pulverize in a spice grinder or with a mortar and pestle.

Tahini: Sesame paste made of hulled and toasted sesame seeds, tahini is beige in color and creamy in texture. Tahini is not to be confused with sesame butter, which is denser, stronger-tasting, and made from roasted and pressed, unhulled sesame seeds. Tahini is widely used in Middle Eastern cooking and is usually available in natural food stores and Middle Eastern and Greek groceries.

Tamari Soy Sauce: Soy sauce is traditionally made with fermented soybeans, wheat, water, and sea salt. The natural foods industry has recently begun labeling their products "tamari soy sauce" to distinguish them from chemically processed soy sauces which often contain sugar, food coloring, and chemical additives. Although the terms "soy sauce" and "tamari" are often used interchangeably, tamari, a by-product of the miso-making process, is an entirely different product. Tamari is the liquid that rises to the top of the miso-making tubs and is then drawn off for use as a condiment. It is stronger in taste and must be used with care as a replacement for soy sauce. It is also wheat-free, a blessing for the allergic. Tamari soy sauce and tamari can be found in most Asian and natural food stores.

Tamarind: The large brown pod of the tamarind tree contains seeds and a very sour-tasting pulp. The pulp is used in Indian, Indonesian, and Thai cooking. Tamarind pulp is sold in concentrated form in jars or dried in brick form. The pods are also available. Dried tamarind must be softened before use: break off a piece, pour boiling water over it, and let it sit for about 30 minutes until soft. Mash and then strain out the seeds and fibers. Tamarind is acidic and is used much like lemon juice. Although lemon juice has a different flavor, it can be substituted for tamarind at a ratio of 2 to 1. Tamarind is available in Indian and Asian food stores.

Tempeh: A staple food of Indonesia, tempeh is made of cultured soybeans. The beans are hulled, split, and pressed into thin amber-colored squares. Tempeh is a unique "meaty" product which facilitates the digestibility of the soybeans. Tempeh can also be made of seeds, grains, and other beans. If you're lucky, you'll find fresh tempeh in your area, but it is available frozen in most natural food stores. Thaw tempeh before using in a recipe. Slice or cube tempeh when it is partially thawed to avoid the crumbling which sometimes occurs when slicing fully thawed tempeh.

Tofu: Tofu is fresh soybean curd, a highly versatile and protein-rich food that has been a staple of Chinese and Japanese cooking for centuries. It is white, has the consistency of a firm custard, and is pressed into cakes. Plain tofu tastes bland, but absorbs flavors readily. Smooth and soft textured, it can be simmered, blanched, steamed, marinated, fried, deep-fried, baked, mashed, or puréed.

Tofu provides complete protein and is a source of iron, phosphorus, potassium, and other minerals and vitamins. Because of the solidifiers used in making it, tofu has 23 percent more calcium by weight than dairy milk. It is low in calories (147 per 8 ounces) and unsaturated fats and is entirely free of cholesterol. It is easily digestible.

Commercial cakes of tofu vary in size and firmness, making it difficult to describe exact amounts in recipes, but generally smaller cakes of tofu are also firmer and so about equivalent to the larger, softer cakes. We use 12-ounce cakes of medium-soft tofu.

To press tofu: Most recipes call for pressed tofu because pressing makes the tofu firmer and more absorbent. To press tofu, place the cakes of tofu between two flat plates or baking sheets. Weight the top with a bowl of water, a stack of plates, a heavy can, or whatever is handy. The sides of the cakes of tofu should bulge out a little, but not split. Let stand for at least 30 minutes, remove the press, and pour off the water.

To blanch tofu: When using tofu uncooked (marinated, mashed, puréed, etc.), blanch it after pressing and before going on with the recipe. To blanch tofu, drop whole cakes or cubed tofu into boiling water. Simmer for about 5 minutes and remove from the water. Blanching firms tofu, keeps it from diluting what it is added to, and makes it more absorbent.

The texture of tofu becomes chewy and spongelike when frozen and thawed. Freeze the cakes whole, thaw, squeeze out the water, crumble, and use in fillings for its chewiness.

Tofu is available in Asian and natural food stores and most supermarkets. Submerged in frequently changed water, tofu will keep, refrigerated, for about a week.

Tofu Kan: Tofu kan is firmly pressed tofu baked or simmered with spices, soy sauce, and barley malt syrup. Five-spice tofu can be substituted for tofu kan in equal quantity. Both are available in Asian and natural food stores.

Turmeric: Turmeric is a powdered spice derived from the rhizome of a plant of the ginger family. It lends its bright orange-yellow color and mild, slightly musty flavor primarily to Indian and Middle Eastern cooking.

Vegetable Oil: We recommend that you use a light, "tasteless" variety of polyunsaturated vegetable oil with no preservatives. For general use we prefer soy and safflower oils.

Waffle: Also known as a "flame spreader" or "flame tamer," a waffle is a round metal plate that sits between the burner and cooking pot. It serves to reduce the heat and to distribute heat evenly. Waffles can be purchased at restaurant or kitchen supply stores.

Wakame: A mild-tasting seaweed especially rich in iodine. Dried wakame should be soaked for 15 minutes in water to soften it and to remove excess salt. Discard the water, cut out the midrib, and chop it into small pieces. Wakame is available in many Asian food stores and in a growing number of natural food stores.

Wasabi: A green Japanese radish with the assertive flavor and sinus-clearing effect you may have enjoyed in sushi. Wasabi is generally available in powdered form in supermarkets and Asian food stores. Mix the powder with water to form a smooth paste, cover, and set aside for a few minutes while the flavor develops fully. Wasabi is very pungent and should be used very sparingly, but adds a wonderful bite to Nori Rolls *(p. 202)* and is an interesting flavoring for soy sauce and dipping sauces.

Wok: A steel skillet with rounded sides used primarily in Asian cooking. Its contour and thin walls allow a large surface area to heat quickly, evenly, and intensely. This enables rapid yet thorough "stir-frying," a method which maintains the color and integrity of the food beautifully. Once only available in Asian food and hardware stores, woks can now be found in the housewares section of most department stores.

When We Say One Medium Onion...

Item	Amount, Raw & Prepared	Approximate Weight
Vegetables & Fruit		
Apple (1 medium)	1 cup, chopped	4 ounces
Avocado (1 medium)	1 cup, mashed	8 ounces
Broccoli (1 stalk)	2 cups florets	6 ounces
Cabbage (1 large)	10 cups, minced	1 pound, 12 ounces
Carrots (2 medium)	1 cup, diced	8 ounces
Cauliflower (1 medium)	2½ cups florets	1 pound
Celery (3 stalks)	1 cup, diced	8 ounces
Eggplant (1 medium)	4 cups, cubed	14 ounces
Green Beans	1 cup	5 ounces
Green Peas	1 cup	5 ounces
Green Pepper	¾ cup, diced	4½ ounces
Leek (1 medium)	3 ounces	
Lemon (1 medium)	2 tablespoons juice	
	1 tablespoon grated peel	
Mushrooms	1 cup, sliced	3 to 4 ounces
Onion (1 medium)	1 cup, diced	4 ounces
Orange (1 medium)	½ cup juice	
	2 tablespoons grated peel	
Parsley (1 bunch)	3½ cups, chopped	4 ounces
Potato (1 medium)	2 cups, diced	8 ounces
	1¼ cups, mashed	8 ounces
Spinach (fresh)	12 cups, loosely packed	10 ounces
	1 cup, cooked	10 ounces (raw)
Tomato (1 medium)	¾ cup, diced	4½ ounces
Canned tomatoes	3 cups with juice	28-ounce can
	1½ cups drained	28-ounce can
Winter squash (1 medium)	4 cups, cubed	1 pound, 4 ounces
Zucchini (1 medium)	2 cups, diced	10 ounces
Nuts (whole)		
Almonds	1 cup	8 ounces
Cashews	1 cup	6 ounces
Walnuts	1 cup	6 ounces
Sprouts		
Alfalfa	1 cup	¾ ounce
Mung bean	1 cup	5 ounces
Other		
Currants (dried)	1 cup	5 ounces
Raisins	1 cup	5 ounces
Tofu (1 cake)	2 cups, ¼ inch cubes	12 ounces

Index